To Johnny & Theresa —
Best wishes
Dave Wright

SPRINT CAR SHOWDOWN

a **Jimmy Wilson** racing adventure

SPRINT CAR SHOWDOWN

Copyright © 2013 Dave Argabright

Published by:
American Scene Press, LLC
P.O. Box 84
Fishers, IN 46038-1075
(317) 598-1263

www.daveargabright.com

ISBN (10): 0-9899426-0-0
ISBN (13): 978-0-9899426-0-7

Front cover image: John Mahoney

Proudly written, produced and printed in the USA

No part of this book may be used or reproduced in any manner whatsoever without prior written permission from the copyright holder, except in the case of brief quotations in reviews.

First printing

SPRINT CAR SHOWDOWN

A NOVEL BY DAVE ARGABRIGHT

Portions of this content appeared previously in
Sprint Car & Midget Magazine from Sept. 2008 to
January 2011

*Dedicated to the memory of
George Wilkins*

*A good friend;
a great man;
and a fine racer.*

11/6/1961 - 12/3/2012

Chapter 1

Jimmy Wilson stared at the racing paper, his blood boiling and anger ringing in his ears. He read the paragraph again, slowly, for the fourth time.

It was just before noon on Saturday, the first day of April. Tomorrow it was time to go racing, a chance for Jimmy to liberate himself from months of off-season blues. He simmered with ambition, desperate to get himself and the Ellison Special sprint car back on top in the quest for the USAC championship.

The racing paper had hit his mailbox an hour earlier, the perfect distraction to take the chill off the spring day. His eyes widened with delight as he discovered this issue contained a preview of the upcoming USAC season, complete with commentary and a prediction of how each driver and team would perform. But he quickly felt his stomach tighten as he began reading.

"Jimmy Wilson and the Ellison crew no longer appear to be a championship caliber team," wrote Barry Kane, a well-known columnist. "The Ellison car was once the most coveted ride on the circuit, but is today merely a second-tier car. Jack Harvey is a mechanic with a great history in the sport, but these are modern times. Can he keep up?

"There is also the fact that Wilson is coming off a mediocre season, dropping to third in last year's standings. Could it be that predictions of his driving talent might have been premature? With some good luck and a couple of race wins, this team will linger around fifth place this season, but it won't be easy."

Jimmy's hands were trembling as he laid the paper on the table.

"I hope that guy is at Shoe's tomorrow," he said aloud. "I'm gonna give him a piece of my mind."

He stood and paced, glancing through his kitchen window at the landscape outside. There were hints of green in the grass, but the nearby fields were bare and drab, not yet awakened from winter's sleep. Spring couldn't come soon enough as far as he was concerned.

He was so eager to resume racing that he could almost feel the familiar sensations. He could almost taste the methanol fumes that would be hanging in the air, feel the tingle of excitement from the sound of racing engines. He could imagine sliding into the seat, feeling the Ellison sprint car in his hands, wearing it like a comfortable, warm shirt.

The memory of the previous weekend brought a sigh. It had been a 10-hour ride in the passenger seat of Bobby Mancini's car, watching the flat landscape of Indiana and Ohio yield to the rolling terrain of Pennsylvania. Jimmy's heart soared as they approached the race track, but he and Bobby hadn't even signed in at the pit shack when a cold rain descended upon the scene and washed out the season opener. The ride home was gloomy and long, with little talking between the two longtime friends and competitors.

Jimmy studied the article again. Kane had named Steve Graffan as the pre-season favorite, saying that he and Bob Strong's team looked to be especially strong. The pick for second went to Bobby, who was back with car owner Fred Otley.

Jimmy was intrigued with the pick for third. Sid Johnson had hired Frank Graham, a 19-year-old from Oregon who won 25 races last year in the Pacific Northwest, driving a car that apparently had never before done much. Kane raved that he was "the future of USAC."

Jimmy felt a pang of resentment welling up in his belly.

"How can that idiot write such stuff?" he huffed. "Doesn't he know that *I'M* the future of USAC!"

He flung the paper across the small room, scattering pages across the floor. Fifth place? If they were *lucky*? Why, he couldn't wait to get in the race car and clean everybody's clock and…

Jimmy paused, and began to chuckle. He looked at the paper scattered across the floor, and bent to begin picking it up.

Man, look at you, he smiled. *Haven't even fired up the race car yet, and you're already throwing things. Gonna be quite the season, looks like.*

It was a glorious Sunday morning at Shoe's Speedway, and

Jimmy felt his pace quicken as he walked through the pit gate. Finally going racing! He couldn't stop grinning.

As he approached their pit he marveled at how nice the car looked. The bodywork was all new, freshly painted in the familiar pearl white. The "Ellison Special" lettering had been moved from the hood to the side panel, with blue pinstripes dotting the body panels. It still carried the No. 49, and the script "Coffman Asphalt" was lettered on both sides of the hood.

Jimmy slowly walked around the car, studying the new look.

"You like it, boy?" Jack Harvey beamed. "Just got the body panels back this week."

For a moment Jimmy stared at the car, shaking his head. "Man, Harvey, all I can say is...it looks great! Like a whole new car!"

"It is new, mostly. Course the frame is the same, and the engine. But most everything is new. Rear end, shocks, all new stuff. I'm kinda excited...I think we'll be pretty good."

"What's with the pinstripes? Your idea? Or Sonny's?"

"No, Coffman. Him and his wife asked us to stripe the car. That's the stripes they use on their trucks, and I guess they wanted it to look the same."

"Great," Jimmy laughed. "Our new look is copied from a dump truck!"

"Hey, color don't matter," Harvey insisted. "Mr. Ellison said their check cleared...that's what matters. You met him yet?"

"Who?"

"Coffman."

"No, not yet. Why?"

"Oh, just askin'. Gonna be interesting, that's all I'll say."

"What do you mean?"

"He has his own ideas. That's all I'm sayin'. We'll see."

Harvey lowered his voice. "That's him, coming right there. In the fancy shirt and the black pointy shoes."

Jimmy saw a blonde man walking toward them, with a gaggle of people following along. He had thick arms and a belly, with broad shoulders. His face was reddened from hours in the sun, and his gait was firm and purposeful.

"This is our car, here," he said to his followers as they approached. "This is the Coffman car. Hello, Jack."

"Mr. Coffman," Harvey nodded, immediately walking to the trailer and milling aimlessly in the top drawer of the toolbox.

"You Jimmy Wilson?" Coffman asked.

"Yes sir, that's me," Jimmy smiled. "It's nice to meet you."

The man stared at Jimmy for a moment, sizing him up. He then offered his hand, saying simply, "Matt Coffman." Jimmy felt like his hand was in a vise, as the man's powerful grip squeezed his hand until it hurt.

"Sonny Ellison says you're our guy," he said. "Says you're quite a race driver."

"Sonny's quite a guy, himself," Jimmy smiled, suddenly feeling uncomfortable. He flexed his fingers, making sure nothing was broken.

"Jack Harvey here, he's our mechanic," Coffman said, turning to his group. "Him and Slim, this fella over here. But I'll be at most races, kind of overseeing things. Sort of like a crew chief. We're going to win the championship this year."

Jimmy smiled. "I didn't know you used to race, Matt. That's cool."

"Call me Mr. Coffman. Me, I never raced. Who told you that?"

"Nobody. But when you said you'd be overseeing things, I assumed you must have some racing experience."

"Well, as far as the race car, I'll figure that out. The main thing is I don't let anybody on my team sit in the rocking chair. I want everybody to perform at their top level. We're not going to tolerate any losing. Last year you were third in the point standings. Well, we're not going to tolerate third place. That's why I'll be with you men, every step of the way. To make sure everybody is performing, and winning."

"I see."

Jimmy glanced at Harvey, who offered a slight shake of his head. This was certainly new; Sonny Ellison's style had always been hands-off when it came to the race car, allowing Harvey—and Jimmy, to a certain extent—to run things they felt they needed to. Jimmy was already sure that he didn't relish the idea of a sponsor "taking charge" of things. He could sense that Harvey had the same reservations.

A dazzling redhead stepped forward from the group, clearing

her throat impatiently. Jimmy guessed her to be in her late 30s. Her dress clung to her shapely figure, and he noticed she had diamond rings on both hands and an expensive necklace.

"Excuse me, Matt, but aren't you forgetting something?"

"Huh? Oh, yeah. This is my wife, Marva."

"How do you do," she smiled at Jimmy, squeezing his fingers in a lingering handshake. She stepped close into his space, and he instinctively backed slightly away, smiling awkwardly.

"You're such a handsome young boy," she purred, turning to the others. "Isn't he just the cutest thing? I think I'll take him home with me."

"Hmmph. Well, let's get going," Coffman said. "I've got some seats reserved in the stands. Boys, I'll be back down here in a little while."

The group turned to walk away, with Marva still holding Jimmy's handshake.

"He's a little bossy, I know," she smiled, lowering her voice. "But his bark is worse than his bite. You have any trouble with Matt, you just let me know and I'll take care of it. Okay?"

She turned to walk away, looking over her shoulder.

"Bye," she smiled, winking at Jimmy.

Jimmy, Harvey, and Slim stared at the group as they made their way across the track.

Jimmy walked to their small trailer, sitting glumly on the ramp. Harvey slowly walked over and sat down at his side, and they looked at each other for a moment without speaking.

"Well, shit," Jimmy said quietly. "What a mess."

Harvey nodded his head, then began to grin. "Well, at least she wants to take you home, boy. Ain't that nice?"

Jimmy walked toward an area in the infield along the front straightaway where a group of drivers were awaiting the start of the driver's meeting. He greeted Bobby Mancini, Rusty Fernandez, Rick Wagner, Steve Graffan and Sammy Caldwell, all seated on the concrete wall. A younger guy in a blue driving uniform walked toward them. He made eye contact with Jimmy, and nodded. Jimmy said hello, just as Russ Witmer asked for quiet.

"Men, I want to introduce your new sprint car coordinator," he said, motioning for Al Petrov to step forward. "He's raced with most of you, and you know him well. His character is unimpeachable, and his judgment is sound. I'm stepping aside to focus on things back in the office, and I'm turning the division over to him. Gentlemen, you all know Al Petrov."

The drivers applauded, a sincere applause that reflected their respect for the man. Al seemed humbled, nodding his thanks to the group. In a moment the clapping subsided.

"There isn't a lot for me to say," Al began. "Russ has this series in tip-top shape. We've got a good following of fans, many great cars, and most of all, a group of racers I'm proud to be associated with. As I look at this group, there aren't many I don't know well. Those who are new here, welcome. I am always ready to hear what you have to say…good, bad or indifferent.

"You won't always agree with me, and that's to be expected. All I can promise is that I'll treat you with the same respect you afford the officials and your fellow racers. Everyone will be held consistent with our rules, with no favoritism. Whether you're a veteran here, or a rookie, the rules apply equally to all of you. Any questions? None? Good, now let's talk about today's program."

He spent the next few minutes outlining the schedule. Soon the meeting was finished, and racers began scattering toward their respective pit area.

"Al will be good," Sammy said. "He's a straight shooter. Sometimes Russ was wishy-washy…you won't get that from Al."

"No doubt about it," Bobby chimed in. "I'm glad it's Al, and not somebody who doesn't know squat about racing."

"Ahhh," Graffan grunted. "I don't like any official…they're just here to mess us up. Just a bunch of crooks."

"I wouldn't want any part of it," Rusty said. "No matter what you do, somebody's mad. I wouldn't be interested in listening to everybody bitch all the time."

"With Al, you know he's honest," Jimmy insisted. "I think he'll do great."

"Sure you do," Graffan sneered. "He's your buddy."

"Yeah, he's my buddy. But he'd have no problem ruling against me, I know that. He's a straight-up guy, period."

"Sure," Graffan said, rolling his eyes.

"Whatever, Graffan. You know, the season ain't one hour old, and I'm already worn out with you. You're an ass."

"You two guys are a joy to be around, you know?" Sammy smiled, putting his arm on Jimmy's shoulder. "Let's at least get through the first race before you're throwing punches, okay?"

Jimmy stopped by Sid Johnson's pit, where he saw the kid in the blue uniform standing at Sid's trailer, cleaning his visor.

"Been a long winter," Sid grinned, offering a handshake. "Did you meet Frank Graham?"

The kid in the blue uniform came walking over.

"You're Jimmy Wilson," he said. "I've heard a lot about you."

"From Sid? Don't believe anything. He's not a good source of information."

They laughed, but the kid was serious. "I figure you're the guy I've got to beat this year. If I can beat you, I can get to Indy."

Jimmy chuckled. "Hell, I can't even get to Indy! If you figure out how to get there, let me know, will you?"

Leon Hartke came hurrying by, shouting in his best official's voice. "First group hot laps, in five minutes! Let's go, gentlemen! Get 'em in the lineup chute!"

"I'm in the first group," Jimmy smiled. "Good luck, Frank. I'm looking forward to racing with you."

Chapter 2

Jimmy's heart soared as he felt the Ellison Special rumbling under his fingertips. Soon he was pitching the car around the banked Shoe's track, feeling the tires spin, feeling the chassis work, feeling the car rolling across the uneven clay surface. In a few moments he was guiding the car back to their pit, where Harvey and Slim waited, with Matt Coffman hanging in the background.

He climbed from the car and pulled his helmet off. Harvey leaned forward, awaiting Jimmy's feedback.

"Runs good, but something's not right in the front end...feels like it's binding up. Makes the car feel twitchy."

"The shock?" Harvey quizzed.

"Could be. We've got a few minutes, let's change it before we qualify."

"Wait a minute," Coffman chimed in. "How do you know it's the shock?"

"We don't."

"Then why change it? Why not get more laps until you figure out exactly what it is?"

Jimmy noticed Harvey's reluctance to reply, so he spoke up.

"Because you've got to sort it out right away," he explained. "If we lay down a bad qualifying lap, we're behind the 8-ball all day. You've got to go with your gut."

"That makes no sense," Coffman argued. "You might be changing something that isn't broken."

"Maybe. But if that's not what's causing the problem, we'll use the shock again."

"Hmmph," Coffman groused, finally nodding his head to Harvey.

"Go ahead," he said.

A few minutes later Jimmy was on his qualifying lap, but the car was no better. He ended up 28th, and he and Harvey and Slim immediately pored over the car, checking the suspension, looking for anything amiss.

He lined up outside the front row in the second heat, and immediately knew he was in trouble. He fought the car at every turn, trying to find the handle. It wasn't terribly loose or tight, but just...*unpredictable*. Just as the car took a nice set, it would suddenly feel completely different, and he fought to stay off the wall and other cars.

With two laps to go he was fourth, clinging to the final transfer position. He had moved to the inside in hopes of staying off the guardrail, leaving the outside lane open. He heard a growing roar in his right ear, and soon saw the front end of Frank Graham's sprint car as they came to the white flag.

Graham pulled alongside as they entered turn one, with a nice run on Jimmy. The Ellison car stayed low, and Jimmy feathered the throttle, trying to keep the car in line, looking for enough traction to hold the kid off.

Suddenly Jimmy felt the car lurch to the right, and before he could catch it he banged wheels with Graham. The Johnson sprinter veered into the guardrail, jumping two feet into the air, slamming back onto the track while the kid struggled to maintain control. As Graham gathered up the car Jimmy drove the Ellison car to the finish, capturing the transfer spot.

He rolled to his pit, cutting the engine and popping his belts. He climbed from the car and tugged his helmet from his head.

"What was that all about, boy?" Harvey said, as much in amazement as anger.

"Jumped out from under me," Jimmy said, quickly wiping his face. "I drove right over that kid. I need to go apologize."

Jimmy looked toward Graham's pit, where Sid Johnson appeared to be trying to calm a very angry race driver. Graham's face was red, and he was shouting and waving his arms as Sid tried to talk to him.

"Let that punk come down here," Matt Coffman hissed. "I'll break his puny ass in two."

"No, you won't," Jimmy said sharply. "I'll handle this myself. You too, Harvey. Both you guys sit this one out."

The kid came charging into their pit with fire in his eyes. A crowd quickly gathered, watching breathlessly.

"What the hell is your problem?" Graham shouted, getting right in Jimmy's face. "You flat ran over me! Is that how you race?"

"I'm sorry," Jimmy said calmly. "Something is wrong with my car and I lost the handle. I didn't mean to..."

"Aw, bullshit! You turned right into me! Just about dumped me! I might be a rookie here, but I ain't gonna take that from you or anybody else!"

"Frank, I'm sorry," Jimmy said again, trying to calm the kid. "That's not how I race. I did not intentionally hit you."

"You try to turn me over, that's how I'm gonna race you!" the kid yelled, oblivious to anything Jimmy said. "I'll dump you on your ass!"

Jimmy suddenly had heard enough. "Get out of my pit," he said firmly.

Graham looked at Jimmy, and Jimmy realized the kid was beginning to regain his composure. He stepped back, glancing at the crowd.

"I don't like this kind of stuff," Graham said, his voice quieting a bit. "I race clean, and I want to be raced that way."

"I race clean, too," Jimmy insisted. "I'm sorry I hit you. I give you my word, it wasn't intentional. Let's talk about it later when you're not pissed off."

The kid turned and walked away, and the crowd quickly scattered. In a moment Coffman spoke up.

"Why'd you let that kid pop off to you like that?" he demanded, hands on his hips. "You even said you were sorry!"

"I *am* sorry. It was an accident."

"Well, you can count on him walking all over you from now on! You should've busted his lip!"

Jimmy looked at Coffman with a mixture of irritation and disdain. For a moment Coffman glared back at him, when Harvey spoke up to break the silence. "Let's change the rear bars."

"That's exactly what I was thinkin'," Jimmy nodded.

They walked toward the trailer when Coffman spoke up.

"Wait, wait a minute," he said, hurrying to keep up with them. "What do you mean, change the bars? Why do you want to do that?"

Harvey paused, but Jimmy waved him toward the trailer, turning to deal with Coffman.

"Mr. Coffman, I've gotta say somethin'," he began. "I appreciate you helping us with your sponsorship, but you've got to let me and Harvey do our thing. That's the only way this deal will work."

Coffman seemed shocked. "Hey, nobody tells me what to do," he began. "I put my name on this race car, I've gotta have some say. Money talks, and that's how it is."

"I get that, but you've gotta let us do our job," Jimmy argued. "Let Harvey do what the car needs. Let me drive it. We know what we're doin'. Besides, you're the sponsor here, not the owner. Big difference."

"That's my name on the car."

"Sure it is. But if you want to call all the shots, you need to be more than a sponsor. You need to buy your own car."

Now Coffman's face was red with anger. "What if I buy this one?" he blustered. "By God, then you'll do what I say. Either that, or you're gone."

"You buy this one, you won't have to fire me. I'll quit, in a New York minute. But until Sonny Ellison fires me I'm the driver."

"Without me, Sonny Ellison is out of the sprint car business," Coffman growled. "Is that what you want? You want me to pull my money out of the deal, and leave Sonny high and dry?"

"Nope. I'll talk to Sonny first thing in the morning. I'm gonna tell him, if this is the deal for this year, I quit. But do me this much, Coffman. Let us run the car today and quit being a pain in the ass."

Jimmy saw the rage in Coffman's eyes, and for a moment he figured the big guy might break *his* puny ass in two. But just as quickly a grudging smile began to play on Coffman's face.

"You got some fire," he said. "I like that. All right, you guys work on the car. I'll go sit in the stands."

Jimmy nodded, and began to step toward the tool box to help Harvey and Slim.

"But one more thing," Coffman said, intensity brimming in his eyes. "You better win. That's all I got to say."

The Ellison car was a rocket in the 30-lap feature, bringing the crowd to their feet as Jimmy sliced toward the front from his last-row starting spot. One of the torsion bars had indeed been their problem, and with that resolved the car was perfect.

Jimmy got no benefit from caution flags, as the non-stop laps were clicking off quickly. He hustled the car on the slick daytime track, and he got some breaks with traffic. Just as he came upon a car and figured where he wanted to go, it seemed the car magically moved just enough to open the lane he needed.

With five to go he was fifth, chasing Bobby Mancini. Bobby was hugging the bottom groove in the Otley sprinter, and Jimmy blasted by him in the middle groove like he was a lapped car. Next up was Frank Graham, hogging the middle. Jimmy simply drifted high entering the corner, and powered by him on the razor-thin cushion that lay inches from the guardrail.

Sammy Caldwell was fighting a fading race car, gamely trying to hang on to second. Jimmy tried him high, but slipped over the cushion, his rear tire brushing the rail. Jimmy hammered the Ellison car, desperately trying to keep the front end from sucking into the guardrail. As they exited the corner Sammy moved to the outside, trying to steal Jimmy's line.

But the Bell sprinter was too tight out there, and Sammy was immediately pedaling, hanging on. Jimmy blasted past on the inside and for a moment thought he had taken the lead. That's when he saw Steve Graffan dead ahead, about a half-straightaway away. Jimmy blitzed into turn one, riding the cushion. He stood on the gas as his rear bumper brushed the guardrail, gaining enough traction to shoot him roaring off the corner. He had dramatically cut into Graffan's lead.

Jimmy could hear him as they passed the flag stand, where USAC starter Mike Rydman was showing the furled green and white flags. *Two laps to go.* He tried the same line into one, but this time was a touch too hot. He hit the rail again, a little harder this time. He clenched his teeth and studied Graffan's tank as they rocketed down the backstretch.

Graffan put the Strong sprinter right on the cushion, as if daring Jimmy to try him low. Jimmy decided to hang back, putting all his chips down for the last corner, following Graffan through the white flag lap.

As they entered turn three Jimmy was 10 yards behind

Graffan, closing rapidly. As they came off turn four Graffan stayed high, and for a moment Jimmy thought he was going to run into the back of his archrival. But with a flick of his wrists he moved alongside Graffan on the inside, both cars clawing for traction. It was momentum that made the difference; as they flashed under Rydman's checkered flag Jimmy was a car length in front. He could actually hear the roar from the grandstand over their engines, and he screamed with joy inside his helmet, pumping his fist into the air. He rumbled down the backstretch, laughing almost uncontrollably, his hands shaking with adrenaline.

He took the car out of gear as he rolled off turn four, rapping the throttle as he approached the finish line. Harvey and Slim were running toward him, their arms raised in triumph. Photographers and officials hurried to the scene, nearly everyone grinning and giving him a thumbs-up.

Jimmy leaped from the car as if his seat had springs; he saluted the crowd as they roared their approval. Harvey grabbed him with a bear hug, the big man nearly cracking Jimmy's ribs as he lifted him off the ground.

"That was a helluva drive, boy!" he hollered. Jimmy put his arm around Slim and the three men laughed and celebrated as photographers leaned in to capture the moment.

The track announcer stepped toward them with a microphone, and tried to interview Jimmy amid the chaos. But Harvey grabbed the man's hand and pulled the microphone close, shouting, "Now, that's how you drive a sprint car! No shit!"

The crowd roared in laughter, and the man grimaced and smiled at the same time. Jimmy shook his head and grinned at Harvey.

"You can't say that on the microphone," he scolded, but Harvey just laughed, feeling his oats. As the man tried the interview again, Jimmy spotted Barry Kane hovering a few feet away, scribbling on a pad of paper.

Jimmy held up his hand to stall the PA guy for another moment.

"Hey, Barry! Barry Kane!"

Kane looked at Jimmy in surprise, and smiled.

"That wasn't bad for a fifth place car, an overrated driver, and a washed-up old mechanic, eh?" Jimmy shouted.

Kane shrugged. "I just write 'em like I see 'em...nothing personal."

"Yeah, that's right...nothing personal. But I'm gonna help you remember that article for a long, long time."

Chapter 3

The Ellison sprint car screamed down the back straightaway at Jefferson Speedway, with Jimmy staring through his visor as the corner approached. He and the car were as one, a seamless machine in perfect synchronization. Behind him, more than a half-lap back, was the second-place car of Sammy Caldwell; on this chilly Saturday night in April, the rest of the field had brought a knife to a gunfight.

Jimmy marveled at how well the car worked. The track was black, heavy, and rutted, a typical surface here at Jefferson. But from the moment they unloaded Jimmy could run anywhere on the track, the car gliding over the holes and ruts.

He found himself on the back bumper of Graffan as they took the white flag, and he wondered what position Graffan was running. Jimmy knew the Ellison car was running well, because he had lapped many good cars as the race clicked off without a yellow.

For a moment he was tempted to try to pass Graffan, just on general principle. But he had a vision of getting himself in trouble with the race in the bag, so he eased up and followed Graffan through the final lap.

It was a different feeling as he rumbled toward the victory lane ceremony. A week ago, when he came from the tail in dramatic fashion to win at Shoe's, he was elated. But tonight he dominated at every turn, so he felt no sense of drama. Quick time, won his heat easily, and romped in the 30-lap feature.

As he climbed from the car he waved to the noisy crowd. Slim was waiting with a cold drink and a grin, and Jimmy wiped his face on a towel and smiled at Harvey.

"Man, that was cruise control," he laughed. "We had 'em covered tonight."

"You were screwin' around!" Harvey growled. "You were half

asleep out there…if anybody else had anything at all, you'd have got us beat!"

For a moment Jimmy stared in surprise. Was he kidding? The stern cast to Harvey's face, his flushed cheeks, and his body language said he was completely serious.

"How far up did we lap 'em, Slim?" Jimmy asked.

"Graffan was fifth."

"So we lapped up to fifth place, and I was asleep? What the hell are you talkin' about?"

"The lapped cars," the big man argued. "You'd follow guys a whole lap before you'd pass 'em. You got to get up on the wheel better than that. Don't be dinkin' around with the slower guys! Wake your ass up and get aggressive!"

Jimmy could only shake his head as someone handed him the checkered flag, and they posed for pictures. Slim smiled broadly, but Harvey and Jimmy simply looked irritated at one another.

Soon they rolled the car back to the pits, and Jimmy saw a throng of fans waiting to greet them. He shook off Harvey's comments and smiled as he chatted with people, signing autographs and posing for pictures.

Matt Coffman came hurrying toward the car, trailed by his usual entourage. What was it, Jimmy wondered, that made people want to cling to the coattails of obnoxious rich guys? *Oh, yeah,* he remembered. *Money.*

"Where's my trophy?" Coffman bellowed. Jimmy could tell from his slurred speech and reddened eyes that he was about half loaded. "I wanna get a picture with my trophy!"

He snatched up the trophy, and stepped in front of the race car. "Get back away from my car!" he demanded. "I want to get a picture!"

Jimmy and Harvey looked at each other, shaking their heads. They stepped away, and Jimmy said to the throng of people, "Sorry, folks. Bear with us just a moment, while we get this picture."

Oblivious, Coffman held the trophy with one hand, and held up one finger. He grinned crookedly as a couple of his leeches snapped photos.

"Man!" he said loudly. "My car was great tonight! We put a whippin' on 'em!"

"Sure did!" said one of the leeches.

"You boys didn't do half bad," Coffman laughed, looking at Jimmy and Harvey. "Maybe we'll keep you on, after all!"

Coffman and his entourage laughed heartily, and he began to walk toward the pit gate, still clutching the trophy.

"C'mon, we're gonna celebrate!" Coffman cried. "I know a good club here in town…we'll see how much booze they have!"

Coffman's shapely wife Marva smiled at Jimmy as the group began to trail behind Coffman.

"You were fantastic," she said, stepping closer.

"C'mon, Marva!" Coffman called. "Let's get goin'! I'm thirsty!"

"Aw, pipe down!" she yelled. "I'll be there in a minute!"

He said something Jimmy couldn't hear, and the group laughed as they walked through the pit gate and out of sight.

"It was fun watching you race," she said, moving so close Jimmy could count the diamonds on her necklace. "I've got to give the winner a hug!"

She reached out to embrace him, and he awkwardly put his arms around her. Over her shoulder he saw Harvey staring at him, shaking his head. Jimmy helplessly returned Harvey's gaze.

"My goodness, feel those muscles," she cooed. "We'll, I've got to go. Give us a kiss."

Jimmy leaned over to kiss her cheek, but she suddenly pulled his arms and kissed him hard on the lips, holding it for a moment before stepping away.

"Hey, I'll see you later, okay?" she grinned. "It's going to be a fun season!"

She shook her hips with every step as she walked away, knowing full well that every guy in the pits was staring. The crowd around the race car was silent for a moment, before finally stepping back toward the car.

Harvey walked to Jimmy's side, lowering his voice. "Boy, you're swimmin' in deep water," he warned. "You better watch yourself!"

"Geez, you think I like that?" Jimmy whispered. "She scares the hell out of me."

A middle-aged lady and a kid of about 12 years old stood nearby, waiting for an autograph.

"He took your trophy," the lady said in amazement. "That guy took your trophy!"

"That's all right," Jimmy smiled. "We'll get another one next week!"

It was late Thursday afternoon, and Jimmy sat on the little porch outside the trailer. He was debating what to do tonight: Hang around home, or hang out at the Anvil. If he went to the Anvil, the end result would be the same as last night, and the night before, and the night before that. He'd drink too much beer, and end up hooking up with a honky-tonk special that brought only regret. The usual contender was Shelby Connor, a wild local woman a few years older than Jimmy. She had quite the reputation around Perkinsville, and while she was lots of fun she offered nothing in the way of a legitimate relationship.

As he sat on the porch, looking at the pretty spring sunshine, he felt a strong urge to try a different direction. He walked to his pickup, and found himself driving west a couple of miles. At the old brick schoolhouse he turned right, and slowed when he approached a small farm on the right side of the road. He pulled into the driveway and cut the engine, slowly walking up the gravel sidewalk toward the house.

Jimmy stepped onto the porch, and reached for the doorbell. He could hear the ringing bell inside, and he stood in silence. A gentle breeze rustled the budding trees in front of the house, and the fragrance of spring gave everything a fresh, new perspective.

The door swung open, and Elaine Carson wore an expression of surprise as their eyes met. She pushed the storm door open.

"Hi Jimmy," she beamed. "What a nice surprise! Won't you come in?"

He stepped inside, and smiled. "I hope you don't mind me stopping by unannounced," he began, realizing he was actually quite nervous. "I don't have a phone, or I would have called first."

"I don't mind at all," she smiled softly. He studied her carefully, trying to get a read. "I'm just sitting here doing some bookkeeping for my dad…I take care of the books for his farming operation. Boring stuff, really. I'm glad you came by, I needed a break!"

"Bookkeeping," he nodded. "That's kind of out of my department, I don't think I'd be detailed enough for that kind of work. Well, are we making any money? Your dad, I mean."

"No farmer would admit to making any money," she laughed, shaking her head. "Maybe next year!"

He noticed how her brown hair cascaded perfectly onto her shoulders. She was nearly as tall as he was, slender and willowy, and her skin was smooth and flawless. She was wearing jeans and a simple plaid shirt, but she still looked wonderful. There was a wholesome quality to her, a girl-next-door purity.

"Would you like to sit down?" she said, motioning toward a chair.

"Oh, thanks, but I can't stay," he said quickly. "I don't want to intrude or anything. I just...I was wondering, would you like to go to dinner sometime? And...maybe a movie?"

She seemed a bit taken aback, like she didn't see it coming. For a moment he figured he'd stepped on it.

"Why...that's really nice, Jimmy. Yes, I'd like that. I'd like that a lot."

"Well...how about tomorrow? Are you available tomorrow?"

She laughed, letting her hair tousle onto her shoulders, and her smile was really bright. She pointed at him, as if she was pretending to be cautious.

"I forgot you were a racing driver," she said. "You move quickly!"

"Oh, well, I didn't mean to...I mean, if tomorrow is too soon, we can..."

She held up her hand gently to interrupt him. "Tomorrow would be great. What time?"

He grinned broadly, feeling a rush of pleasant excitement sweep over him. "Is 5:30 too early?"

"That's perfect," she said. "I'll be ready at 5:30. Sure you can't stay for a minute? I can make us some lemonade."

"Nah, I better get going. Well, it's nice seeing you, Elaine. I'll see you tomorrow night."

She walked him to the door. He let himself out, and she stepped onto the porch as he walked down the front steps.

"'Bye," he said, waving over his shoulder. She stood smiling on the porch, her arms crossed, watching him walk away.

"See you tomorrow," she waved. He carefully drove around the small turnaround, and glanced over his shoulder to see her walk back into the house.

Dang, he said to himself. *I wish it was tomorrow...*

It was an hour later when he leaned back in his recliner, reading a book. A plate sat on the stand next to the chair, with a few bread crumbs and a couple of leftover chips.

He glanced up to see headlights in the driveway, and felt his belly tighten. He wasn't in the mood to deal with Shelby, not tonight.

Jimmy turned on the outside light and saw Shirley Morrison walking onto the small porch. Her husband Gene employed Jimmy at his full-time gig, driving a truck hauling grain throughout the area. Shirley and Gene made the little house trailer available for Jimmy as part of the job. They were middle-aged folks with grown children, and they had taken a liking to Jimmy as if he were one of their own kids.

"Well, hello," Jimmy grinned. "Quite a surprise to have company tonight, especially a beautiful lady like you!"

"Oh, you're the charmer," she smiled, kissing him on the cheek as she stepped inside. "I saw your light and figured I'd visit... haven't seen you for a while! Say, you're keeping the old place nice and clean!"

"Aw, it's the least I can do," he said, motioning toward a chair. "You guys are kind enough to let me stay here, I should at least try to keep it nice."

"What are we reading?" she said, nodding toward his book. "Oh, wait...maybe I don't want to know."

"Just an old Zane Grey western," he grinned. "I like cowboy stories."

She smiled, that kind of motherly smile that tells you she's got something on her mind and you're going to hear about it in just a minute.

"I've got an idea," she said, and he sensed she was getting right to it. "We haven't had you over for dinner in a while. Would you like to have dinner with Gene and I?"

"Of course I would, Shirley. I've had your cooking, remember? Sensational."

"Thank you. Is it okay if I invite someone to join us?"

"Oh, I get it," he nodded. "This is one of those fix-up-Jimmy-because-you-feel-sorry-for-him setups."

"Oh, no," she insisted. "It's just that, well, Gene wanted to play cards afterwards, and we need a fourth player. Hard to play cards with just three."

"I see," he said. "How about if I invite somebody?"

Her eyes narrowed. "Who?"

"How about Shelby Conner?"

He studied her reaction, trying not to laugh. She was aghast, and she shook her head plaintively. "Oh, Jimmy, please don't," she groaned, then she realized he was teasing her. She shook her head again, shaking her finger at him in her most motherly way.

"That girl is trouble," she insisted. "Big trouble! I wish you didn't associate with her."

"Aw, we're just friends. Nothing wrong with a guy having friends, is there?"

"Hmmppph," she said.

"So who were you thinking?" Jimmy asked, and he already knew the answer.

"Well, Elaine Carson loves to play cards…"

"Gee, not Elaine," Jimmy interrupted. "She's a beautiful girl, her dad has a big farm, and she's not interested in a lug like me. She's out of my league, Shirley."

"She most certainly is not! She's a very nice girl, and you two would get along fine. I know you would."

"Well, I'm sure she'd have no interest in going out with me."

"You might be surprised. She thinks you're just fine."

"She does? How do you know?"

"She sat with us last Sunday at church, and she mentioned your name three times. She said you seem very nice. She even said you were handsome."

"Me? Handsome? C'mon, Shirley, quit playing around," Jimmy said, letting his voice raise slightly as he played her along. "Listen, I don't like being made fun of, okay? It hurts my feelings!"

"I'm not playing around," she insisted. "That's the truth! She said you were handsome! I wouldn't kid you about something like that. Really, I wouldn't!"

"Hmmm. Aw, I don't know, Shirley. Maybe it would be okay. Having dinner with you and Gene, I mean. And if Elaine was to happen to be there…I guess that would be okay."

"Really!" she beamed. "That's great, Jimmy! I know you'll have a real nice time!"

"But listen," he interrupted. "I absolutely, positively won't do it tomorrow night, Shirley. You can forget that, right here, right now, because it won't happen. Okay? Just get any ideas about tomorrow night out of your mind! You got that?"

She seemed startled, shaking her head. "Well, for heaven's sake, okay! If you don't want to do it tomorrow, I understand! That's fine!"

"Well, okay," he said sullenly. "Just wanted to make that clear."

"Don't get upset, Jimmy. Is everything all right? What's going on tomorrow?"

"I'm going out with Elaine, that's all."

She was stunned for a second, and he couldn't hold back his laughter any longer. She jumped from her chair and playfully began batting at his head and ears with her purse as he held his hands up to defend himself, almost falling over with laughter.

"You're rotten, is what you are," she said, making a face. "I've raised three sons, young man, so don't you think for one minute I won't pin your ears back when you mess with me!"

Then she stepped back, clenching her hands together in excitement. "Are you really?" she gushed. "Are you two going out?"

"Yes, we are," he said, very seriously. "We're going to dinner, and then maybe a movie. Is that all right, mother?"

"Oh, how exciting!" she shouted. "It's wonderful! You two are just going to hit it off so well! You wait and see, Jimmy! This is just going to be wonderful! The girls at the Dorcas Circle are going to be so excited!"

"Now, it's just a date," Jimmy insisted. "Don't be thinking this is some big serious thing, Shirley. It's just a date."

"I know, I know, but it's wonderful. You two are perfect for each other. You'll see! She is the sweetest girl, and you're such a sweet boy! Oh, my goodness! This is great news. Well, I'm going home now. Listen, I might stop by Saturday morning, just to check in! I'd kind of, you know…"

"You want a detailed report of how it went," Jimmy interrupted, shaking his head. "No dice, Shirley. I keep a low profile on that stuff. You want any info, you'll have to get it from Elaine."

"That's fine," she grinned. "Because I'll call her first thing Saturday morning!"

She stepped through the door, stopping to give him a hug. She reached up and put her hand on the side of his face, clasping it warmly.

"You're such a nice young man," she said. "I'm so happy you're going out with such a wonderful girl."

He watched her back the big Oldsmobile from the driveway and speed toward their farm. He closed the door, feeling the chill of the spring night.

A nice, nice young man, he mused. *I wonder what she'd think of some of the discussions me and Shelby have late at night?*

Chapter 4

The next morning Jimmy headed for Central City. He wasn't running Gene Morrison's truck today, and he hoped to visit with Sonny Ellison about the situation with Matt Coffman. He climbed into his pickup, and headed south. The sprawling countryside eventually yielded to the suburbs, then the busy city streets. He navigated to the west side, listening to the radio, relaxing.

He stopped by Sonny's office but found he wasn't there. He walked back to the small race shop, but it was locked. Glancing at his watch, he decided to stop by Pop's for something to eat.

Pop's was a popular hangout for racing people, and Jimmy spotted Sammy Caldwell and a couple of mechanics seated near the entrance. He joined them for lunch, catching up on plenty of racing gossip. After lunch he drove back to Sonny's paving business, and this time noticed the race shop door was open. First he tried Sonny's office, but he was still out. He turned to walk back toward the shop.

He saw Harvey working on the car, and he hollered as he entered the shop so he wouldn't startle the man too badly.

"Hey, boy, what you doin' here? Ain't you still driving the truck?" Harvey smiled, wiping his hands on a rag.

"Just part-time, at least for the time being. What you workin' on?"

"Just going over things, getting ready for Sunday. Car's been ready since Wednesday. I'm just killin' time, pokin' around."

"Where's Slim?"

"He ran over to Columbus, Ohio. Pickin' up some parts for a paving machine. Want a soda? Look here, we got us a little fridge! When you want a cold drink, you just reach right in to get one. Ain't that nice?"

"You're getting awfully modern, Harvey. Next thing you know

you'll have a TV in here, watching daytime soap operas."

"Now, that ain't a bad idea," Harvey grinned, propping himself up on the workbench.

"Say, where is Sonny? He hasn't been to either of our races, and he isn't here today. Is everything okay?"

"Yeah, but his mother is kind of sickly, and he's been dealin' with that a little bit. She lives down south somewhere, and he's tryin' to get her moved up here to some nursing home. Plus, I guess they been real busy with the paving business, weather was bad this winter so there's lots of fixin' on the roads."

"Have you told him about Coffman? About how he's acting?"

"Yeah, I told him how Coffman thinks since we put his name on the hood, it's his race car. Sonny said don't worry about it, that's just how Coffman is. If it gets too bad, he'll say something to him. But for now, I reckon we'll just have to ride it out."

Harvey opened his bottle of soda and leaned back. He looked at Jimmy and smiled.

"We sure are goin' good, boy. Two in a row, to start the season. Can't beat that."

"Nope. Let's keep it going, Harvey. Its fun when we're goin' this good. Of course, you'll still find some reason to bitch me out, but that's to be expected."

Jimmy grinned playfully, but Harvey just shook his head. "I was just tellin' it like it is," he insisted. "You were dinkin' around."

Harvey took a big drink of soda, then belched loudly. "Listen, boy, we keep winning, we might have some trouble."

"What kind of trouble?"

"Bob Strong. He and his boys are starting to raise hell. They think we're cheatin'."

"Are we?"

"That ain't your concern. But if you hear people talkin', just…"

"It *is* my concern," Jimmy insisted. "It's my reputation, Harvey. I want to beat 'em, but I want to do it right. I don't want you to cheat the car up."

"That's my worry, not yours."

"If you're cheating, sooner or later we'll get caught, and they'll take the money and points away. That makes it my worry, too."

"Do you think the car is cheated up?" Harvey asked.

"The thought has crossed my mind."

"You're kiddin'…why?"

"The car is so strong," Jimmy said, shaking his head. "I figure we've either got a big motor, or you finally sorted out the injection. Remember how you struggled with it last year? Now the thing pulls like an ape, all the way through the power band. My guess is that you got the injection absolutely nailed down. But it's also possible you put together a big motor."

"Either way, I ain't sayin'," Harvey said quickly.

"I know. But if the motor is big, Harvey, they'll catch us. It's not exactly rocket science."

"The good news is, we've got 'em thinkin', boy. And I got an idea. What if we was to REALLY get 'em thinkin'?"

"What do you mean?" Jimmy said, giving him a curious look.

"Well, what if we was to start actin' funny, like we're hiding something?"

"What good would that do? They'll just protest us."

"Sure they will, boy! But never forget this: The more time they spend thinkin' about our car, the less time they spend thinkin' about *their* car. That's what I want…get 'em all flustered, tinkering with their car, and they'll jack themselves right out of the ballpark."

Jimmy thought for a moment.

"You know, that's not a bad idea, Harvey. It might be fun, too. Okay, I'll play along. Just let me know what you want me to do."

"That's good, boy," Harvey grinned.

Jimmy got up to leave. "That's pretty impressive, Harvey," he said seriously.

"What's impressive?"

"That you actually had a good idea."

"Hmmppph," he grunted. "Real funny, boy. Like you're some kinda deep thinker."

Jimmy glanced at his watch.

"I've gotta go…I don't want to be late."

"Late? For what?"

He smiled proudly at Harvey, and puffed out his chest.

"I've got a date, Harvey. How 'bout that?"

Harvey's eyes widened, and he shook his head.

"Not with that Marva Coffman broad, I hope."

Jimmy laughed out loud. "Oh, wow," he said, shaking his head. "Can you imagine that? Man, that lady would hurt you. Hurt you bad! Listen, I'll see you Sunday over at Franklin."

Jimmy looked across the table at Elaine and smiled. She looked great, wearing a colorful blouse and tight jeans.

"This is really a nice restaurant," she said, looking around. "I've never been here before…it looks expensive."

"Gene said it was one of the best in town," he explained. "I won a couple of races the past two weeks, so we can celebrate."

"Really? You won a race?"

"Two, actually. Two in a row. We've got a great start to our season. I'm excited."

"I guess I don't know anything about racing," she admitted sheepishly. "I've never even been to a race."

He smiled in amazement. "Never been to a race??!! Wow."

"Well, other than the 500, I mean. My parents and I go every Memorial Day. But that's the only one. It's very exciting, but I don't know much of what's going on."

"The 500…that's where I want to race someday. That's my goal, to make the Indy 500."

"Wow! Wouldn't that be something! Do you think it will happen?"

"I hope so…I'm trying!"

"Why do you race?" she asked. He liked the way her questions were so sincere, and how she listened intently to his answers.

"That's a good question," he said, thinking it over. "Well…I guess I just do. It's hard to explain…it's kind of like, why does your dad farm? Why does a guy play music? It seems natural, I suppose. Ever since I was a little kid, I wanted to race."

"But isn't it…dangerous? I mean, I've always been amazed that people would want to drive a racing car, knowing it's so dangerous. How do you deal with that?"

He laughed. "Just like every race driver," he explained. "It isn't going to happen to me. And really, it isn't as dangerous as somebody might think."

"Have you ever gotten hurt? Have you been in a crash?"

"Yeah, I've crashed a few times. I've cracked my shoulder,

cracked some ribs, bunged up my foot, got my neck burned a little bit in a fire. But never anything serious."

"Not serious!" she exclaimed. "All those things sound pretty serious to me!"

"Not really. I mean, you try not to crash, try to be smart, and hope you're lucky. That's about it. If you thought about getting hurt, you couldn't do this."

"Are any of the men married? Do they have families? The people you race with, I mean."

"Sure, most of 'em do. Wife, kids, the works. If you've got a family, usually you also have a trade, a line of work. Racing is seasonal, and it's hard to make it through the winter without some other kind of work."

"My goodness, how do their wives deal with all that danger? I would think they'd be a nervous wreck."

"But it isn't as dangerous as you think," he insisted. "Yes, somebody might get hurt, but it's not likely. Not every week. So you don't think that much about it.

"You can get hurt in any line of work. Well, the guy working in the flower shop is probably safe. But take farming, for example. Has your dad ever been hurt on the farm? Stitches, burns, broken bones?"

"All of the above," she admitted.

"And I'll bet you know somebody in your area that's been killed in a farming accident. Right?"

"Yes."

"See, it's the same deal. You're a smart girl, I can tell. You know something could happen to your dad, but I'll bet you don't spend much time worrying about it, because you know he's careful. Am I right?"

"You're right," she smiled.

"It's the same way in racing. You don't waste your time worrying about it."

"Let's talk about something a little more upbeat," she laughed. "How do you like working with Gene?"

"He's swell. And Shirley, too."

"Aren't they adorable? I've known them all my life, and they're so much fun. Shirley definitely keeps him in line."

"She thinks a lot of you," he smiled. "She talks about you all the time."

"You, too," Elaine nodded. "She's been telling me all about you."

"The matchmaker," he laughed.

"I was kind of wondering about that," she said. "I was hoping you didn't invite me to dinner just to placate Shirley. I'd feel bad if that were the case."

"Are you kidding? I invited you to dinner because you're a nice lady, attractive, and the conversation is interesting. But I'll turn the question around: Did you come to dinner just because Shirley wanted you to?"

"Oh, no," she insisted. "You seem like a nice guy, and you're fun to talk to. I enjoy meeting someone new."

He looked at her and smiled. "But you're not sure about this racing thing, are you?"

She laughed, kind of a nervous laugh.

"Well, to tell you the truth, I guess I don't understand the lifestyle. I'm a practical person, kind of traditional. When you talk about the danger, the uncertainty, the traveling, I have a hard time relating to all that.

"I can't even offer much in the way of conversation when you talk about racing…I don't even know what you're talking about."

"That's okay," he insisted. "In a way, I like keeping things separate sometimes. Sometimes you can get too much into racing, and it wears you out. If I can separate a little bit through the week, I'm actually more focused on the weekends."

"When do you race again?"

"Sunday, over in Franklin."

"Do you think you might win?"

"Actually, I'm *sure* I'm going to win."

"Wow! That's awfully confident!"

"Yep. We're on a roll, Elaine. And nobody out there can stop us."

Jimmy looked out across the dark racing surface, studying the thousands of tiny puddles dotting the racing surface, watching as the warming sunlight turned the smallest puddles into a rising mist. It was going to be a typical Sunday afternoon at Franklin; wet and muddy in the beginning, with lots of speed and bravado. Then would come the deep holes and ruts, when it would *really* get exciting. Franklin on Sunday afternoon could bring spectacular satisfaction, or bone-crushing disappointment.

Jimmy walked to the tail of the Ellison Special sprint car, leaning over to press down on the rear bumper, feeling the tension of the suspension. His eyes looked over the car, studying every detail. Harvey had the car ready; every bolt had been gone over multiple times, and the car was impeccably clean and polished.

"Boy, that's some race car," Mike White said, awe in his voice. "That's about as good as it gets, a piece of equipment like that." Mike was an Indiana State Policeman who lived a mile or so from Jimmy's trailer, and he was also a racing fan. He had introduced himself to Jimmy at a local restaurant and the two had become friends.

"It *is* a great car," Jimmy nodded. "It's a privilege to get to drive it. But don't tell Harvey I said that, huh? He'll get the big head."

Mike nodded down the way, and Jimmy turned to look.

"Is that Al Petrov, in the official's shirt? Boy, I've seen him race a few times down through the years."

"Yeah, that's him. He's a great guy, I'll introduce you."

"Where'd he lose his arm, anyways? He's had that hook as long as I remember."

"Ah…I dunno. He told me once, but I don't remember. Happened when he was pretty young. Hey! Hey, Al!"

Al turned and smiled at Jimmy, offering a wave.

"Well, you ready to race?" he said, extending his left hand. "Going for three in a row, Jimmy. That's pretty good."

"'Course I'm ready to race…and I'm not going for three in a row, Al, I'm *doing* three in a row. You watch and see."

Al laughed, and nodded. "Little bit cocky, eh? That's all right. A good racer needs to be cocky."

Jimmy nodded toward Mike and introduced him to Al. They continued to chat for a moment before Al turned to hurry away.

"Better make my rounds and say hello to everybody," he said.

"Go down and hassle Graffan or something," Jimmy teased. "Find some reason to disqualify him."

Al raised his eyebrows. "I'm surprised you'd even bring something like that up."

"Whattya mean?"

"You know what I mean. I can't walk ten feet in this pit area without somebody asking if we're going to inspect your car."

"They think we're cheating?"

"Well, I don't know if they really believe it, but they're beginning to wonder."

Jimmy turned serious. "Al, be honest. Do you think Harvey would cheat? Do you?"

Al thought for a moment, then slowly shook his head.

"Honestly? I don't know, Jimmy. I will say this: I raced against him for at least 15 years and in all those years I don't recall him once being caught cheating."

Al looked directly at Jimmy with a piercing stare. "You know, Jimmy, if anyone protests, it's strictly by the book. Our friendship, it doesn't figure in. You know that, don't you?"

Jimmy returned Al's direct gaze. "Absolutely. You got a job to do, and I expect you'll do it."

Al nodded, and smiled. "Well, I'd better get the driver's meeting started. Don't be late."

Al started to walk away, and Jimmy called his name. Al turned back toward the Ellison pit.

"You tell Graffan and Bob Strong's boys to get their money out," Jimmy said, his eyes twinkling. "They think we're cheating, they can put up the dough to find out."

Chapter 5

Harvey leaned into the cockpit, looking squarely into Jimmy's eyes as he prepared to pull on his helmet.

"She's liable to slick off, boy," the big man said. "Just run your race, and watch out for the holes. Gonna be rough on somebody, and I don't want it to be you. Remember, we got the best car out here. You hold up your end of the deal and bring it home."

He stepped away, bending down to check the rear tire pressure one last time. Slim handed Jimmy his helmet, and in a moment was giving Jimmy's lap belt a final tug.

They rolled the car to the push-off chute, and Jimmy felt a truck bump him from behind. He waved his arm and in a moment the Ellison Special was rumbling around the rutted, rough half-mile. Even at idle, Jimmy could feel the uneven bumps and rises in the track.

It had been another sterling day thus far. Quick time in qualifying, then grabbing the last transfer in his heat race with a breathtaking move off the fourth corner coming to the finish.

The field quickly formed up, and Jimmy lined up on the outside of row three alongside Bobby Mancini. Directly ahead was Graffan, with Sammy on the pole. The new kid from out west, Frank Graham, was on the outside of row one in Sid Johnson's car.

They survived two false starts before the race got underway, with brown dust churning under their tires. The track was drying out more quickly than Jimmy had anticipated, but the vicious holes and ruts remained. The Ellison car was still decent, and he immediately fell in behind Bobby and Graffan.

The three cars were nose-to-tail for the first dozen laps, steadily moving forward. Graham was leading, and Jimmy couldn't see Sammy and figured he must have dropped out. The Ellison car was a bit loose, but Jimmy could see Graffan fighting the same condition.

Several monster holes began to develop in three and four, making passing difficult. Everybody moved low through the corner, with only a few brave souls churning through the bone-jarring middle and top.

A couple of cautions had kept the leaders bunched up, and just past halfway Jimmy turned it up a notch, pulling alongside Graffan. The Strong sprinter was equal to the task, and the two raced side-by-side for two laps, their fight carrying them to the tail of Graham, who three laps earlier had relinquished the lead to a determined Bobby Mancini.

This had been the best run yet for the rookie, and he was in no mood to drop any more positions. He was clearly struggling on the slickening track, and now he had his hands full with two tough racers. Graffan got a brilliant run off four and blasted alongside Graham, beating him to the corner and leaving him even more desperate to hold off a charging Ellison sprinter.

Jimmy carried more momentum into turn one and thought he might make the pass as well. But Graham crowded him down and Jimmy had no choice but to yield the line. Jimmy managed to keep his revs up through the turn, and quickly pulled alongside as they hit the back straightaway.

Jimmy heard the scream of Graham's car slowly fade from his right ear, and he knew he would lead him to the corner. As he began to lift and turn in, the screaming sprinter suddenly roared alongside him on his left, trying desperately to steal the coveted inside line.

Jimmy instinctively realized the kid was in over his head, and he gently got on the brakes. Graham's momentum was much too great to make the corner, and Jimmy watched as he crossed just in front of the nose of the Ellison's sprinter. Graham plowed into a massive hole in the middle of the track, and Jimmy sucked in a breath as Graham's car leaped three feet into the air, then cartwheeled wildly over the steel guardrail, bounding out of sight as Jimmy steered his car down along the inside rail.

The starter was furiously waving the red flag, and Jimmy looked for Harvey and Slim along the pit rail. He saw the big man wave, and he rumbled to a stop. The two men quickly jumped the rail and approached the Ellison car as it fell silent.

Harvey was all business as Jimmy pulled off his helmet. "I'll tighten 'er up a little," he said quickly. "How much?"

Jimmy thought for a moment. "Just a turn or two, not much. Hey, Slim, is Graham okay?"

"Ain't heard. Busted his ass, didn't he?"

"Man, he cleared the rail by 15 feet," Jimmy shivered. "Poor Sid…ain't anything left of that one."

Mike was standing at the rail, and he stepped over to offer a cup of water and a towel. Jimmy drank deeply from the cup as he heard something on the P.A., pausing to try to get what they were saying. Suddenly the crowd roared loudly, applauding.

"He's walking to the ambulance," Mike repeated. "Just shook him up."

Jimmy nodded. His mind was racing, trying to think of a strategy to deal with Graffan, then Bobby. Suddenly Slim whispered, "Hey, look…they're changing a tire!"

They all looked toward Bobby's car, where Fred Otley was using a wheel hammer as a helper jacked up the rear of the car.

"That's a break, boy," Harvey said quickly. "That'll put him to the back…you gotta figure out how to get by Graffan."

"How many laps left?"

"Ten…you gotta get up on it, boy. We can win this thing."

The starter displayed the yellow flag, and Jimmy quickly donned his helmet. His crew stepped away, and soon the car was re-fired. He fell in behind Graffan, and as they approached the start he studied the leader intently, trying to match his start.

Graffan stepped on the gas, but the Strong sprinter spun the tires. The Ellison car gripped the track beautifully, and Jimmy swept past on the inside, immediately pulling to an advantage of several car lengths. As they passed the flag stand Jimmy realized the starter was simply holding the green flag; this one was coming back.

Jimmy cursed under his breath, and sure enough the yellow light blinked on as they roared down the backstretch. Jimmy eased up on the throttle, allowing Graffan to move back in front, and as they approached the flag stand the starter was pointing a furled black flag at Jimmy as a warning. Fellow official Leon Hartke shook his finger ominously at Jimmy as he slowly idled past.

"I didn't jump, you idiots!" Jimmy muttered. "He spun his tires!"

The last thing he needed was a penalty, so he played it conservatively on the next try. This time Graffan had a better start, and Jimmy followed him to turn one. It was soon evident that Harvey had helped the Ellison sprinter more than Billy Hobbs had helped Graffan. The question was, would it be enough?

Jimmy noticed that Graffan was struggling to get the car into turn one, becoming slightly more cautious with each lap. As they moved down the front straightaway, Jimmy allowed his momentum to carry him alongside Graffan as they approached the corner. By the time Graffan realized Jimmy was coming, it was too late. The Ellison car edged ahead of Graffan coming off turn two, and in a moment Jimmy could no longer hear him.

Now, just keep him back there, Jimmy thought, wrestling the car through three and four. He concentrated on hitting his line perfectly into one, listening carefully for Graffan. Through the corner, down the backstretch, again through three and four, past the flag stand, still no sign of him. Jimmy began to breathe, determined not to make any mistakes.

As he came off turn two he saw the caution lights blink on, and he immediately eased up on the throttle. He rumbled carefully through three and four, when he spotted a car sitting in the outer regions of the track in turn one, facing the wrong way. Bobby Mancini.

He flexed his hands, stretching and clenching his fingers. After a couple of laps under caution he saw an official waving at him on the front straightaway. As he drew closer he could see the official waving Graffan back into the lead.

"No way!" Jimmy screamed inside his helmet. "We made a full lap! No way!"

Graffan quickly moved past, but just as quickly Jimmy raced back alongside him, shaking his head vigorously. Another official walked onto the track on the backstretch, emphatically waving Jimmy back to second place.

The two cars were still side-by-side as they approached the flag stand, where several officials waved at Jimmy to yield the point.

Jimmy caught sight of Harvey, who had walked clear out onto the track to confront Leon Hartke.

When they next approached the front straightaway, the starter had climbed from the flag stand, and was pointing the furled black flag at Jimmy. His message was clear: Get back in line now, or you're done. Jimmy clenched his teeth and slowed, pulling behind Graffan. He waved at the official in disgust, so angry he was shaking.

The race quickly got back underway, but this time the savvy Graffan was ready for him. He moved around and found a faster line, and Jimmy was unable to make a run on him in that corner.

The next few laps saw a torrid duel between the archrivals. Jimmy was faster, but Graffan used all his tricks to stay out front. His drive was superb, his talent helping make up for his steadily slipping race car.

With three laps to go Jimmy had enough momentum to get alongside, and Graffan fought back desperately. They raced into turn three where Graffan managed to pull slightly ahead. Their momentum carried them both a couple of widths off the inside line, and Jimmy's eyes widened as he saw a cavernous hole approaching. He instinctively lifted the throttle and steered toward the hole, trying to hit it straight on.

Graffan wasn't so fortunate; his car slammed into the hole with such force his hands were torn from the wheel, and Jimmy saw Graffan's head lurch violently. His car bicycled wildly, and for a moment Jimmy thought Graffan would collect him, but just as quickly Graffan grabbed the wheel and regained his composure.

But the stumble had cost Graffan dearly, and the screams of the Strong sprinter quickly faded as Jimmy drove the last two laps alone in the lead. He flashed under the checkered flag, raising his fist in celebration of three straight wins.

He rumbled to a stop on the front straightaway, where Harvey and Slim awaited. Harvey was still incensed about the restart, but finally offered a handshake and a relieved grin. Jimmy climbed from the car, waving as the crowd saluted him with a loud cheer.

"You were dead-on with that wrench," he told Harvey. "You helped the car a bunch on that red."

"Don't I always?" Harvey grinned.

"No," Jimmy laughed. "Not always."

Jimmy saw Al Petrov approaching, and before Al could open his mouth Jimmy and Harvey both were vigorously voicing their displeasure.

"Good God Almighty, Al," Jimmy said, shaking his head. "Could they screw us any worse than that? What's the matter with you guys?"

"The entire field didn't get a lap in," Al said calmly. "That's a fact, Jimmy. The call was right."

"Aw, bullshit," yelled Harvey. "They damn near made TWO laps! If you'd get your head outta your ass, you'd a seen it! You guys are a bunch of damned crooks!"

Al started to speak, then shook his head. He simply looked at Jimmy as he turned to walk away.

"You drove a great race," he nodded. Then he walked back toward the infield, crowding through the gaggle of people who had begun to congregate.

Jimmy and Harvey looked at each other and shook their heads.

"It's gonna be like this, boy," Harvey insisted. "We're winnin' races, and we ain't gonna get a break. They'll make it as hard as they can for us."

There was a buzz of activity surrounding the Strong sprinter, parked on the track a few feet away. They turned to look as people crowded around the car, chattering excitedly.

"What's goin' on over there?" Slim wondered.

"He hit that hole a ton," Jimmy said quickly. "I wouldn't be surprised if he busted a rib or something."

Jimmy was approached by the P.A. announcer, who moved in for an interview.

"My goodness, that's three straight wins," said the announcer. "What's the secret behind your great start this season?"

Jimmy pointed to Harvey and Slim.

"No secrets," he insisted. "These guys…Jack Harvey and Slim MacDonald…they gave me a great car. We're all pretty confident, and things are just falling our way, I guess. We're working real well right now."

"Tell me, could you have passed Steve if he hadn't gotten in trouble there in three? Looked like he almost turned over."

"Yeah, he sure did, that was a nasty hole down there. I think I would have got him…our car was better, he was awfully loose. If I hadn't gotten him down there, I'd have done it at the other end."

The announcer seemed surprised by his answer, and Jimmy heard a smattering of boos in the stands. The reaction caught Jimmy off guard, and he looked at Harvey and Slim and shook his head in amazement.

"Well, Jimmy, you're always an honest interview," the man continued. "Now, tell me…next up is Sunset Park, one week from today. Can you win again? Four in a row?"

"Absolutely," Jimmy smiled. "We're going to keep winning. We'll just race as hard as we can, and see if they can catch us."

The crowd offered a mixture of cheers and boos, and Jimmy waved. He smiled broadly, but deep inside he was surprised and hurt by the boos. Why would anyone be against him? He hadn't done anything bad to anyone.

Third-place Rusty Fernandez stood nearby, and several track officials quickly organized a winner's photo.

"Is Steve coming?" one of the officials called, looking toward Graffan's car. "Oh…yes, here he comes!"

Graffan was slowly making his way toward them. He had ice packs on his neck and shoulders, and he gingerly grasped the ribs on the right side of his chest. Jimmy almost felt sympathy pains as Graffan carefully walked with slow, plodding steps.

He looked up at Jimmy, shaking his head.

"You're lucky," he groused. "If I hadn't hit that hole, you weren't gonna win this one."

Jimmy just chuckled. "Oh, I don't know," he mused. "I was a bunch faster than you, Graffan. It was only a matter of time."

"No way," Graffan said, wincing. "First Mancini has a flat, then I hit that hole…you were just lucky. That's all."

Jimmy grinned, and the officials herded the three men close together. Jimmy cradled the trophy in his right arm, extending his left hand out with the checkered flag. Before the photographers began clicking their pictures, Jimmy leaned toward Graffan.

"Why, thank you, Steve…I'm glad you care so much…here, I'll let you hold my flag if you ask real nice." As soon as he spoke Jimmy realized he was probably getting over the line a little bit, and he wished he hadn't said it. But he was just having some fun. Graffan slapped the flag to the ground, getting in Jimmy's face. "That's it," he snarled. "Keep runnin' your mouth…I'm gonna knock you on your ass."

Suddenly it didn't seem funny to Jimmy, and he felt his cheeks and ears redden. He quickly sat the trophy down and stepped close to Graffan.

"Mister, I'm right here," he said through clenched teeth. "Any time you want to try me on, I'm ready. I've been waitin' for this."

The officials quickly stepped in, and Rusty placed one of his massive paws on Jimmy's shoulders and gently coaxed him away.

"C'mon, man," Rusty chided. "Can't you two guys even do a picture without getting in each other's face?"

Jimmy saw Al Petrov standing a few feet away, giving them both a withering stare. Jimmy picked the trophy back up, and stood a couple of feet from Graffan.

"You want a picture, take it," he barked at the photographers. "I'm outta here."

Harvey stood nearby, leaning on the cage of the Ellison sprinter. The big man was grinning, eyes surveying the tense scene.

He looked at Slim, nodding his head.

"Got 'em right where we want 'em, Slim," he laughed. "Right where we want 'em."

Chapter 6

The Ellison sprinter clawed at the steep banking of Sunset Park as Jimmy roared through turn one. It was only warmups, and already Jimmy was grinning.

"Perfect," he whispered to himself. "This car is perfect."

After a couple of laps the starter waved the checkered flag, and Jimmy rolled to their pit and cut the engine. Harvey was waiting, and as Jimmy climbed out they both stared at the car for a moment.

"Feel okay?" Harvey finally offered.

"Pretty good," Jimmy nodded. "Probably don't need to touch it."

Harvey nodded, a smirk playing cross his lips. "I got it perfect, didn't I? C'mon boy, tell it like it is...'ol Harvey did it again, didn't he?"

"Ahh...it's okay," Jimmy grunted. "I'll make it work."

Harvey leaned his head back and guffawed. "You won't say it, 'eh? That's all right, boy. I'll look for fast time here in a little bit."

Jimmy walked to the pickup in front of the little open trailer and opened the door. He poured some cool water from a jug, drinking deeply from a cup.

"So, you gonna make it four in a row?" came the voice of Barry Kane, a well-known writer with a racing paper.

"Yep," Jimmy smiled. "I hope so. How you doin', Barry?"

"I'm fine. You've definately got the other boys thinkin', I'll say that. Rumor is that your car will be protested today."

"Is that right?"

"That's the talk. Jimmy, people think you're using a big engine. Any truth to that?"

Jimmy laughed. "Barry, think about that...if Harvey had some kind of secret, would he tell me about it? C'mon, you know better than that."

"Well, you're the driver. Is it possible?"

Jimmy thought for a moment. "Ah," he scoffed. "I gotta get ready to qualify."

He immediately slid into the seat. Harvey and Slim rolled the car toward the push-off lane, and soon Jimmy was pulling onto the fearsome high-banked half-mile. He bobbled slightly on his first lap, missing his mark going into turn one. But he quickly recovered and his second lap was a scorcher.

Moments later as Jimmy wheeled into their pit Slim playfully batted his helmet. Even though the words were muffled through the helmet, Jimmy couldn't mistake his message or emotion.

"New record," Slim shouted. "Took almost a tenth off the old one!"

Jimmy nodded, climbing from the car. He noticed how quickly onlookers had congregated around their pit, just as he saw Harvey approaching after watching the run from turn four.

"Glad you could make the old pig work," Harvey said soberly.

"Took everything I had," Jimmy said, trying not to smile.

The track announcer asked Jimmy to come to the front straightaway for an interview, and soon he found himself looking across at the grandstand, packed with people on a sunny Sunday afternoon. As he was introduced he again heard a smattering of boos, mostly drowned out by applause.

The announcer asked Jimmy why they had been going so well. Jimmy gave him the usual line about working together as a team, and the announcer pressed a bit.

"Jimmy, you're three-for-three this season. I have to say, there's lots of talk that you folks have found some speed secrets, if you know what I mean. Things nobody else has. What about it?"

Jimmy looked at the man for a second, then smiled. "Well, you never know," he said coyly. "Say, isn't this a beautiful day? I'm just glad all these folks came out to watch us race. We'll try to give 'em a good show."

He heard laughter in the crowd, and applause. Jimmy waved, and the interview was over.

"Harvey, I just realized something," Jimmy said as they hung around their car.

"What's that?"

"Coffman...he hasn't come to the last couple of races."

Harvey paused thoughtfully. "Say...you're right! I ain't seen him since Jefferson!"

"Maybe Sonny talked to him...I'm glad you told him what was going on. Coffman and his sleazy wife were unbearable."

"I didn't tell him," Harvey insisted. "I thought you talked to him."

"No, never had the chance. Hmmm...maybe Coffman got bored and moved on to something else."

"That's probably it," Harvey agreed. "That's how it is with rich people...they move around so they can be a pain in everybody's ass."

"Doesn't matter to me what the reason is," Jimmy nodded. "I'm just glad they aren't here. That whole bunch was a pain. Still...kinda weird how he just disappeared."

An official walked past their pit, calling the first heat to the lineup chute. Jimmy stepped to the car and in a moment they were on the track.

It was a competitive heat, and Jimmy found himself battling Bobby for the lead on the final lap. Bobby was giving Jimmy fits; Jimmy had him passed two laps ago, but Bobby stormed back by with an aggressive move to the inside.

Jimmy felt his car slip as he pulled alongside going into turn three. Bobby gave him just enough room as they came off the corner. Jimmy instinctively drifted left to avoid clipping the oncoming wall, watching helplessly as Bobby pulled three feet ahead at the finish.

He drove back to his pit, where Harvey and Slim waited. Jimmy climbed from the car and wiped his face, catching his breath.

"Looked loose," Harvey said, waiting.

"Yeah, but not bad," Jimmy answered. "I wouldn't change much, Harvey. Matter of fact, leave it alone. The problem was me."

Harvey looked shocked. "Whad'ya mean, you?"

"I just didn't get into a rhythm. It was only 10 laps, and the feature is 40. We'll be all right...the car doesn't need anything. Trust me."

Harvey eyed him suspiciously, saying nothing for a few moments. "Well, okay," he said grudgingly, turning away.

Jimmy walked a few cars down, where Bobby and his car owner, Fred Otley, were deep in conversation. Jimmy didn't want to interrupt, so he stood several feet away, waiting.

"There's the old sandbagger," Fred called out.

"Sandbagger?" Jimmy said, shaking his head as he walked toward them. "What'ya mean?"

"You know what I'm talkin' about," Fred said emphatically. Jimmy was surprised at the sharpness to his tone. "You drove by us, then let up. Ain't hard to see what you're up to."

Jimmy looked at Bobby, then back at Fred. "I don't get it."

"Aw, bull," Fred countered. "Don't play innocent, Jimmy. It's obvious you guys are easing up, trying not to show too much. It ain't workin', though. Somebody is gonna put up the money to check you, sooner or later. And then they'll find out what's goin' on with that race car."

For a minute Jimmy just looked at him with surprise. Fred was normally easy and laid back, and Jimmy wasn't sure how to reply. Fred just snorted and walked away, busying himself in his tool box. Bobby nodded in the other direction, and he and Jimmy began walking away.

"What's eatin' him?" Jimmy asked his friend.

"Aw, he's just uptight. You guys goin' good, that's got everybody thinking something's going on."

"Do you think we're cheating?"

"You must be," Bobby laughed. "If a no-drivin' SOB like you can win three in a row, you must be cheating."

"Yeah, sure," Jimmy nodded. "I can always count on you to give it to me straight, Bobby."

The afternoon seemed to pass quickly, and soon Jimmy was rumbling around the track, watching as the field fell into order for the feature race. He made his way to the outside of row three, then prepared himself for the start.

The field moved down the backstretch, and Jimmy saw the yellow light go out. Taut with anticipation, his right foot trembled slightly as he waited for exactly the right moment to accelerate.

As the cars rolled through turn four they suddenly screamed in unison, and Jimmy felt his tires slip slightly as he pressed the throttle. It was a nice, smooth start, and Jimmy flashed into turn four staring at the back bumper of Sammy Caldwell.

He quickly passed Sammy on the outside, then moved by Bobby on the front straightaway. Five laps into the race, he was right behind leader Steve Graffan.

He bided his time, studying Graffan. He noticed how Graffan had to wait on the car in the middle of the corner, and he planned his move. As they entered turn one he carefully laid back, then came on strong in the middle of the corner to gain momentum going into turn three.

The Ellison car moved to the left of Graffan, forcing him to yield the inside line. The car stuck beautifully in the lower groove, and as they came off the corner Jimmy could no longer hear the Bob Strong-owned Sprinter.

In no time Jimmy was into traffic, trying to maintain his rhythm. He was stuck behind Rusty Fernandez and a car unfamiliar to him, a yellow 66. They raced hard, side-by-side, with Jimmy helpless but to ride behind them. Finally Rusty managed to pull ahead, and the yellow car dropped back to the inside.

Jimmy prepared to pass, but hesitated. Something told him to wait, something he couldn't exactly explain. As they entered turn one, Jimmy saw the yellow car suddenly snap sideways, then spin wildly across Jimmy's nose. Jimmy had left himself plenty of room to brake, turn left, and miss the car as it spun to a stop.

The remainder of the race was uneventful as Jimmy cruised to the finish. He rolled to a stop on the front straightaway, climbing from the car to see Harvey and Slim hurrying over.

Jimmy noticed how they seemed so complacent. There was no celebrating, no shouting, just a matter-of-fact tone that they had done what there were supposed to do: win the race.

"You're still dinkin' around with traffic," Harvey said flatly. "You're not aggressive like you need to be."

"I'm exactly as aggressive as I need to be," Jimmy argued. "Look at where we finished, Harvey."

"Hmmmph. Whatever."

"You're getting greedy," Jimmy insisted.

"And you're gettin' soft," Harvey countered.

Jimmy shrugged, turning to see the PA man approaching. As he began the interview, Jimmy noticed that Harvey and Slim had quickly moved the car toward their pit. In a moment they had the car on the trailer, quickly stowing their gear.

As the victory ceremonies concluded Harvey had backed the trailer out and was trying to leave. He was parked right at the track gate, waiting for it to be opened.

Jimmy walked toward him, wondering what was going on. He gave Harvey a curious look as the big man stared.

"I left your stuff where we were pitted," he told Jimmy. "We need to get goin.'"

He winked at Jimmy, who was now a little confused. Suddenly Jimmy saw Bob Strong, Graffan, Fred Otley, and several racers approaching, trailing USAC officials Al Petrov and Leon Hartke.

"What's your hurry, Harvey?" Strong shouted. "Trying to make a quick getaway?"

"Al, tell 'em to open this damned gate," Harvey yelled. "I'm ready to go."

The men all began talking at once, clearly agitated. Al held up his hands to quiet them.

"Jack, there's been a protest filed," he said to Harvey. "We'll need to check your car."

Harvey looked at his watch, then back at Petrov. "You're too late, Al. They had their time after the race, and it's too late now. We're free and clear."

"No, they came to me within the allotted time," Al said, his tone calm and even. "Their protest is valid, and we'll have to check your car."

Harvey hesitated. "We're already loaded. Let's check it next race."

The men began shouting in anger, and Al shook his head.

"You know better than that, Jack. Just turn around and drive back to your pit, and we'll get started."

The lights in the barroom were dim as Jimmy and Bobby sat across from each other in a booth. A jukebox played country tunes, and a haze of cigarette smoke hung in the air. They talked about sports, they talked about women, they even talked about the weather; it was clear they were trying to stay away from talking about racing.

"Sandy's a great cook," Jimmy offered. "Thanks for such a great dinner. And thanks for letting me stay over this weekend."

"Ah, no problem. Figured you'd be bored, sitting out in the sticks on an off weekend. Besides, it gave me an excuse to get out of the house on a Friday night."

"Like you need an excuse...hey, is that your buddy Whitey?"

"Where?"

"Over there, at the corner table. Got two chicks with him."

"Wow...now that's a nice set. Let's go check it out."

They grabbed their beer and walked over. Whitey waved when he spotted them, and they each grabbed a chair.

Whitey was an avid sprint car fan who lived down the street from Bobby. He was something of a hippie, with long hair and a beaded necklace. Whenever anybody asked what he did for a living, Whitey was always vague; Jimmy suspected he sold pot.

"Hey, what happened with the deal at Sunset," Whitey quizzed Jimmy. "Were you guys legal?"

"A hundred percent," Jimmy said with satisfaction.

"No kiddin'...I'll bet ol' Strong was hot, after putting up the money to have you checked. Nothin' else came of it?"

"We still think he's cheating," Bobby laughed, pointing at Jimmy. "We just don't know how. C'mon, killer, tell us your secret!"

Jimmy shook his head. "I'm tellin' you, Bobby, I don't have a clue. I just show up and drive."

Bobby nudged Whitey. "Aren't you gonna introduce us?"

The two girls with Whitey were good-looking, and young. Jimmy quickly figured out that the dark-haired girl was with Whitey, and Bobby had already zeroed in on the blonde.

"We're only gonna be here a minute," Whitey explained. "There's a blues show at Zaks, and we're headin' over there as soon as we finish our drinks."

"Really? I love the blues!" Bobby offered. "We'll come along!"

"Far out!" Whitey nodded. "It would be cool to have two sprint car brothers with us. You can follow us over!"

"No, no, no," Bobby said quickly, nudging closer to the blonde. "Let's leave my car here, and we'll ride with you guys."

Jimmy laughed under his breath, wondering how in the hell Bobby had stayed married this long.

Chapter 7

The club was old, and crowded. It was located in a tough neighborhood on the north side of Central City, and they grabbed the last open table, near the back. Soon they were enveloped by the raw, rich blues music.

"These guys are great," Jimmy said over the loud music to Bobby, but his words were unheard. Bobby and the young blonde were all over each other, and Jimmy was amazed at Bobby's brazen behavior.

He leaned back in his chair, sipping his beer and enjoying the excellent music. He looked casually around the room when his eyes fell upon a crowded table across the way. For a moment he felt an instinctive tightness in his stomach before he allowed himself to relax.

Steve Graffan was seated among a half-dozen people, none of whom Jimmy had seen before. They were laughing and enjoying the music, when Graffan happened to look up and their gazes met.

Graffan's face turned hard, and he stared. Jimmy gently lifted his beer in hello, offering a slight smile. Graffan's expression was unchanged, and Jimmy turned his attention back to the stage.

For the next half-hour Jimmy tried not to look their way, focusing on the show. Bobby reached over and tapped him on the shoulder.

"Did you see him?"

"Yeah, a little while ago."

"You want to leave?"

"Nah. There won't be any trouble. It's cool."

They had been at the club nearly an hour when the band took a break. The house lights were up just a bit, and they talked about the great band.

Bobby nudged Jimmy. "Don't look now, but our friend is coming over."

Jimmy nodded. In a moment Graffan was standing at their table, and Jimmy could see from his vacant look that he was loaded.

"You're a cheat," he slurred, looking directly at Jimmy.

"Go away," Jimmy said quietly. "We don't want any trouble."

"You're a cheat and a liar," Graffan persisted. "I'm gonna knock your head off, right here."

Jimmy felt his cheeks flush, and he tried to stay calm. "I told you to go away," he said, staying in his chair.

Graffan leaned over him menacingly. "I'm gonna do something I shoulda done a year ago," he slurred. "You want it in here, or outside?"

"You ain't gonna do nothin' in here," came a powerful voice behind them. A large black man in a white shirt and black vest stepped closer. "You guys have a problem, take it outside."

For a minute they just looked at the man.

"I'm not askin'," the man insisted. "Either go outside, or get back to your seat."

"You're a chicken shit," Graffan grinned. "Just like I figured."

"Outside," Jimmy barked, rising from his chair. He pulled his wallet from his pocket and dropped a bill on the table.

Graffan nodded and headed for the door. Bobby put his hand on Jimmy's shoulder.

"This is a really bad idea," he said, shaking his head. "Really bad."

"Doesn't matter," Jimmy said, his teeth clenched. "I'm sick of just thinking about it."

They walked to the back door, stepping down two worn concrete steps. Cars were parked all around, with a small open area along the alley near the back of the lot. Graffan walked to the clearing, and Jimmy followed.

Jimmy slipped his watch off and handed it to Bobby. He saw Graffan's two friends leaning against a car.

"Watch my back," he whispered, and Bobby nodded.

Jimmy stepped toward Graffan, who swung wildly and missed. Jimmy stepped inside and delivered a sharp right to Graffan's mouth, drawing blood. Graffan answered with a left that landed solidly, and the two men were quickly locked in a clench, falling to the ground.

They rolled into the alley, where small bits of gravel cut at their backs and elbows. Jimmy had him in a head lock, but before he could land any solid punches Graffan escaped, his fingers scratching Jimmy's face.

The two men grunted, gasping for air, their struggle the only sound as the others looked on. Jimmy used his left forearm to push Graffan away, and drilled him in the nose with a hard right. Blood began running down Graffan's face, small red droplets dotting both men.

Jimmy again tried to get Graffan in a head lock, but when Graffan jerked upwards his skull smashed hard against Jimmy's chin, clouding his vision with bright white splotches. Jimmy felt the warm taste of blood in his mouth, and felt Graffan's body stiffen as he swung. The first punch glanced harmlessly off the side of Jimmy's head, but the second landed squarely on Jimmy's cheek.

The taste of blood enraged Jimmy, and he managed to get on top of Graffan, trying to bounce his head on the ground. The two men wrestled, their arms locked together as they got to their knees.

As they grappled Jimmy heard the sound of cloth tearing. He opened his eyes to see Graffan's chest and belly, uncovered through his torn shirt. Jimmy brought his right hand back and delivered his fist hard into Graffan's gut, feeling the man almost gag from the blow. He drew back and hit again, and Graffan fell to the ground, their arms still entangled.

Graffan was really sucking air, yet he fought wildly. The two men rolled across the alley, along a grassy berm, rolling over and over until Jimmy felt small, piercing pangs of pain in his back, then his knees. He realized they were now lying in loose dirt.

Graffan was on his back, trying to connect with punches that were growing weaker. Jimmy grabbed Graffan's left arm and pushed it away, landing a glancing punch on Graffan's chin.

He could sense that Graffan was fading. He tightened his grip on Graffan's left arm, holding it so the man's face was wide open.

Jimmy tried to speak, but had to catch his breath. "You...had...enough?" he wheezed.

Graffan offered only a profanity, and Jimmy hit him solidly on the mouth. For a moment he thought he had knocked him out, but Graffan squirmed and tried to break free of Jimmy's hold.

Suddenly a door from a nearby home burst open, and an elderly black woman came rushing outside, followed by two small dogs yapping their heads off.

"You get out my garden," the woman screamed. "Look at my plants! Y'all stop fightin'! Get out right now!"

Jimmy strengthened his grip on Graffan's arms, and his foe vainly struggled. Jimmy drew back his fist, ready to hit him again.

"I'm done," Graffan panted. "Don't hit me anymore."

"You young fools! I gone go call the po-lice right now," the woman shouted, disappearing into the house.

"C'mon, man, she's callin' the cops!" Whitey shouted excitedly. "We gotta split!"

"Say it louder," Jimmy commanded, his fist still drawn. "I want them to hear it."

"I'm done," Graffan said loudly. "Just get off me...somethin's stabbing my back."

Jimmy stood, swaying from exhaustion. He leaned down to grasp Graffan's hands, helping him to his feet. Jimmy turned Graffan around, and he discovered a small wire cone hanging from his shirt. Graffan's buddy steadied him while Jimmy untangled the flattened cone and dropped it to the ground.

Jimmy looked around, and saw they were indeed in the woman's garden. A dozen tomato plants were smashed, along with small wire cones. That explained the piercing pain he felt each time they rolled over.

"Please, man, the cops are coming," Whitey pleaded. "I'm leaving right now...if you guys are coming, let's get it on."

Jimmy looked at Graffan, both men still struggling to catch their breath. Jimmy and Graffan stared at one another as they gasped.

"This is over," Jimmy said. Graffan just nodded, turning to follow his buddy to their car.

They hurried toward Whitey's car and jumped in. Whitey quickly cranked the engine, squealing his tires as they tore from the lot. They hadn't gone a mile when two police cruisers raced past, headed toward Zaks.

"That was a close one," Whitey breathed. "It would be, like, so totally not cool to have the cops searching my car, man."

Jimmy leaned back in the front seat, suddenly realizing that every part of his body was hurting. He looked at his bloodied hands, gently rubbing his throbbing knuckles. His lower lip was badly swollen, and his right cheek burned. He knew there would be a shiner by tomorrow.

"I'm so totally bummed out by you, Jimmy," Whitey lectured. "I thought you were, like, a peaceful brother, dude. But you acted like a redneck, man. That's so totally not cool."

Jimmy leaned his head against the headrest, his body trembling with fatigue. "Shut up, Whitey," he said quietly. "Just get us home."

"Sorry I messed up your night," Jimmy said as they stood at Bobby's car. "That little blonde was cute."

"Ah, don't worry about it," Bobby said, examining Jimmy's face. "Probably kept me out of trouble. You sure you're okay?"

"I think so," Jimmy said, managing a weak smile. "Boy, if it feels this bad to win, I'd hate to think what it feels like to lose."

"You don't do this often?" Bobby teased.

"Not since, oh, fourth grade," Jimmy said, wincing as he touched his lip. "How bad is my lip busted?"

"It's not split. But you're gonna have a helluva black eye."

"Hey, something really hurts back here," Jimmy said suddenly. "The back of my head, and along my lower back."

Bobby turned him around, and laughed. "You got gravel stuck all through your hair," he said, gently brushing it away. "It's inside your shirt, too. There, that should do it. Let's go get something on those cuts."

A few minutes later they walked in the front door of Bobby's place. Sandy Mancini looked up from her magazine and gasped in surprise. "Oh, my gosh," she nearly shouted, jumping from her chair. "Jimmy, what happened?"

"Said the wrong thing about you, and I took care of him," Bobby said, puffing out his chest. "Look, honey, not a mark on me!"

"Stop being funny! For heaven's sake, Jimmy, get in the kitchen here where I can look at you. Did you have an accident?"

"You might say that," Bobby smiled.

"Just a fight," Jimmy said, embarrassed.

"A fight! Are you serious? That's not like you at all, Jimmy! What happened?"

"Aw...Graffan."

"You...you got into a fight with Steve Graffan! Are you serious? That's terrible! Why on earth would you do such a thing?"

"He didn't have a choice," Bobby insisted. "Graffan started the whole thing...it's better this way, anyhow. It's been brewing for a long time, and it was time they got it out of their system."

"I don't see how fighting helps anything," Sandy said, wiping Jimmy's face as he winced in pain. "Where did it happen?"

"A place called Zaks."

Sandy's eyes narrowed and she looked sharply at Bobby. "Why'd you go over there? I thought you and Jimmy were just going to Bernie's for a couple of beers."

"We did," Bobby said casually. "Ran into Whitey, and he told us about a really good blues band at Zaks. Rode over there with him."

"Just Whitey?"

"Naw, he was with a couple of friends of his. You know, fellow hippies."

"Hmmm. Here, Jimmy, take your shirt off. My gosh, look at all those little cuts. You're going to get some infection if we don't clean them out. Let me get some soap and water."

She hurried to the bathroom, and came back with a washcloth. "This is going to sound silly, but...who won?"

Jimmy looked at Bobby, and shook his head. "He quit first," he said softly. "But...right now it sure doesn't feel like I won anything."

"That's exactly right," Sandy said quickly. "Now, this is going to hurt, Jimmy....sorry...here, I'm almost done, just a few more with the iodine...there, that's it. Seems funny, you guys hanging around with Whitey. Who were his friends?"

Bobby looked blankly at Jimmy. "I didn't catch their names," he said quickly. "Did you?"

"Nope," Jimmy answered. "I was too busy rolling around in the gravel."

Jimmy wheeled from the hardware store parking lot, steering his truck onto the wide city boulevard. He drove past aging old homes and overgrown lots, past graffiti-covered fences and vacant buildings.

He slowed as he eyed the intersection. This one? No, maybe the next. Then he saw the familiar sign, and turned into the alley.

He rolled to a stop in the parking lot, empty and peaceful on the sunny Sunday afternoon. He walked across the alley and up the front steps where he knocked on the door.

Instantly there was feverish yapping, and a moment later the door opened. The two little dogs jumped against the screen door, barking furiously at the stranger.

The woman eyed him suspiciously through the screen, and Jimmy felt her gaze linger on his blackened eye.

"I'm sorry to bother you, ma'am...but I was one of those guys in your garden the other night, and I thought..."

"What 'chu want?" she said quickly.

"Well, we tore up your plants, and I figured...well, I got some more tomato plants to replace the ones we damaged. If you'll show me what to do, I'll plant them in your garden."

She stared. "Don't you go messin' wit' a helpless old woman," she said. "I'll go upside yo' head."

"I'm not kidding," Jimmy insisted. "I've got the plants, here in my truck. I wanted to make it right, and tell you I'm sorry."

She stared intently at him, and her gaze began to soften. "You sho'nuff tellin' the truth, child? You gon' replace my tomato plants?"

"Yes, ma'am, but I don't know if I remember how to plant them. Just show me how, and I'll take care it."

She hesitated a moment, then smiled. "You bring those plants over here, honey. I'll meet you in the back."

He hurried to the truck, and lifted the tray of plants. She came out the back, walking from her tiny yard into the large, unfenced garden.

"Why, you *is* tellin' the truth," she grinned broadly, examing the plants. "These is fine plants, honey. Let me get my tools, and we'll get 'em right into the ground!"

He looked at the garden, and saw where she had tried to straighten some of the plants in an effort to save them. She had also tried to repair the flattened wire cones, but they remained bent and crooked.

The woman chatted happily as she showed Jimmy how to set the plants, her weathered hands making it look easy. He slowly followed her lead, trying to get the plants straight and at the right depth.

"This is quite a garden you've got here," he said, wiping his brow. "Do you eat all this stuff?"

"This here is the Lord's bounty, child. He sees me through the winter with this...God hisself blessed this dirt, black and rich. Tomatoes, corn, beans, radish, potatoes, it's a gift. You like to eat bread?"

"Bread? Sure."

"I done baked some bread, and we'll have some. Coffee, too. You done good on those plants, they nice and straight. C'mon in and wash yo' hands."

"Oh, just one second," he said, trotting to this truck. He carried several new wire cones back, handing them to the lady.

"Yours got all bent up," he said.

"Well, you really is an angel," she beamed. "These are right fine, child. Mine was old as the sun."

"They might've been old, but they were sure still sharp," Jimmy said, rubbing his back and wincing.

She leaned her head back and laughed easily, her eyes flashing with good humor. Jimmy followed her into the small house, and she pointed toward the sink.

"They's soap right there," she said. "How you like yo' coffee?"

"Black," he smiled, leaning over the sink. The warm scent of fresh-baked bread filled the room, and he was soon seated at the small wooden table. The little dogs pestered him for attention, and he patted their heads.

"Shoo, you dogs," she said. "Mind yo' manners. Child, I don't even know your name."

"Jimmy," he smiled, lifting the knife to spread some preserves on his bread.

"My name is Nadeen. You such a good boy...what you doin' hanging around that devil's house over there? They ain't nothin' there but fightin' and sin, every night. Loud music and noise, and fightin'. Why such a good boy like you, hangin' roun' a place like that?"

"Aw...me and that other guy, it's been coming for a long time. But it's all right now. We got it over with, and there won't be any more problems."

"Well, that's good, honey."

He studied her peaceful expression as she ate the bread. She broke away small bits of it now and then, dropping it to the begging dogs.

"This bread is fantastic," he nodded. "And the preserves...what kind is this?"

"Rhubarb," she smiled. "Right from this yard, child. I tol' you, this here is the Lord's bounty. He always provides."

Jimmy nodded. "I need to get going," he said finally, petting the dogs as they put their paws on his leg. "I've got an hour drive home."

She walked him to the front door, carefully stepping down the steps to the sidewalk. She put her weathered hand on his face, and smiled broadly.

"I declare, the Lord done sent an angel to fix my plants. You like tomatoes, child?"

"I love 'em."

"Well, you come back here and have some tomatoes later this summer. Remember, the good Lord gives us our rewards from what we plant. All right, honey?"

"All right," he laughed. "I'll see you later, Nadeen. And thanks for the bread."

He slowly eased out of the parking lot, steering back onto the wide street. She waved as he drove away, her apron blowing gently in the breeze.

Somehow, he felt better. Except for his busted lip, black eye, sore neck, and burning cuts on his back and shoulders, that is. He felt better.

Chapter 8

Jimmy leaned against the porch railing, grinning as the two small children clamored for his attention. The older Mancini boy was telling Jimmy about his new goldfish, while the smaller child grinned and offered Jimmy a bite of his sandwich. Jimmy hoisted the kid into his arms, and pretended to take large bites from the sandwich as the child laughed.

"Guys, easy on our friend," Sandy Mancini smiled. "Sorry, Jimmy, but they get so excited when they hear you're coming over. You're like a long-lost uncle or something."

"I don't mind," Jimmy insisted. "They're good kids…besides, I'm not around kids much, so it's kind of fun."

"Really? I'll remember that next time they're wearing me out. I'll call you and you can take 'em for a while."

"Fine by me. Where's your biggest kid? Isn't he ready?"

"He's upstairs. Running late, as usual."

"Hey, Bobby!" Jimmy shouted into the house. "C'mon, we need to get on the road!"

"Yeah, yeah," came the voice from inside. "Hey, Sandy, where's my blue driving suit? Didn't you wash it?"

She looked at Jimmy and rolled her eyes. "Hanging in the closet, where it always is!" she called out. "Yes, I washed it."

In a moment Bobby burst outside, leaning down to kiss the two children, then Sandy.

"Win the race, daddy!" said the older boy.

"Nope, sorry," Jimmy teased. "Daddy isn't allowed to win any races this year…I'm gonna win 'em all."

"Hey!" the boy protested. "No fair! My daddy says you're cheating!"

Jimmy laughed out loud. "Wow! Is that right?" he said, feigning hurt feelings. "You told your kid I'm cheating?"

Bobby held up his hands defensively. "I didn't say that…what

I said was, if a slug like you can win four races in a row, there must be something awfully special about that race car."

"Yeah, well, thanks, ol' buddy."

"C'mon, let's get rolling," Bobby said anxiously. "I'm not even sure how to get to the race track. Do you know?"

"Yep, ran there a few times, in the bad old days. It's about 60 miles the other side of the Illinois state line. Thanks for driving, by the way."

"No problem. What's wrong with your truck?"

"I think a U-joint is going out. I didn't want to risk trying to fix it off the side of the road somewhere in the middle of the night."

They climbed into Bobby's car, and he started the engine and pulled the shift lever into reverse. Sandy leaned into the window and gently put her finger on the tip of his chin.

"You behave, Mr. Mancini," she smiled. "No monkey business."

"Aw, quit worryin', will ya? I got Jimmy to look after me."

"Hmmm...well, you behave, the both of you. Be safe, and good luck."

He nodded, and backed out of the drive. The children shouted and waved as they drove away.

Jimmy stared at the young family, the smile fading from his face, replaced by an empty, yearning look. "That's a nice-looking bunch, Bobby," he said quietly. "You're pretty lucky."

"Yeah, I guess I am. But it ain't always what it's cracked up to be."

"How so?"

"I dunno...I guess I just got married too young. I was only 18...I never got a chance to be a kid, really. Next thing you know, you've got two kids and a house payment and sometimes the walls close in on you."

"Why'd you get married, then?"

"She was pregnant...what else you gonna do?"

Jimmy nodded. "I still say you're lucky. She's a good lady, and it would be cool to have kids."

"See, that's what's funny," Bobby laughed. "I kind of envy you... you got lots of freedom, and nobody nagging at you."

Jimmy stared out the window for a moment. "I wouldn't mind a little nagging sometimes," he said. "I spend a lot of quiet nights."

"Yeah? Well, that's your own fault. You could circulate a lot more if you wanted."

Jimmy rode quietly, watching the urban sprawl of Central City yield to the countryside. Farmers were busily sowing their crops, and the trees were filled with blossoms on the warm spring day.

"So what's this track like?" Bobby quizzed. "What's it called… River Glen?"

"River Ridge," Jimmy corrected. "It's a nice place. I'd call it a big quarter, maybe even a third. I ran a modified over there once, and later I ran a sprint car there maybe three or four times. They've had a Saturday night program there for years."

"Do you think it's a good idea, Al taking us to these smaller tracks?" Bobby was referring to their friend and current USAC official, Al Petrov.

"Yeah, I'm all for it," Jimmy nodded. "I like the bull rings, that's where I cut my teeth. It'll make for some exciting racing."

"I'm probably gonna be a little rusty," Bobby admitted. "It'll be interesting, that's for sure."

Jimmy sat on the right rear tire of the Ellison Special, watching people file into the big wooden grandstand across the way.

"So you and Graffan finally tangled," Harvey beamed. "Hot damn! Tell me all about it, boy! Did you knock him on his ass?"

"Not much to tell," Jimmy shrugged. "Just a plain 'ol bar fight, nothing more. I hit him a few times, he hit me a few times, and we both looked like idiots."

"Aw, I wish I coulda seen it," Harvey said gleefully, rubbing his hands together. "I've wanted to bust that crumb myself for three years."

Jimmy gave Harvey a funny look. "How'd you hear about it?"

"Hear about it? Hell, everybody in this pit area heard about it. You're the hot topic, boy. I've already heard 20 stories…you both went to jail, he broke your jaw, you pulled a knife, he pulled a gun, all that good stuff."

Jimmy laughed. "Nope, nothing like that…more like a couple of school kids, bloodying each other's noses."

Try as he might, throughout the night Jimmy couldn't duck the topic of the fight. Everybody who stopped by his pit asked about the scuffle, eagerly wanting to know the details. Jimmy was polite, but he was growing tired of explaining that it really wasn't that big of a deal.

He was glad each time he climbed into the race car, because there he didn't have to face any questions. Soon his focus was consumed by matters at hand, because they timed well off the pace in 16th.

Harvey was fit to be tied. "Maybe Graffan hit you once too many times in the head," he groused as Jimmy climbed from the car. "You're all over the place!"

Jimmy shook his head. "Don't start on me," he insisted. "This thing is way tight, and I was doing is trying to shake it loose. You're still thinkin' we're on a half-mile, Harvey. We've got to get busy."

"The car is fine," Harvey said, crossing his arms. "You just need to drive it right."

Jimmy tossed his helmet in the seat and walked to the tool box. Harvey stared in amazement as Jimmy grabbed a handful of wrenches. He walked back to the car and stopped, staring at Harvey. For a moment they just looked at each other, until Jimmy finally spoke.

"Well? You gonna help me fix this thing, or you gonna stand there with your thumb up your butt?"

Harvey stared for a moment, leaning close enough hat Jimmy could see the tiny red veins in his eyeballs. "Hmmph," he groused. "You get into one fight, and now you think you're a big shot. Gimme those wrenches…I'll loosen the damn thing up, you crybaby."

Their heat race was much better, although they were still struggling. Their poor qualifying time gave them a good starting spot, and Jimmy held on to finish third and make the transfer.

"We're geared wrong," Jimmy said as he climbed from the car. "It's too slow off the corner, and we're not getting enough RPMs on the straight."

Harvey nodded. "That's what it sounded like to me, too. Slim, let's change the gear. We're a ways off, so let's go a couple of points."

Jimmy watched Slim pull the cover, and in a moment he and Harvey had the gear changed. They had just put the cover back on when Bobby came walking over.

"It's not as bad as I thought," he offered. "I had to think about it a little, but it feels natural, already. I like this place!"

"Well, you can have it!" Harvey chimed in, wiping his hands on a rag. "This is stupid, racing at this little rat hole. We don't belong on these bull-rings...sprint cars should only be on the half-miles."

"Why?" Jimmy asked.

"Whattya mean, 'Why?'. Because they do, that's why. Midgets on the quarter-miles, sprint cars on the half, and Champ Dirt cars on the miles. That's how it's supposed to be."

"Who says?"

"Nobody HAS to say...that's just how it's supposed to be."

"If they can pay the purse, why not? I like the smaller tracks," Bobby insisted. "Gives us more variety."

"You want variety, go race those po-dunk outlaw races. This is USAC, and we ain't got no business on these little rat holes."

Jimmy laughed. "You see why I'm always in such a good mood?" he said to Bobby. "It's from Harvey's happy personality. It's a joy just to be around him."

Harvey gave him the one-finger salute. "There's your personality, right there," he growled.

Jimmy looked up to see Al Petrov and Leon Hartke approaching. Hartke had the siphon pump and a small plastic container.

"We need to check your fuel," Al said to Harvey. "Just be a minute."

"Check our fuel?" Harvey bellowed. "We qualified 16th! You're thinkin' we need nitro to qualify 16th??!!"

"Just need some fuel," Al repeated. "You've won four in a row, Jack, and we're just trying to keep everything above board."

"Go ahead," Harvey said dismissively. "You won't find any dope in our fuel...and we're still gonna kick their ass."

"We just need some fuel."

"So, how many more rat holes like this are we gonna see this year, Al? Let's just run all of 'em on these little dumps."

"This is a nice track, Jack. Look around. And there's the best reason of all for running here."

He motioned toward the packed grandstands.

"Well, when everybody tears their cars up, you ain't gonna be very popular," Harvey argued. "You wait and see."

Al looked over at Jimmy and grinned, a twinkle in his eye. "There he is, Muhammad Ali," he teased. "Or are you Joe Frazier?"

Jimmy just smiled, trying to ignore him.

"He's a badass," Bobby chimed in. "I saw it with my own eyes!" Jimmy shot an annoyed glance at Bobby.

"Floats like a butterfly, and stings like a bee," Al chuckled.

"He's like a bee sting in the ass, is what he is," Harvey snorted.

Jimmy lined up mid-pack for the feature race, right behind Graffan. At the start Graffan moved to the outside, with Jimmy right behind, and together they began making their way forward. At the midway point of the 40-lapper they were just outside the top five, helped by a couple of cautions that kept the leaders in check.

The last 20 laps were frantic and eventful. Graffan had a fierce battle with Bobby for second before moving up to race hard with leader Sammy Caldwell, the savvy veteran. Jimmy had his hands full with a wild local kid, a young racer who stirred up a hornet's nest in his heat race by spinning Rusty Fernandez.

Jimmy and the kid banged wheels several times. Jimmy didn't mind racing hard, but he was irritated that the kid kept bumping him when there was plenty of room to avoid each other.

In the waning laps they came upon a lapped car, with Jimmy on the inside and the kid alongside. The slower car moved to the middle, and immediately the kid moved left, trying to crowd Jimmy into the infield.

That was the last straw, and in one deft move Jimmy caught the kid's left rear tire and spun him out.

On the restart Jimmy made a run at Bobby for third, but didn't have enough to make a clean pass. At the finish it was Sammy, Graffan, and Bobby, with Jimmy trailing in fourth.

He drove the Ellison sprinter to their pit and climbed out. He noticed that both nerf bars were badly bent, with the right one actually dragging the ground.

"Look at our car!" Harvey said, his hands on his hips. "That's what you get on these little tracks, everybody just beatin' the piss out of each other! I can see right now, I'll be makin' lots of bars this season!"

Jimmy shrugged, and took a long drink of water. Slim nodded up the way.

"That kid is coming over. Got lots of friends, too."

Jimmy saw the young racer walking briskly toward their pit, followed by a dozen onlookers. Jimmy just stood and waited, looking the kid in the eye.

"You spun me out!" the boy said, glaring at Jimmy. "What's the deal?"

"You spun yourself out," Jimmy said quietly.

"No way! You turned right into me, and spun me out! All my friends saw it! You know you did!"

Jimmy shook his head. "You spun yourself out. You tried to crowd me down, and there wasn't any room. You did it to yourself."

"That's bull! I was faster, and you should have given me some room with that lapped car!"

Jimmy just shook his head. "You know what happened, and I'm not going to argue with you. Just leave my pit, right now."

The kid snorted in disgust, and began to walk away. "You got a payback coming."

"Whatever. Just leave."

As quickly as they dispersed, Barry Kane approached Jimmy, notebook in hand, covering the event for his racing paper. Two other reporters tagged along, and Jimmy figured they must be from the local paper.

"Got a minute?" Barry smiled.

"Sure I do. How you doin', Barry?"

"I'm fine. So, the win streak is over, at four. Are you disappointed you didn't win tonight?"

"I'm disappointed we didn't qualify better. Starting that far back made it tough, although we did move up. Just not enough."

"If you'd had some more laps, could you have won it?"

"No, I don't think so. We were too tight, and I think Sammy and Graffan were just better. I might've got Bobby for third, but that would have been it."

"What happened with Donnie Watkins?" asked one of the other men. "Did you spin him out?"

"No, we just banged wheels and he got turned around. It was just tight racing, we got caught behind that lapped car and got together, and he got the worst of it. Just hard racing, really."

"Do you like racing on these smaller tracks?" Barry asked. "Should we be here?"

"Oh yeah. This is sprint car racing, right here. Hardcore racing on these smaller tracks, and I like it. This is where I grew up."

The men folded their notebooks closed, and the two local men turned and walked away. Barry hung around until the other reporters were out of earshot.

"Okay, what's the deal with you and Graffan? Is it true you guys got into a fight?"

Jimmy said nothing, standing with his hands in his pockets, smiling at Barry.

"You're not going to comment?"

"I've just got nothing to say about that."

"Look, Jimmy, it would be better for you if you did…with all these rumors floating around, you could go a long way toward setting people straight if you told the real story."

"Print the rumors, then. I don't care. Far as I'm concerned, it's nobody's business."

"Oh, so you did get into a fight? And a fight is a private matter?"

"I don't have anything to say about Steve Graffan or anything that happens away from the race track."

"But, Jimmy…people saw you with a black eye last week, and Steve's face is still all scratched up. C'mon, be reasonable. Just tell the readers what happened."

"Why don't you go ask Graffan?"

"I did…he won't talk, either. Said whatever happened is between you guys."

"Well, there you go. Sounds like there isn't a story to write."

"All right, then, this is on the record. Jimmy, did you and Steve Graffan get into a fight? Yes or no."

Jimmy stood there smiling, saying nothing. Finally Barry began to chuckle.

"You're not going to answer…why are you so stubborn, Jimmy? I'm trying to help you."

"Oh, *help me*. I see. Well, I'll tell you what, Barry. You're a nice guy, and I like you. But why don't you go help somebody else, okay? I've got all the help I need right now."

Chapter 9

Jimmy stood at the back of his car, greeting a long line of fans. He signed programs and posed for photos, and an hour after the races the line finally began to dwindle.

Slim and Harvey had the car on the trailer, and prepared to get on the road back to Central City.

"You drive over by yourself?" Harvey asked. "We're gonna stop and get some eggs, if you're hungry."

"No, I rode with Bobby. I already got my bag out of the truck, so you guys can go ahead. See you next week."

Harvey and Slim waved as they climbed into their pickup, and Jimmy shouldered his helmet bag and walked toward the infield concession stand.

He saw Bobby approaching, with a broad smile on his face and two attractive women in tow. The girl alongside Bobby was a leggy blonde in tight jeans, while the other woman was a stylish brunette wearing corduroy pants and knee-length boots. Both ladies smiled at Jimmy.

"Hey, Jimmy, I want you to meet some friends of mine...this is Brenda, and this is Joy. They're from around here, and they invited us to go out for a few drinks. You in a hurry to get on the road?"

"Why, no," Jimmy smiled. "I've got all the time in the world...everybody should have a little Joy in their lives, don't you think?"

The girls laughed, and Bobby rolled his eyes.

"Let me go get changed, and I'll be ready," Jimmy said, nodding toward the building. "Maybe five minutes."

"Hurry up," Bobby grinned eagerly. "These ladies are thirsty."

Jimmy walked to the building and into the small rest room. He stripped off his uniform, and reached into his bag for a washcloth. There was no hot water, so he shivered as he washed himself as best he could, then dressed in his jeans and shirt.

A few minutes later they were headed for a local watering hole.

Bobby had the blonde in his car, while Jimmy rode with Joy in her Mustang. They turned into the parking lot to discover the place was closed.

"Let's just go to my house," Joy offered. "I can make us some drinks."

The boys agreed, and they headed out of town on the state highway. Jimmy and the girl made small talk, and she flicked on her turn signal as they approached a crossroad, a darkened gas station sitting silently on the corner.

Four miles later they turned into the driveway of a nice ranch home, the night breeze blowing softly as they walked to the front door. Bobby turned in behind them, and in a moment they were seated in the living room.

Joy put on some music and mixed some drinks. Jimmy soon got up to find the bathroom, and when he came back he discovered that Bobby and the blonde had disappeared.

"They ran away," Joy giggled. "Here…you can sit here beside me." She coyly patted the seat alongside her on the sofa.

"Sounds like a winner," Jimmy smiled, reaching over to flick the lamp off.

He wasn't sure how much time had passed when he noticed the light flickering through the picture window. Joy suddenly sat up on the sofa, peeking outside.

"Oh, my gosh," she said frantically. "He's here."

Jimmy didn't at all like her tone. "*Who* is here?" he asked cautiously.

"My husband."

"Husband!" he hissed. "You didn't say anything about a husband!"

"Well…we're kind of separated. He doesn't actually live here right now."

Jimmy glared at her in the dim light, raising himself from the sofa to peek out the window. He saw a county police cruiser sitting in the driveway, headlights off, the driver sitting behind the wheel.

"Good God, that's a cop," Jimmy said, his eyes wide.

"Yeah, I know," she said, nodding her head. "He's not supposed to come around, but he's jealous. He must have seen your car. Maybe you should go."

"Go? Not while he's sitting out there, I'm not. We've got to get rid of him, and fast."

Jimmy tried to think. He looked quickly at Joy.

"I've got an idea...where's your phone?"

"In the kitchen."

"Okay. Now, what's the name of this road? And what's the name of that gas station back on the highway, on the corner?"

"It's 400 East. And the station is Deeter's."

"Go get Bobby and your friend, and tell them what's going on. Tell Bobby we have to leave in about 60 seconds, and if we don't we're probably both gonna get shot. Can you do that? And don't turn on any lights, whatever you do."

She nodded and hurried away. Jimmy grabbed the phone book, and a moment later was dialing the phone.

After two rings a woman answered. "Sheriff's department."

"Hello? Hey, listen, I need to report...well, I don't know what I'd call it, but I need an officer. It's an emergency."

"What's your location, sir? And what is the problem?"

"I'm out here on the state highway, at road 400 East. There's a little gas station, the sign says, 'Deeters.' I'm on the pay phone. And...well, you aren't gonna believe this, but there are three women out here running down the highway without any clothes on."

"I beg your pardon?"

"Yes, that's right, naked as a jaybird, and I almost hit one of 'em with my car. They're drunk or stoned or something, and they're right in the middle of the road! Can you please get somebody out here right away before one of 'em gets killed?"

"What is your name, sir?"

"My name is Steve Graffan, and I'm from Central City, Indiana. I'm a race driver, and I'm driving home from River Ridge Speedway, we raced there tonight. Call the promoter, he'll vouch for me."

"Yes, Mr. Graffan. Will you please stay on the line while you wait for the officer?"

"Aw, man, now they're trying to break into my truck! I've gotta go, but I'll stay until he gets here! Hurry!"

He quickly hung up the phone, just as Bobby walked into the darkened kitchen.

"Oh, man! That guy is a cop! How we gonna get out of here?"

"If we're lucky, we might have a chance," Jimmy said, inching toward the picture window and peering outside. "You ready to go? If this works, we'll have to make a run for it."

The driver's door of the cruiser opened, and Jimmy saw a tall man step out. He began to take tentative steps up the sidewalk, but stopped. After a moment he walked back to his car, leaning against the fender with his arms crossed. He started up the walk once more, but suddenly hurried back to his car. He climbed inside, and Jimmy could see him talking into the radio handset. His headlights came on, and he quickly began backing out of the driveway. His tires screeched as he turned north toward the highway.

"Wait about 30 seconds," Jimmy insisted, his hand on the doorknob. Bobby nodded, standing right behind him with car keys in hand.

Jimmy looked at Joy, her eyes wide with anxiety. "Sorry 'bout all this," she said.

"Listen, if I were you I'd go someplace else for tonight," Jimmy said. "When he gets back here in a minute or two, he's not gonna be in a good mood."

She nodded, and grabbed her shoes and keys. Jimmy watched the fading taillights through the window, then shouted, "Go!"

He and Bobby ran to their car, and were inside in a flash. They backed onto the lawn, then hurried to the road and turned south.

"No headlights," Jimmy cautioned. "He'll see us."

Bobby nodded, and pressed the accelerator.

"Turn east at the next crossroad," Jimmy said. "Then you can hit your lights. And haul *ass*, Bobby."

They rolled through the countryside, Jimmy watching for headlights behind them. They studied the signs at the country intersections, each road number growing higher. Finally came an intersection with two signs, the new set slightly different than the others.

"There's the county line," Jimmy said, finally beginning to relax. "Go one more mile, then turn back north and we'll get on the highway."

Bobby looked over at him and shook his head. First they grinned at each other, then began to chuckle, and got more carried away until they were both laughing uncontrollably. After a minute or two they finally settled down and began to catch their breath.

"Well, killer, looks like I got you out of trouble again," Bobby nodded.

"OUT of trouble? You're the one who gets me INTO trouble."

"Aw, what's life without some adventure, huh? It's good to get things stirred up, ain't it?"

"You like all this excitement?"

"Yeah! I'm all for some excitement!"

"Well, that's good, Bobby, because that cop is going to remember your license number for a while."

The color drained from Bobby's face, and he stared intently through the windshield, considering the possibilities.

"Damn," he whispered. He was quiet for a moment, as Jimmy tried not to laugh. "Listen, killer," he finally spoke up. "Hurry up and fix your damned truck…from now on, you're drivin'!"

They rolled through the night along the two-lane highway. Jimmy could have used a nap, but he chatted with Bobby to help keep him awake. They were about 10 miles west of Central City when they saw red lights far into the distance.

"Aw, man, must be a wreck," Bobby groaned. "I hope the road ain't closed."

As they drew closer they saw several cars pulled off the side of the road, including several race cars and trailers. They looked at each other and Bobby slowed. A cop with a flashlight stood in the road, waving them to stop.

"What's up?" Bobby called to the cop. "Wreck?"

"Yeah, road's closed. You'll have to turn around and detour."

"Everybody all right?" Bobby asked.

"You'll have to detour," repeated the cop.

"Say, that's Sid Johnson's trailer, and there's Fred's outfit," Jimmy pointed out. "On up a ways I can see Bob Strong's trailer…pull off the side there and let's see what's going on."

Bobby began to back up. "We're just going to stop for a minute," he said to the cop. "We've got some friends driving through here, just want to be sure they're all right."

They walked toward the accident scene. It was a lonely country crossroad, and as they drew closer Jimmy's heart began to pound, and suddenly his breath came in sharp, short bursts.

It was the Ellison tow rig.

The race car was still on the trailer, in the ditch off the right side of the road. The pickup was a few yards away, the left front corner badly smashed. Broken glass littered the pavement, and the flashing red lights made the night seem surreal. A fire truck was idling nearby, and the police radios cackled in brief bursts, mingling with the sounds of the emergency workers and onlookers.

A Cadillac sat in the center of the intersection, the front end crushed nearly flat. Jimmy heard the sound of broken glass crunching under his feet as he looked around, trying to get a handle on what had happened.

Then he saw it, a few yards away.

A body lay at the edge of the pavement, covered by a white sheet.

He stood in stunned silence, staring at the body, when he felt a man's arm drape over his shoulder.

"You okay?" Sid Johnson said softly.

Jimmy looked at Sid, his voice caught in his throat.

"That's not Harvey or Slim," Sid assured him, patting Jimmy on the back. "I think that's the guy from the other car."

"Where…"

"They took 'em to a hospital, about ten minutes ago."

"How bad?"

"Well…Harvey is beat up pretty bad, he was unconscious. Slim apparently got pitched out, he's lucky to be alive. They found him in the field there…how he didn't get taken apart on that fence, I'll never know."

"What…what happened? Anybody see it?"

"No, evidently Billy Hobbs and Steve Graffan were the first ones here. They were behind him a mile or so, and they came up on the wreck. Farmer up the road must have heard it, because after a minute or two he came down with a flashlight and said he'd already called for an ambulance."

Hobbs and Graffan came walking up.

"They're both pretty lucky," Hobbs said somberly. "Just as we got here the truck had caught fire under the hood, and Steve grabbed an extinguisher from our trailer and put the fire out. This guy here, the dead guy, was right there where he's layin'. I think he got pitched through the windshield."

"The Cadillac evidently ran the stop sign and plowed into 'em," Graffan explained. "Looks like he was headed south, and he just blasted 'em in the left front. Harvey never saw the guy coming, his skid marks ain't but six feet before the impact."

"Did you talk to Harvey? And Slim?"

"Harvey was out cold," Graffan said, shaking his head. "His pulse was good, but he never moved or talked. They had a hard time getting him out of the truck, his foot was stuck up under the dash.

"Slim was layin' out in the field, we were shinin' the flashlight all over the place tryin' to find him. He sat up and said something about washing the car, he was completely goofy. He's all cut up, but he started coming around a little bit when they put him into the ambulance. He knew his own name, and he was askin' about Harvey."

"I've got to get to the hospital," Jimmy said, trying to stay calm. "And I need to call Sonny Ellison. Hey…where will they take the truck, and the race car? Anybody know?"

"I'll find that out, and I'll call you at the hospital," Sid offered. "Let me know if you need to, and we'll use my trailer to get the race car back to the shop."

"Take my car," Bobby offered. "I can catch a ride with Sid."

Jimmy began to walk away, and he stopped.

"Anybody know which hospital?"

"St. Elizabeth," Hobbs and Graffan said in unison.

Jimmy climbed quickly into the car and turned around in the roadway. He began the detour around the country mile, his mind racing, trying to remember the exact location of St. Elizabeth Hospital.

His hands were trembling, and he felt like he was going to cry.

Get hold of yourself. You gotta be strong. It ain't the end of the world.

Yet, somehow, he wondered if it was.

Chapter 10

The hospital waiting area was quiet, and Jimmy dozed as the early-morning sunshine warmed the small room. He began to dream, his subconscious rolling through a bizarre series of images of flashing red lights, a demolished Ellison tow rig, Harvey being cut from the cab, and a dead man covered with a white sheet.

A sound startled him, and he woke with a jump. He saw Sonny Ellison walking into the room, and he managed a weak smile.

"Hey, Sonny," he said, extending his hand. "Sorry to call so early in the morning with bad news."

"You look tired, Jimmy. How are Jack and Slim? Any word?"

"No, the nurse said Harvey would be in surgery for a while, and they'll tell me when they have some news. Slim is getting admitted, but they wouldn't let me see him yet."

Jimmy briefed Sonny on the details of the crash, including the death of the other driver. Sonny sat quietly for a moment as he digested the news.

"Wow…"

"The truck is junk, but it looked like the race car was okay," Jimmy continued. "The trailer broke free from the truck, but the car stayed on, and stayed upright. I just saw it from 20 yards away, and I don't have any idea of whatever might have been damaged. I'll take a look at the race car maybe later today, and I'll have a better idea what it needs to be ready to race."

Sonny moved his hands dismissively. "I don't care a thing about the car, or the tow rig. As far as I'm concerned, the car is parked until Jack and Slim are up and about. Don't you agree?"

Jimmy studied him for a moment before answering. "Sure," he said quietly, his voice sounding tired. "You want a cup of coffee?"

They said little as they sipped the vending machine coffee. Suddenly the doors opened and a middle-aged man with salt-and-pepper hair and blue scrubs stepped into the waiting area.

"Are you here with the two gentlemen from the car accident?" the man asked.

"Yes," Sonny spoke up.

"I'm Dr. Shapiro," he said, giving them a serious look. "Are you…family members?"

"They don't have any family," Sonny explained. "They're my employees, and …well, they don't have anybody else."

The doctor seemed skeptical. "The information I have is that they were with a racing car…I assume they have no insurance?"

"Why would you assume that?" Sonny replied. "Just because they don't have family, doesn't make them destitute. They have insurance through my company."

"Well, someone is going to have to be responsible," the doctor said, warily crossing his arms. "We'll need someone to take care of some paperwork."

"Never mind the paperwork," Sonny argued, and edge to his voice. "I'll take care of that. Can you give us an update on their condition?"

The doctor paused, as if studying them. Finally he spoke. "Mr. Harvey suffered a serious blow to the head. He regained consciousness briefly on the way in here, but only for a moment. He also looks to have a serious fracture in his lower left leg, which I expect will require surgery. I'm waiting on the x-rays right now.

"Since he isn't awake, he can't tell us what's hurting. But the primary concern is that head injury, and right now I can't give you much of an assessment. We need time…the next 24 hours are important. If he can get through today and tonight, that will tell us a great deal."

"Are you saying Harvey might not make it?" Jimmy spoke up.

The doctor looked at him calmly, then back at Sonny. "We'll have to be patient, and see what the next 24 hours brings."

"How about Slim? Mr. MacDonald, I mean." Jimmy asked.

"He's got a number of bumps and bruises, but it doesn't look as though he's seriously hurt. He's complaining of back pain, and a sore shoulder, but his x-rays revealed no broken bones. We've stitched up a couple of lacerations, and he's got a nasty bump on his head. He'll probably be released sometime Monday morning."

"When can we see him?"

"Mr. MacDonald will be in a room later this morning, and will be allowed to see you. But we're going to watch him closely for a few hours."

For a moment it was quiet.

"Any questions? I'd like you to go to the admissions office and talk with the receptionist, so we can collect some information. In the meantime, we'll let you know if there are any changes."

Jimmy motioned as Sid Johnson backed toward the small shop. The race trailer creaked and groaned, and Jimmy held up his hand and shouted, "Whoa! That's good!"

Sid cut the engine, and climbed from his truck. Jimmy unhooked the ramps and placed them on the ground, then set about unhooking the tethers that held the car in place.

"I could have done this by myself," Sid smiled at Jimmy. "You didn't have to leave the hospital just for this."

"I needed to get out," Jimmy shrugged. "Hospitals give me the willies. Besides, we couldn't see either of 'em yet. Sonny's still up there, and I'll get back as soon as we're done here."

"I'm amazed the car's in one piece," Sid marveled. "The truck was wrecked, the trailer's bent all to hell, yet the car isn't hurt at all. You guys are lucky."

He caught himself, and smiled. "I don't mean 'lucky,'" he said quickly. "You know what I mean."

They rolled the car off into one bay and unhitched the trailer.

"Look how the tongue is all wrenched," Sid pointed out. "The dolly and crank are junk, too. Sonny might have a welder capable of fixing it, but in my opinion this thing is finished."

"It doesn't matter much for the time being," Jimmy said quietly. "We're not going to race again for a while, sounds like."

Sid looked at him with one of those fatherly looks, saying nothing. Finally he leaned against the rear tire of the car.

"Sonny's kind of lost interest for the moment, hasn't he?"

"Yeah, from the looks of it. He's pretty upset about those guys layin' in the hospital."

"I'm not surprised. This kind of thing happens takes the wind out of your sails in a hurry. Like they say, it's all fun and games until somebody gets hurt."

Jimmy nodded gamely, and Sid looked at him and smiled.

"And, since you're the typical self-centered, blood-and-guts race driver, you want to keep racing, right? And you're feeling pretty guilty about that."

Jimmy glanced up and him with a sheepish look on his face. "Something like that."

"Don't feel bad about it. Matter of fact, any racer is going to feel that way. You want to race, no matter the circumstances. But since Sonny doesn't feel the same way, that leaves you without a ride."

"Geez, am I a heel for thinking about it already?" Jimmy asked. "I mean, we've got a great year going, and I hate to throw it away. Plus, if things were reversed, Harvey would be the last guy in the world to quit. If that was me layin' up there, he'd already have another driver lined up by now. And I wouldn't blame him, not one bit. Life goes on, man. It doesn't stop for anybody, and I wouldn't want it to stop for me. Neither would he, I'll bet."

Jimmy leaned against the roll cage. "I've got nothing but respect for Sonny, and he's been the best owner I've ever raced for," he said, the stress evident in his words, as if it was a strain to say them. "But, man, I don't get him not wanting to go on. I'm leading the driver points, he's leading the car owner points, the car's not hurt bad…there is no reason for us not to race."

"Except for the fact that one of his lifelong friends might be on his deathbed," Sid offered, crossing his arms. "You know, you might want to think about this for a little bit before you pass judgment."

"Hell, I'm not judging him," Jimmy said quickly. "I just don't understand why he wouldn't let me race the car. This should be automatic…you keep racing, no matter what."

Sid sat there for a moment, saying nothing. He studied Jimmy's expression, then broke the silence.

"You know, Sonny has been a friend of mine ever since he first got a race car. He's always been a first-class guy, even when we didn't see eye-to-eye. We've loaned each other stuff, we've cried in each other's beer when our cars got tore up, and we've been a ways down the road together.

"I can't think of anybody in racing that's been together as long as Sonny, Harvey, and Slim. Some of that is because Harvey and

Slim have no family to speak of, and Sonny's tried to look after them, if you know what I mean. That whole bunch is tight, real tight.

"Harvey isn't just Sonny's mechanic. Neither is Slim. So give him a little room on this one, Jimmy. He's all upset right now, but maybe after some time passes, he'll feel like keeping the car going."

Jimmy nodded. "Aw, I'm not down on Sonny. I know this deal is real, real tough for him. But in the meantime, I'm kinda stuck. Should I go out looking for a ride? Or should I watch my point lead go away while I sit out? Plus, and I hate to say this, but I gotta think of the money. I need to race to pay my bills. So what should I do?"

Sid nodded in understanding. "You know, there might be another option. I've got another car I could finish up, but I don't have a motor. If Sonny doesn't want to keep his car going, maybe he would let us use his motor in my spare car, and you could run it. We'd run it as car No. 49, and list Sonny as the owner. I'll run the car out of my pocket, but he can have the points."

Jimmy thought about it and nodded his head.

"That's a great idea, Sid. I'm going back to the hospital right now, and I'll talk to him."

They stepped outside, and Jimmy pulled the door down and checked to make sure it latched. Sid opened his truck door and paused.

"I could have the car finished up by Thursday no problem, but we'll need some more help this weekend. Our timing isn't very good, because this weekend coming up is probably the toughest weekend of the year. On the dirt at Shoes on Saturday night, then the pavement at Sunset Park on Sunday. That means changing the car over between races, and that's a thrash. Could you line us up some more help?"

Jimmy nodded. "I've got a couple of guys who will help us...I'll check early in the week to be sure."

"Just let me know what Sonny wants to do," Sid said, starting the engine in his truck.

"I will," Jimmy nodded. He reached over and patted Sid on the shoulder. "That's a real nice thing you're offering, by the way."

"Sonny would do the same for me," Sid insisted. Then he smiled.

"You oughta go home and get some sleep, Jimmy...you're gettin' bags under your eyes."

Jimmy knocked gently on the door of the room, peeking inside.

"Hey, Slim," he said softly. "How you feelin'?"

Slim's head was propped up slightly on a pillow, and his eyes were nearly closed. He managed a weak smile as Jimmy gave his hand a squeeze.

"I'm beat all to hell," he sighed. "How's Harvey?"

"Well, his signs are strong. He'll be all right...he's a tough son-of-a-gun, and if I know Harvey he'll get through this."

"Boy," Slim said, his voice so quiet Jimmy had to lean close to hear him clearly, "I don't remember a thing. What happened?"

"A car ran a stop sign and nailed you, about 10 miles west of town. You got thrown out, and were laying in a field alongside the road. Harvey was still in the truck, knocked out."

"I...I don't even remember riding home. How did we do at the race? Did we win?"

"Fourth."

"What day is this?"

"It's Sunday afternoon. Do you remember us coming to see you this morning? Me and Sonny?"

" I don't remember seeing anybody. When can I get out of here?"

"Probably tomorrow morning. You'll be awful sore, I'll bet. Sonny wants you to come stay with him for a couple of days."

Slim nodded slightly, beginning to drift off. Jimmy sat quietly with him, until he was sleeping soundly.

Jimmy slipped from the room, riding the elevator to ICU. He sat in the waiting area, and a few minutes later Sonny came walking in.

"I stopped by Slim's room, but he's sleeping," he said.

"I talked to him," Jimmy smiled. "He sounded pretty good, actually. He's already asking about going home."

"Any news on Jack?"

"Nothing."

Sonny slumped into the chair next to Jimmy. "Boy, what an

ordeal...we never think about the possibility of something like this happening, do we?"

Jimmy nodded. He wondered if it was too soon to bring up the topic of the race car, but he figured he'd at least feel him out.

"We got the car and trailer back to the shop...car doesn't have a scratch, but the trailer is pretty badly bent."

Sonny nodded, and said nothing.

Jimmy waited a moment, then started to speak. Just as he did, Sonny spoke at the same time.

"It's kind of soon to..."

"Jimmy, I was thinking..."

They smiled.

"We've both got something on our mind," Sonny nodded. "You go ahead."

"No, you first," Jimmy insisted.

"Well...I realized we've got an issue to resolve, at least in the short term. I suspect you're going to want to keep racing, but to be honest, right now I don't think I can. I'm worried about Jack, and I don't feel right spending any energy on the race car while he's laying up here."

Jimmy listened, not saying anything.

"I have never once raced without Jack taking care of my race car. And, I don't think I want to. That's no offense to you, Jimmy. But Jack's the guy who got me into this sport.

"At the same time, I don't want to leave you high and dry. Frankly, I'm torn. I want to do right by you, but I don't have much appetite to go racing right now."

"I understand," Jimmy said quietly. "And, you know, Sonny, I'm with you. I'm worried about Harvey, and I feel kind of guilty thinking about racing with him laying up here. As far as you not wanting anybody else to take care of your car, I'm cool with that, too. You two guys go back a long ways.

"But here's another idea. Sid helped me get the race car and trailer back to the shop a couple of hours ago, and he had a suggestion. He's got another car, but it needs a motor.

"I could pull the motor out of our car and put it in Sid's spare car, and we'd run it as No. 49. You'd be listed as the car owner, but it would really be out of Sid's pocket. He'll get the money, and you get the points. Later on, when Harvey's ready to get back at it, we haven't lost the whole season.

"Would that be something you'd consider?"

Sonny sat quietly for a moment, deep in thought. He shifted in his chair, and nodded his head.

"I like that idea...it would take a load off my mind, because I know you'd have a good race car. Sid's a good friend, and I'm not surprised he offered to help.

"Yeah, let's do that...get with Sid, and make it happen. You know, there's one other issue that clouds things up a little."

"What's that?"

"Matt Coffman," Sonny explained. "His sponsorship was based upon us running every race. We'll have to see if Sid is willing to put Matt's name on the car. If not, I'm not sure I can agree to do this."

"I didn't even think about that," Jimmy replied. "I've been meaning to ask you about Coffman, but hadn't had the chance. When the season started he came to the track and bossed us around something fierce, like he owned the car. We had words a little bit, and he stayed up in the stands after that. Then all of a sudden we didn't see him at all. I figured maybe you had a talk with him."

"Hmmm," Sonny said. "Matt can be awfully overbearing, I know. But I wasn't aware he had been a problem with the race car. I have to tell you, though, Matt's kind of a mystery right now. Seems he has disappeared, and nobody knows where he's gone."

"Disappeared?"

"For lack of a better word, yes. Rumor around town is that he's in some kind of trouble. His asphalt business was closed for a week or so, but finally reopened. He apparently owes money to several of his suppliers. There's also a rumor he's got some tax trouble. I've had to switch to a different vendor for my materials, and apparently nobody knows what's become of Matt."

"Wow," Jimmy replied. "All I know is that he was a real pain. I can't say I'm sorry he quit coming to the races."

"Regardless, he paid me for the entire season's sponsorship," Sonny added. "I have a responsibility to keep his name on my car for the rest of the season. So if we're going to do this deal with Sid, we really need to get Matt's name on the car. Tell Sid I'll give him some of the money Coffman gave me at the start of the year. That's only fair."

"Okay, I'll ask Sid when I see him tomorrow."

The ICU nurse approached them. "If you'd like to see Mr. Harvey, you may do so. You're allowed 10 minutes with him, but you'll need to scrub beforehand, and wear a gown. You'll find a sink and supplies right around the corner."

"Any change?" Sonny asked.

She shook her head. "Try to keep very quiet, and please keep it limited to 10 minutes."

In a moment they were led to Harvey's bedside. The big man looked drawn and pale, and Jimmy was shocked at his pallid color. His leg was in a temporary cast, and tubes and wires connected him to a host of nearby machines.

There was no sound, just the rise and fall of his breathing. Every now and then one of the machines would beep, and Jimmy and Sonny spent the 10 minutes in silence. There was only the gentle heaving of Harvey's chest, and a face that was completely devoid of expression.

Jimmy walked into the small mobile home, tossing his keys on the kitchen table. He grabbed an overnight bag and tossed in several changes of clothes and a few pairs of socks. He stared into the bag, trying to remember anything else he would need for the next few days.

"Shaving kit," he said out loud, stepping into the tiny bathroom. He grabbed the small bag, but it caught on the spigot for an instant and turned upside down, spilling the contents all over the floor.

He cussed, and knelt to pick up the mess. As he finished he felt a rush of exhaustion sweep over him, and he stepped back into the bedroom. He fell across the bed, closing his eyes.

I can't go another minute without some sleep…instead of driving back to Central City tonight, I'll go down first thing in the morning.

He immediately drifted into sleep. He imagined hearing a knock on his door, and he pictured Harvey standing there, ready to yell at him for catching some rest. After the second knock he realized he wasn't dreaming, and he summoned enough strength to rise from the bed.

He weaved unsteadily as he opened the door, leaning back on his heels as he looked outside.

Her hair was blowing softly in the evening breeze, and she looked spectacular standing on the small porch with a bronze sunset as a backdrop. She smiled broadly and waved as he opened the door, and he realized she was wearing a dressy outfit.

"Oh, my gosh, Elaine, I am so sorry," he said wearily. "I completely forgot…we were going to have dinner tonight."

"That's all right," she said, still smiling. "Did something else come up?"

He managed a weak smile. "The past 24 hours, you just won't believe," he said, motioning toward the sofa. "C'mon in, and let me tell you about it."

He explained the accident on the way back from River Ridge, and her expression turned from light happiness to genuine concern. She leaned forward as she listened, with Jimmy describing the day at the hospital. He finished the story and shrugged.

"That's about it…we're just hoping and praying Harvey will be all right. That's all we can do at this point."

"How awful," she said, shaking her head. "Just think, if you'd been riding with them, you would have been in the wreck!"

He stopped suddenly, almost recoiling at the possibilities. "Wow, I never thought about that…guess I was fortunate, riding over with Bobby. Say, I really am sorry about dinner. I'm so exhausted, I'm about to fall over. Can I get a rain check?"

"Of course you can. But aren't you hungry?"

Jimmy suddenly realized he hadn't eaten all day. "You know, now that you mention it, I'm starving. I guess I hadn't realized it."

"Well, let me fix you something," she said rising to her feet. "Do you have anything in your fridge?"

"Yeah, some baloney. But don't worry about it, Elaine. You don't have to go to all the trouble…"

"It's no trouble," she smiled. "Besides, I'm hungry!"

He smiled, looking admiringly at her slender figure as she walked into the tiny kitchen. In a matter of moments she had a couple of sandwiches on a plate, and had made some lemonade.

They sat at the small table, and Jimmy realized he was getting his second wind. He explained that he planned on spending a couple of days at Bobby Mancini's home so he'd be close to the hospital.

"Are you going to Central City tonight?" she asked.

"I was, but I'm so tired, I'll just drive down in the morning," he sighed.

She smiled and reached over to hold his hand.

"You need to get some rest," she said softly. "How about I get going, and let you get some sleep."

"No, stay a few minutes," he said. "I need some company… it's kind of nice to have some quiet time, here at home. Let's go sit down."

She stood and walked to the small sofa, and sat at one end. He followed, and sat at the other end, and she patted her lap.

"Here, lay your head down," she smiled softly. "Just relax a little bit."

He leaned back, feeling his neck press against her leg. He looked up into those chocolate brown eyes, and felt his insides shiver. She was beautiful in a perfect, pure way, and he loved how her hands gently wove through his hair, caressing his scalp. Her gentle touch soon moved to his neck and face, and he found it so pleasant and relaxing he felt he could float away.

"Gee," he whispered, "that feels really nice."

"You're exhausted," she nodded. "I can see it in your eyes. You poor guy, you've been through the wringer."

Her words trailed off in his dreams. His eyes closed firmly and he finally began to sleep.

Sheesh...*what a day.*

Chapter 11

It was just past seven when Jimmy quit for the evening. He showered and shaved before heading up to the hospital to see if Harvey had improved.

It had only been three days since the accident, but it seemed like forever. Slim was feeling better, but they had discovered a broken rib and he was on a strict regimen of rest. Sonny brought him by the race shop earlier that afternoon and Slim relaxed in a chair and visited while Jimmy installed their engine in Sid's car.

Jimmy found a parking spot and entered the building, pressing the button to call the elevator. He rode up to ICU, turning the corner into the waiting area.

Sonny saw him and rose quickly to his feet. "He woke up!" Sonny nearly shouted, vigorously shaking Jimmy's hand. "He just popped his eyes open, and…woke up!"

"Fantastic!!" Jimmy beamed. "How long ago?"

"About an hour…he's really weak, but he knew his name, and asked what had happened. The nurse sat and talked with him, and I got to see him for just a couple of minutes."

"Wow…so what's next?"

"Well, they want him to get stronger, and then he'll have surgery on his leg. They're hoping to do that by Friday. After that, it's just a matter of getting him better."

They both sat down in the waiting area, Sonny excitedly clenching his hands together.

"Boy, do I feel better," he raved. "This is like a big weight lifted off my shoulders."

"Sonny, is there any chance…I mean, did they say anything about there being any…well, you know…brain damage?"

"They'll try to assess that in the next couple of days," he explained. "The doctor said there was no way to know, and he couldn't give me any odds of whether or not that had happened.

Sometimes things are fine, and sometimes they're not. Either way, at least he's awake, and we can figure out where we are."

Jimmy nodded. "I'm glad Harvey has you for a friend," he said. "You're a loyal guy, Sonny. I appreciate you looking after Harvey like you have."

"He's been my friend since school days," Sonny said quietly. "I'm not gonna abandon him now."

They said nothing for a few minutes before Sonny spoke again. "You know, this might change him. With a head injury, sometimes people are…well, different. Sometimes it's really subtle, but it's… different. We'll need to be patient."

Jimmy smiled. "I can see it now…Harvey will be quiet and calm, and ask me how I want the car set up. He'll apologize if the car isn't right, and when I make a mistake, he'll say, 'That's all right, Jimmy! You did your best!'"

They both laughed out loud at the thought.

"That wouldn't be Harvey," Sonny said, shaking his head.

"Nope," Jimmy agreed. "I'll settle for getting him back just like he was."

"You know, I probably over-reacted, asking you to park our car for a while," Sonny said. "I should have just let you get some help and run it like it was. I'm sorry I made so much work for you, taking our engine out and putting it one of Sid's cars."

Jimmy shook his head. "Of all the things you shouldn't be worrying about, that's the one," he insisted. "I'm sure not gonna second-guess you on that. Let's not even bring it up again. We'll run Sid's car for a few weeks until Harvey is ready, and then we'll get back to normal. Don't give it another thought."

Jimmy steered his pickup across the countryside, glancing in the mirror at the race car and trailer riding behind them. Slim sat in the middle seat, while Mike White rode shotgun.

As the miles clicked away Jimmy could feel a nervous tension in his stomach, and he wondered if it was because he was now responsible for much more than just driving the race car.

"I'll bet we could drive this road in our sleep," Slim chuckled, studying the familiar landmarks along the state highway. "Wonder how many times we made the ride over to Shoes."

Jimmy started to reply when he heard a loud noise—CLUNK!—and felt the truck lurch slightly. His fingers tightened on the wheel and he tried to figure out what was happening when Mike suddenly pointed to the left.

"Lost a wheel!" he shouted. "There it goes!"

Jimmy guided the truck off the edge of the highway, which luckily offered a wide, flat berm. He had already realized it was a trailer tire, and his mind was racing with possibilities: Was it just a matter of losing the lug nuts? Could they get it bolted back on? Did it damage the trailer? Is the wheel going to hit anything?

They watched the wheel bound over the fence along the road, still carrying plenty of speed as it disappeared into a wooded area well back off the road.

"Boy, look at that thing go," Slim marveled.

"I saw where it stopped!" Mike shouted. "I'll run get it."

He glanced for oncoming traffic, then darted across the highway, scurrying over the fence and running into the woods. Jimmy and Slim walked back to the trailer, surveying the damage.

"Doesn't look like anything is hurt," Jimmy said, kneeling next to the trailer. "Looks like the lug nuts just came off. My own danged fault…I was so busy thinking about the car, I didn't check the trailer wheels."

He stood up, offering a half-hearted grin to Slim.

"Let's get this thing jacked up," he said. "Oh, wait a minute: I'LL get it jacked up. You take it easy, Mr. Broken Rib."

Slim objected, but in a moment Jimmy had the jack in place and was beginning to lift the trailer when he heard a cry from the nearby woods.

"Hey!" Mike shouted. "Gimme some help here!"

Jimmy rose quickly and instinctively moved in that direction. Mike was carrying the wheel and tire, running awkwardly, and 20 yards behind him—and gaining fast—was a massive black Brahma bull, charging after the intruder. Mike glanced over his shoulder and when he realized the beast was gaining, dropped the tire and burst into a sprint. He could almost feel the bull's hot breath on his neck as he vaulted the fence, landing in a pile in the ditch.

Jimmy and Slim laughed mightily in spite of the situation, hurrying over to help Mike to his feet.

"Why'd you drop the tire!" Jimmy teased. "Now what are we gonna do?"

"Man..." Mike panted, "He was gaining on me! Wow, one of his horns poked a hole in my t-shirt! Am I stabbed?"

"You hooked it on the barbed wire," Jimmy scoffed, shaking his head. "Wouldn't have happened if you would've left him alone."

"Hey, I just got the wheel and was walking back, and I heard him snort...geez, the ground shook when he started running!"

They looked out across the field, where the tire and wheel lay some 25 yards from the fence. The bull paced impatiently, staring at them, and you could hear his snorts.

"Hmmm, this will take some thought," Jimmy mused. "Slim, walk down the fence a ways, and see if he follows you. If you can draw him away, I can get across the fence and get the tire before he gets back."

The bull seemed to know what they were after, and he refused to budge. Jimmy finally became impatient.

"I'm not lettin' some bull make me miss a race," he growled, climbing the fence. "C'mon, you porterhouse! I'm not afraid of you!"

The bull snorted, pawing at the ground. He suddenly charged, head lowered, sending Jimmy scrambling back across the fence.

"He means business," Slim said. "Think we could make it with just one wheel on that side?"

"No, we'd just blow out the other tire," Jimmy panted. "Hey, here comes somebody."

They looked up to see a new Chevy pickup towing a red No. 2 sprinter, driving slowly past. Harry Bell waved, steering the truck off the side of the road just in front of Jimmy's outfit.

In a moment Harry and another man climbed from the cab, walking across the road toward them.

"Stop to look at the cattle?" Harry kidded. "I thought we were goin' racing tonight!"

Jimmy grinned. "Got a minor problem," he explained. "Our friend here has our trailer tire, and he ain't keen on giving it back."

Harry studied the situation. "Well...why'd you give it to him in the first place?"

"It came off the trailer. Bounced into the woods, and must

have stirred him up. You're a farmer, Harry. He looks pretty mad... what should we do?"

"He's a rank one, for sure," Harry agreed. "I think I've got something he'll be interested in."

He walked back to his truck and retrieved a long, chrome electric cattle prod. Harry quickly scaled the fence, waving his arms, whistling and calling out to the bull as the animal paced a few yards away, snorting in rage.

"Hey, Harry...if he kills you, do you still want Sammy to run your car tonight?"

"Yeah, may as well...but don't let him take more than his 40 percent!"

Harry crept toward the wheel, and the bull edged closer. He was finally within range of the prod, and Harry jabbed his flanks, giving him the business. But the massive animal seemed oblivious, and Harry quickly retreated back across the fence.

"He's too damn big," he said, shaking his head. "This prod ain't got enough juice. Well, just one more idea, Jimmy. Unhook your truck from the trailer."

"What?"

"Go ahead and drop your trailer."

Jimmy just shrugged, and in a moment it was done. "What are we doing, Harry?"

"See that gate down there? You drive into the field, and I'll lay in the bed of your truck. Drive close to the wheel, and I'll grab it. Okay?"

"Sounds like a plan," Jimmy agreed, firing up his truck. Everett manned the gate, and in a moment Jimmy was easing across the field, closing in on the tire. The bull paced frantically, retreating and charging, retreating and charging, his nostrils wide with anger.

Jimmy drove to the left of the tire, getting it as close to his truck as possible. He eased to a stop as the bull stamped at the ground, not ten feet away. He was close enough that Jimmy could see the tiny red veins in his bulging eyes.

"Okay, Harry!" Jimmy yelled. Harry scrambled over the right side of the truck, grabbed the wheel, and scurried back into the bed. Jimmy gunned the engine, and just as he engaged the clutch the bull lunged. They were almost eye-to-eye when the bull rammed his head into Jimmy's driver door, and for a moment Jimmy thought the truck was going to turn over. But he managed to get going, and they quickly slipped back through the gate as Mike frantically latched it back in place.

Jimmy backed his truck in front of the trailer, getting out to examine his door. The sheet metal was completely caved in, although the mirror wasn't broken. Jimmy cussed his luck as he surveyed the damage.

"Didn't know you'd be in a rodeo, did you?" Harry laughed, looking at the door. "Yeah, sometimes those damn things ram right into you. Seen it happen before."

"Why didn't you tell me that?" Jimmy groused.

"You got your wheel, didn't you? Besides, that's why do we used *your* truck. Mine's too new for that kind of stuff."

A few minutes later they were back under way, easing down the road. Jimmy fumed as he thought of the smashed door. He looked over at Slim.

"Okay, Slim," he quizzed. "How would Harvey handle that deal?"

Slim thought for a moment. "Well, first of all, the wheel would never have come off," he said, giving Jimmy a scolding glance. "And the bull, that's easy. Harvey would have stared him down, and sent him back to the barn. He's meaner than any ol' bull I ever saw."

Jimmy felt a sense of being overwhelmed from the moment they unloaded the car at Shoes Speedway. Although they pitted next to Sid and had plenty of help, Jimmy felt a constant, nagging feeling that something had been overlooked.

He continually studied the car, making sure everything was right. He rolled out to qualify, and after timing fourth-quick he heard a rattling vibration as he drove back to their pit. He recognized the sound: One of the headers had worked loose.

Jimmy quickly got things tightened up, and his spirits were buoyed a bit when he won his heat from the back. Now he was consumed with adjusting the car for the changing track conditions. He walked the track after the heats, and he was certain the track would improve in the chilly late-spring night air.

He had already realized how much he missed Harvey. Despite

their constant arguments, the big man had become a solid presence for Jimmy, and most of the time—despite his unflinching tone and grouchy demeanor—he was right about what the car needed.

Jimmy's call on the setup turned out to be completely wrong. He was hopelessly loose for the feature, fighting the car the entire way. He slogged along in ninth, when the red light flashed on with just three laps remaining. Bobby Mancini and Steve Graffan had been battling for the lead when they got tangled up in three, sending both vaulting wildly over the fence. After a few anxious moments both men climbed unhurt from their machines.

In addition to stepping up to help Jimmy, Sid had made some changes of his own in recent weeks. He had parted ways with Frank Graham, with the young racer heading home to the west coast. Sid reconnected with Rick Wagner, the longtime Ohio veteran who had driven for Sid through several stints in the past. Tonight their collaboration paid off, as Wagner won in Sid's primary car. The win provided a lift to the mood in their pit, and Jimmy loaded his car and hung around as he waited for Sid to get the payoff.

"How 'bout we just settle up for both races tomorrow evening after Sunset Park?" Sid suggested. "That would be simpler, and you wouldn't have to wait around tonight."

"Uh, well, I hate to admit this, Sid, but I'm a little short," Jimmy explained. "I'll just take tonight's money now, if you don't mind."

"Don't mind a bit," Sid nodded. "I'll go get in line and be back as quick as I can."

A short while later Sid returned, and they went to the front of the truck where they could count out the money less conspicuously. Jimmy hated for anyone to know he was broke; but facts were facts. Whatever he made tonight was going to be welcome company for the six dollars in his wallet.

Sid counted out his 40 percent, and Jimmy nodded.

"Say, I owe you some more," Sid continued. "Gas for your pickup."

"Oh," Jimmy said, surprised. "I never thought about that. It's no big deal."

"Sure it is. You shouldn't pay the tow rig out of your 40 percent. It's my car, and I'm responsible. Do you have a guess on what you'll use in gas this weekend?"

Jimmy pondered the question. "Maybe twenty bucks."

"Here's a twenty. That even us up?"

"Yep, we're even."

Thirty minutes later they were checking into the Flying Carpet Inn, their pickups parked side-by-side in the parking lot.

"You guys wait out here, and I'll get the room," Sid said, heading for the front desk.

In a moment they were packed into the little room, with everyone looking longingly at the two beds. They left the door open, and in a few minutes Rick Wagner came driving up.

"Okay, we'll draw for the beds," Sid said, pulling out a deck of cards. "First Ace gets the first bed, second Ace gets the second bed."

"Wait a minute," Jimmy said quickly. "Slim's got a broken rib, he shouldn't sleep on the floor. I vote to give him one of the beds."

Sid looked around. "Everybody agree? Yes? Okay, Slim, you're in this one. We'll draw for the other bed."

"I ain't takin' a bed without drawin'," Slim objected. Jimmy cut him off with a wave of his hand.

"Listen, I'm too tired to argue with you, and I don't want you all gimped up in the morning, slowing us down. Get your butt on the bed and go to sleep, it's a short night already."

Slim grumbled but began taking off his shoes. The others quickly drew cards, and Howard, the mechanic who helped on Sid's car, smiled with satisfaction as he displayed his card.

"One clover," he said, handing the card back to Sid. Jimmy took a quick shower and rolled out his sleeping bag, and within minutes the light was off and they were settled in. Jimmy and Mike were crowded on the floor near the door, while Sid and Wagner parked on the floor at the end of each of the beds.

"Leave the drapes open, so we can see if anybody is messing with the cars," Sid said. The room was quickly filled with the sound of men snoring, and Jimmy quickly drifted off, visions of angry bulls darting through his mind.

Chapter 12

Sid was awake first, a little after six. As he rustled his way into the shower the others began to awaken. Jimmy brushed his teeth and dressed, walking outside to piddle with the race car. Soon they were headed for the car wash, where the two cars were rolled off the trailer and cleaned.

They walked across the street to a small café for some breakfast. The other men filled one booth, and Jimmy and Mike grabbed another. As they waited on their food, a group of men wearing racing caps filed into the booth behind them, apparently not noticing Jimmy.

"Hey, that's Rick Wagner sitting over there," one man said, his voice low. "He was the big man last night, wasn't he?"

"Yeah, didn't you see their cars across the street? Rick's car, and that new 49, the one Wilson was in last night."

"Hey, what was the story on that?" a pot-bellied man asked. "His mechanic got hurt?"

"Yeah, Jack Harvey. Had a wreck on the way back from River Ridge. From what I hear, he's still in a coma, and he'll never walk again. Sonny Ellison has quit, so Sid Johnson is running the 49 to get his owner points. Hired Wilson to run the car."

"Wasn't so good last night."

"He won't win another one this season," the tallest man said, puffing a cigarette. "Without Harvey, he's lost…you could see it last night. I've never been much on him, anyways."

Mike and Jimmy listened and exchanged a grin.

They ate quickly, and Jimmy laid some money on the table when they had finished. They rose quietly, and Jimmy made it a point to not look at the men seated in the next booth. He couldn't help but notice how they quieted when they spotted him, and he and Mike joined the other men as they crossed the street.

Jimmy had always liked Sid, but this episode cemented his respect for the man. Sid had put in long hours helping get the second car ready, and had readily agreed to have Coffman's name lettered on the hood.

"I appreciate you doing this for us," Jimmy told Sid. "I'm not kidding, it means a lot."

"Ah," Sid smiled. "I just wanted to go racing. I've always wanted to see how we'd race together, and this was a chance to try it. And Sonny is a friend of mine, and so is Harvey. Harvey is a hard case sometimes but he's done me a lot of favors down through the years."

"I hope I can start running a little better," Jimmy smiled. "I need to hold up my end of the deal."

"What the heck happened to your truck door?" Sid asked. "Meant to ask you last night."

"Aw, it's a lot of bull," Jimmy answered. Sid gave him a funny look, and Jimmy simply smiled and shook his head.

They quickly rolled the cars back off the trailers and got busy on the changeover from dirt to pavement. Slim insisted he felt good enough to help switch the shocks, while Jimmy changed the torsion bars. They then pulled the rear end cover to change the gear. Mike hung close by, chasing tools and watching, trying to learn without getting in the way. Jimmy then moved the Pittman arm to slow down the steering, and rolled a set of pavement tires off the rack on the front of the trailer.

"What time you got?" Jimmy asked Sid as he hammered the wheels in place.

"Little after nine," Sid answered, wiping his hands on a rag. "You guys about done?"

"Ready to roll in five minutes," Jimmy called, suddenly feeling a sense of confidence come over him.

He timed second-quick at Sunset Park, reminding himself how much he enjoyed these steep banks. Plenty of racers disliked this fast, daunting place, but from day one Jimmy loved it.

He ran second in his heat, and would line up fifth in the feature. Sid came over to help him look over the car.

"Let's make sure everything is tight," Sid suggested. "You don't want things falling off at this place. Plus, you've got a good shot at winning today."

"I can't believe you like this place," Wagner smiled. "Man, I hate it. I don't mind pavement, but this place, I guess it spooks me. Nothing three feet of dirt wouldn't cure!"

"I dunno, I just always felt good here," Jimmy insisted. "'Course, Harvey always put a great car under me, and that probably made it a lot easier in the beginning. Hey, they're callin' for the feature."

In a few minutes he was idling down the backstretch, intently focused on the start, staring at the tail of Sammy Caldwell's red No. 2. As they roared off the fourth corner, Sammy moved to the right, opening up a full lane to the inside.

Jimmy had a good run, and he pulled nearly alongside, trusting that Sammy heard him. But as they approached the corner Sammy began moving lower, and Jimmy yielded as much ground as he could, trying to avoid contact. As he braked, Sammy's left rear banged into his right front, and Jimmy felt the car cut sharply to the inside.

The back end quickly came around, and for a moment Jimmy thought he might slide right out into the oncoming traffic. He gassed the throttle sharply and turned hard to the left, sending him spinning harmlessly across the grass.

He pounded the steering wheel and cursed, actually saying very a few sharp words for his ol' buddy Sammy. He could temper his anger with the fact that over the two or three years they had raced together, it was the first time he could recall contact between them.

In a moment Jimmy was restarted, and he felt the car out as he caught up to the field, making sure everything was all right. Now his odds were long, and he knew it.

"Let's see how many I can pass," he said, gritting his teeth and clenching the wheel.

Despite the contact the car was very good, and he quickly began cutting through the field. A couple of cautions came at the perfect time, and with each restart he gained several positions.

He caught Sammy and was right on his tail when he saw the flagman showing them five fingers. As quickly as they passed under the flag stand the caution flag waved for a stalled car on the backstretch. As they slowed and the field fell into restart order, Jimmy realized Sammy was leading the race.

"Well, well, well," he said, nodding his head. "What a nice situation this is."

He knew Sammy hadn't yet heard him, so he thought about a strategy. He definitely had a better car than Sammy, but it was hard to outsmart the veteran racer. Jimmy debated waiting until the last lap to show his hand, but decided to try an all-out run on the restart.

As they rolled the backstretch the caution light went out, and Jimmy's foot tensed on the throttle. By instinct he knew where Sammy would start, and a fraction of a second before Sammy took off, Jimmy hammered the throttle. His jump was perfect; early enough to gain some momentum, but late enough to escape a penalty.

He was alongside Sammy as they entered turn one, and he felt his car skitter slightly in the high groove. He lifted and felt the car turn nicely, and was right back on the throttle. In a moment the roar in his left ear lessened, and for the next four laps there was only the sound of his own screaming engine.

Jimmy pumped his fist as he crossed the finish line, and he could see the big crowd standing and saluting him as he sped past. After an insurance lap he rolled to a stop on the front straightaway, where Sid and the guys were waiting, broad grins on their faces and their fists in the air.

Sid leaned in close as Jimmy unbuckled, grinning widely.

"That's about as good a drive as I've seen," Sid shouted. "I don't know what got into you, but you did a helluva job!"

Jimmy peeled off his helmet and saluted the crowd, which responded with a thundering roar of approval. The PA announcer moved in with a microphone, and shook Jimmy's hand. Jimmy was so excited he had no idea what the guy asked him.

"I just want to dedicate this win to Jack Harvey and Slim MacDonald," he said, his voice quaking. He tried to catch himself, but he was pretty sure he was going to cry. He waited a moment and managed to gather his emotions, and he continued.

"This has been real tough week, and this helps us keep going… Sid Johnson helped us out with this car, and I can't thank him enough. The car was great, and the cautions came right when I needed them.

"Most of all, I want to thank you great fans!" Jimmy shouted, and they again cheered. "I want everybody to come by and see us after the races, and help us celebrate!"

The announcer moved over to interview a disappointed but poised Sammy Caldwell, then third-place Rusty Fernandez. As soon as he had finished the interview, Sammy hurried over to Jimmy.

"Didn't aim to hit you there on the start," he said. "Did I pinch you down too much? I thought you had room, then I felt us hit."

Jimmy tensed for a moment, then relaxed. It was hard to stay mad at a classy guy like Sammy.

"I thought you saw me. I figured I was far enough alongside, and when you came down I got on the brakes but you kept coming. I was in the grass, man. I gave you as much room as I could."

Sammy hesitated before answering. "Well…I didn't expect you'd come that hard on the first corner. You're usually more patient than that."

"You gave me an open lane," Jimmy said quietly. "You give me that, and I'm going to take it, just like I expect you to. Whether it's the first lap or the last lap."

"If I'm in the wrong, I'm sorry," Sammy said simply. "I like racing with you because you're clean, and that's how I race. I didn't intend to hit you."

"I know you didn't," Jimmy said, and he meant it. "It happens."

They stood quietly for a moment, in the middle of one of those awkward moments. "So we're okay?" Sammy finally spoke up.

"We're okay," Jimmy answered.

"If I'd known it was you back there, I sure would've played it different on that restart," Sammy laughed, shaking his head. "Man, how do you get such a jump like that?"

Jimmy grinned. "Just lucky, I guess."

They posed for victory pictures, and the gate from the grandstand was opened. Fans poured onto the track and into the pit area, and Jimmy found himself nearly mobbed by happy people, shaking his hand, patting his back, raving about what a great race they had seen.

As he greeted the throng he happened to see the four men from the nearby booth at breakfast. One man looked toward Jimmy and said something to the others, and they nodded.

Jimmy looked at the tall man with the cigarette, and they made eye contact. A sheepish smile crept onto the man's face, and he brought his hand up to the bill of his hat in a token salute.

Jimmy smiled, and nodded in return to the man. He felt like his feet were four feet off the ground as the stream of people closed in around him, caught up in their passion and excitement. He was tired as hell, but right now it was easy to feel good.

Chapter 13

Jimmy steered his pickup into the hospital parking lot, making his way up the elevator to room W-121. As he approached the room he heard loud voices inside.

"I don't give a damn what your orders are, get away from me with that thing," Harvey bellowed at the two nurses. "You ain't gonna do it."

"Mr. Harvey, you need this," the nurse pleaded. "I promise it won't hurt, and if you'll just relax, we can get this over with."

"Get the hell out—" Harvey stopped suddenly when he saw Jimmy. "Oh, hello, boy."

The women turned as Jimmy entered the room, their faces drawn with exasperation.

"Oh, good, you're here," the older nurse said quickly. "Maybe you can talk some sense into him. He's being awfully difficult—"

"You're the ones bein' difficult," Harvey roared. "I told you, I ain't doin' it. Just give me that bedpan and get out. I don't need your help."

"What's the argument?" Jimmy asked.

"Mr. Harvey needs an Enema, and he refuses," the younger nurse explained. "According to our charts it's been three days since—"

"I get it," Jimmy interrupted. "Sounds like he isn't keen on your idea."

"Ain't no way," Harvey said, crossing his arms. His leg was extended straight out, encased in a big plaster cast, hanging from a cloth device. But Harvey seemed oblivious, as he emphatically wiggled around as he shouted.

The older nurse nodded for Jimmy to step out into the hallway.

"Don't be talkin' behind my back," Harvey yelled. "Damn it, get in here! Boy! Get in here!"

"Try not to get upset when you see him act like this," the nurse explained in a whisper. "Many patients who have suffered a serious head injury sometimes act like this, shouting and such. So try to be patient, and don't let it alarm you. With time they'll usually get back to normal."

Jimmy gave her a wry smile, slowly shaking his head. "Ma'am, I hate to tell you this, but for Harvey, yelling and raising hell *is* normal. Matter of fact, I'm excited. This is the most normal I've seen him since the accident!"

"HEY!" Harvey yelled. "Get in here! This nut case is messin' with me!"

"Will you try to talk to him?" the nurse pleaded.

"All right. Give us a couple of minutes."

The nurses quickly left, and Harvey began to settle down. "If they think I'm gonna let them…well, ain't no way," Harvey huffed.

"How's the leg?"

"Good. Doc says I'll get out of here when I can walk on crutches. Some young punks came in here this morning and said I'll have to do 'rehab,' whatever that is. Boy, I'm ready to get out. Didn't you race today?"

"No, we had the weekend off, remember?"

"No you didn't," Harvey insisted. "We have to run Sunset Park today, because we ran Shoe's yesterday."

"That was last weekend," Jimmy gently corrected. "You just got your weeks mixed up."

Harvey was quiet as he struggled to remember. Jimmy could see the frustration in his eyes as he tried to make sense of what Jimmy told him.

"And you're running Sid Johnson's car," Harvey said slowly, like he was trying to piece it all together. "You quit Mr. Ellison for a while."

"No, I didn't quit," Jimmy explained. "Sonny didn't want to race without you. We put our motor in Sid's spare car, and we're running as No. 49 so Sonny keeps getting points. We'll do that until you're feeling better."

"Yeah, that's right," Harvey nodded. "Just till I'm feeling better."

He suddenly looked drained, and weak. He sagged back into the bed, looking at Jimmy with sad eyes.

"I'm thirsty. Where's Slim?"

"Slim will probably be here a little later. Here, have a sip of water."

Jimmy held the small glass close, gently putting the straw between Harvey's lips. The big man filled his mouth and swallowed, then relaxed his head back on the pillow.

It was quiet for a moment when Harvey reached up, clasping Jimmy's hand. His grip was firm, but Jimmy could feel the tremble.

"How come I'm here? How'd I hurt my leg? Where's Slim?"

"There was a crash on the highway," Jimmy said softly for the umpteenth time. "You busted your leg. You had surgery on it. You bumped your head. You're getting better, every day."

Harvey began to cry, and Jimmy was so uncomfortable he wanted to run from the room. But he forced a reassuring smile, and kept squeezing Harvey's hand.

"How come I can't remember? I want to go home. Where's Slim?"

An hour later Jimmy sat by Harvey's bed, reading a newspaper while the big man slept peacefully. He heard someone coming, and looked up to see Sonny and Slim come through the door.

"How's he doing?" Sonny said softly. "I'm surprised he's sleeping this early."

Jimmy nodded, pointing to the hallway. They stepped outside, closing the door behind them. Jimmy explained the exchange with the nurses, and told of Harvey's confusion and outburst of emotion.

"Well, that's how they said it might be," Sonny said, his voice low. "Almost like putting a puzzle back together, isn't it? But at least we know he's improving. Yesterday we had probably a half-hour talk where he was sharp as could be, perfectly normal. Then 10 minutes later he was asking where he was again."

"It's hard, seeing him like this," Jimmy admitted. "You know how proud he is, he'd be crushed if he knew this was happening. But he is getting better, I can see it. He's a lot stronger today than when I was here on Thursday. Every time I'm here I can see progress."

"They start the therapy for his head injury this week," Sonny said. "I guess they have ways to help him with his memory, and help him get his confidence back a little bit. I'm anxious to see if that helps him."

"Nothing we can do but try," Jimmy nodded.

They started to step back inside when Sonny suddenly stopped short.

"Holy cow, I almost forgot," he said. "Hey, you won't believe this! I've got great news, Jimmy. GREAT news! Yesterday I ran into Lou Warren, my buddy with the Meteor Foods championship team. Remember him? The Speedway opens in two weeks, and he said they were getting everything ready."

"Sure I remember Lou. But what's the news?"

"He asked about you, and told me he'd be interested in you taking some laps in one of their backups and maybe try to make the 500, if they get their primary cars in on the first weekend. Isn't that great??!! A chance to race at the Speedway!"

Jimmy said nothing, feeling like his knees were wobbling. The hallway suddenly seemed brighter by ten times, and he leaned against the wall as he tried to grasp what Sonny was saying.

A shot. At the Speedway. With a big team. Could it really be possible?

Chapter 14

Jimmy eased his foot onto the clutch pedal of his truck, reaching up to cut the engine. He sensed the butterflies in his stomach, fluttering and flitting and making him feel like he was short of breath.

Knock off the nervous stuff, he chided himself. This is just another race shop, and just another bunch of racing mechanics.

The sign over the door was colorful, with a logo Jimmy had seen at the grocery store since he was a kid. "Meteor Foods" was lettered on the window, and as Jimmy stepped inside he heard the familiar sounds of a race shop. The clang of wrenches, the sharp report of an air tool, the chatter of mechanics, and a radio in the corner playing a Rolling Stones song. Several Indy cars were situated throughout the shop, giving Jimmy's butterflies another jolt.

A shaggy-haired mechanic looked up at Jimmy and smiled in recognition. "Looking for Lou?" he called out, pointing toward a small office in the back. "He's in his office, probably on the phone. Here, I'll show you."

He laid his ratchet on the floor and stood up.

"You're Jimmy Wilson," he said, offering a handshake. "I've seen you run sprint cars plenty of times."

"Yeah, that's me," Jimmy smiled.

"I'm Mike, but everybody calls me Wart. I'm one of the mechanics here, and I do tires on the weekends. So you're gonna run one of our cars?"

"Well, I hope so. I talked to Lou on the phone and he told me to come over. I guess I need to get fitted for a seat."

"Cool! Here, he's off the phone now. You can go on in."

Lou Warren looked up at Jimmy as he hung up the phone. Jimmy guessed Lou was in his 40s, with a balding pate and a deep tan that suggested a lot of days at the race track. Lou smiled when he saw Jimmy, rising to walk around the desk and shake his hand.

"Wow, was it even 30 minutes ago that we hung up the phone?" Lou laughed. "You weren't kidding when you said you'd come right over!"

Jimmy felt his face redden, and he grinned sheepishly. "Yeah, well...I guess I didn't want you to change your mind."

Lou laughed again. "That's what I like to see, Jimmy. You're determined, and that's good. Here, have a sit."

Jimmy eased himself into a small chair in front of Lou's desk.

"Well, here's the program," Lou said, repeating what he said on the phone. He had a style of looking you right in the eye, and Jimmy imagined that he could be a tough customer if you fired him up. But there was also a sincerity there that immediately put Jimmy at ease.

"We've got three cars, and I want 'em all in the race. We run Johnny Nichols full-time on the championship trail, and he's our primary guy. We've got a second car with the Englishman, Ian Montgomery. And you'll be in our third car."

"So I'll only get into the car after the first weekend of qualifying?"

"You're in luck," Lou said, pointing to the phone. "That call I just got was from my guy at Meteor, and he confirmed that they want another car in for sure. They came up with a little more money, so we'll do a three-car deal, from day one.

"Our only issue is that we're stretched thin on parts and people to do this. If one of my other guys hurts his car, or if we run short somehow, you might have to give up your seat. But right now we want three in the race."

Lou leaned back in his seat, studying Jimmy. "You're a rookie, and I'm taking a big chance here. I know you can race, because I've seen it. But that's not the real reason I'm putting you in the car... it's because everybody tells me you've got a good head on your shoulders. I'm counting on that. With three cars we don't have any margins on pieces and parts, and we cannot—I mean cannot— bend any equipment. You know what I'm saying?"

Jimmy nodded solemnly. "No crashes," he said, almost whispering.

"Exactly. Now, you're going to be under a ton of pressure. That's normal, and you'll just have to deal with it. But what's most important is that you listen. You listen to me, and to your crew chief. Everybody else, you ignore. The first time I see you trying to be a star, trying to do too much, not listening, we'll have a big problem."

Jimmy looked right at him.

"I mean it," Lou repeated. "That's the deal going in. As long as you do what I tell you, we'll get along great. Understood?"

Jimmy nodded, allowing a small smile to break across his face. "Absolutely."

Lou suddenly stood. "Well, let me show you around and introduce you to the guys. Indy opens on Saturday, and we've only got three more days to get squared away and get our stuff over there. Let's get started fitting you up."

On opening day Jimmy spent a sunny Saturday afternoon getting through his rookie test. Four separate runs at a controlled speed, the first three under the watchful eye of the USAC observers. The final segment came with four veteran drivers looking on, one stationed in each corner. Jimmy finished the last segment and walked to the official's stand on the front straight.

"Go meet them in your garage," said an official. "They said they needed to talk to you in private."

Jimmy's heart dropped. Why do they need to talk to me? Didn't I do all right? I was smooth, and I think I hit the speed marks right on the button…what's this all about? He hurried toward the garage area, forcing himself not to break into a run.

He felt his knees shaking as he stepped into the garage. There stood Johnny Cole, Lee Baxter, Joe Newton, and Dick Hawkins. Normally he'd be excited to be in the same room as such legends; now, he was nearly consumed with anxiety.

The four men looked solemnly at Jimmy as he stopped cold.

"Did I pass?" he blurted, his voice an octave higher than normal.

"Close the door," Cole said quietly. "It's better that way."

Jimmy thought he was going to throw up. "What did I do wrong?" he said, trying not to faint. "Where did I mess up?"

The men looked at each other, and back at Jimmy.

"Son," Hawkins began quietly, "are you sure you've actually driven a race car before? I mean, really?"

Jimmy's mouth hung open, but no words would come out. He heard only the silence of the room roaring in his ears, and he felt his entire life turning to ashes right before his eyes.

Suddenly the four men burst out laughing, their guffaws echoing in the small space.

"You did great, kid," Newton grinned, slapping him on the back. "We're just having some fun with a rookie, that's all!"

The other men tried to control their laughter as they nodded, falling about the room.

"Boy, if you coulda seen your face," Cole said, wiping tears from his eyes. "You were a dead duck!"

Jimmy managed a weak, defeated grin, and he leaned over the workbench, shaking his head.

"Man," he panted. "That was cruel and unusual punishment!"

"Now we're ready to get busy," said his crew chief, Willie Moore, looking at his watch. "We'll take the car back to get fueled, and then we'll get some more laps before six. Everything feel all right?"

Jimmy nodded.

"Hey, Jimmy," a voice called out from along the concrete wall near their pit. "Let's get some photos of you taking the rookie stripes off!"

He turned to see John Flanders, a free-spirited photographer who followed all the USAC sprint races. Flanders was fishing a big camera from his bag, quickly changing lenses.

"Do we have time?" Jimmy looked at Willie.

"Yeah, go ahead and take a minute. You should enjoy this… taking the stripes off the car, that's a big step!"

Jimmy was beaming as he slowly peeled the pieces of tape off the rear wing of the car as Flanders snapped photos. Several other photographers hurried over to capture the scene, and Jimmy posed several times with the car, and with Willie, after the final stripe had been removed.

A mechanic sat in the car, steering it while another crewman on a small garden tractor began towing it toward Gasoline Alley.

Jimmy looked at the big crowd gathered behind the mesh fence located a few yards from the pit area, realizing that while many stared, nobody had any idea who he was.

A few minutes later Jimmy was back in the car, ready to resume practice. Willie leaned over the cockpit, his face so close to Jimmy's that he could see the tiny pores on his forehead.

"Just concentrate on the markers in the corner, and be smooth," Willie explained. "Check your mirrors every few seconds, because cars will be coming up on you. When you get into the corner, keep your groove. Don't be moving around.

"Now listen," Willie said, moving even closer. "This thing's got *waaaayyy* more horsepower than your sprint car. When you get back on the throttle, roll your foot into it real smooth. Jump on it too fast, and you'll lose the back end.

"I want you to back off when you get to the '4' marker on the straightaway. Let's lay some laps down with you backing off there, and see where we are. Okay? Now, let's get back out there. Be smart."

Jimmy rolled one lap slowly, getting some temperature in the tires. Soon he rolled into the throttle, hearing the turbocharged Offy screaming behind him, feeling the air rush over his head as he zoomed along the front straightaway.

Any illusion that he was going fast vanished as a car roared past on his right side. Check those mirrors, he reminded himself.

He watched for the first marker along the outside fence, the "4" looming larger as he approached. He lifted the throttle and gently eased into the brakes for only a moment, feeling the car scoot close to the ground as his helmet tugged to the right. Midway through the corner he eased back into the throttle, gradually picking it up and finding himself along the short chute.

After several laps he saw a crewman leaning out over the inside wall on the front straight, holding up a signboard that simply said, "IN." He finished the lap, lifting halfway down the backstretch to steer into the pits coming off turn four. Willie and the crew were waiting as he cut the engine, hearing the Offy burp and burble before falling silent.

"Nice and smooth," Willie nodded, leaning in close. "Your lap times are consistent, and that's what we're looking for."

The crew looked over the tires and studied the car, looking for anything amiss.

"Let's pick it up a little. I want you to carry the throttle in deeper, about halfway to the next marker. Know what I mean? Okay? Good. Just use your foot to control your speed, but don't do anything quick...not with the wheel, not with the gas, not with the brakes. The car doesn't like anything quick or disruptive. Let's get some more laps in."

The next two hours seemed to rush past in a matter of moments. Jimmy steadily picked up speed, carefully pushing the car farther, growing more comfortable. His numbers increased with each session: 166.5, 166.8, 167.7, 168.1, 168.5. His last run was his best, flirting with 169.

He was on the track when the closing gun sounded, and the yellow light flicked on. Soon he was idling into this pit, climbing from the car as he tugged his helmet from his head. He saw Lou standing with Willie, and both men nodded at him.

"Real good day," praised Willie. "Every lap was better, and you were smooth."

"Thanks," Jimmy said, swallowing a swig of cold water. He was surprised to discover how tired he was, because the afternoon seemed so easy.

They were blessed with great weather as the weekend drew closer, and each day Jimmy made slow progress. He was learning the nuances of the track, trying to follow Willie's coaching to the letter. Still, he had to admit: If he heard, "Watch your mirrors" once more, he thought he might puke.

He was now able to stay flat on the throttle all around the race track, and with each lap he was growing more confident. He felt good about everything but his speed; it was indeed going to take at least 180 to make it, but they were stuck at 175. He and Willie and Lou talked about things that morning before rolling the car from the garage.

"I think we've got too much drag," Willie mused. "Our trap speed is 185, and everybody else is at least 10 mph over that. We're going to have to trim the car out and get that trap speed up there, and concentrate on getting him through the corner."

"What's 'trap speed?'" Jimmy asked.

"At the end of the straightaway they have a couple of scoring lights, and it measures your speed through the trap entering the corner. It helps us figure out a lot of things, including how well you're getting down the straightaway."

"You have no choice but to start taking wing away," Lou nodded. "But, boy, be careful. Jimmy, this is where you earn your money, son. I realize this is new to you, but you're going to have to concentrate like you never have before.

"When they take wing out of the car, you'll carry a lot more speed into the corner, and you'll have a much greater chance that the rear end will step out. That's bad news here, real bad news. It isn't like a sprint car where you can catch it. Once the ass end jumps out from under you, by the time you realize it you're already gone. So you've got to really feel this thing in the corner, and hit your turn-in marks exactly right."

Jimmy nodded, and they began rolling the car out for practice.

The next three hours were plenty difficult, as Jimmy scared himself a half-dozen times. The stability he had grown accustomed to was gone, and Jimmy struggled to stay consistent. His trap speeds were improving, but now he was struggling to get through the corners, and about half the time had to lift the throttle.

Jimmy climbed out after a brief run as the mechanics puzzled over the car. He looked up to see Lloyd Fisher, a guy who had raced here at least 15 years, sitting on the concrete wall as his crew worked on his car. They made eye contact, and Fisher waved him over.

"You're the sprint car boy," he said in a Georgia drawl, sticking out his hand. "Gettin' this ol' place all figured out?"

"Man, I'm not figuring anything out," Jimmy said, slumping his backside on the wall. "This place…it's spooky! I'm trying to do exactly the same thing every lap, but instead of picking it up I'm actually getting slower!"

"That's just Indy bluffin' y'all," Fisher smiled. "Don't let it buffalo you, son. Just stay after it, and don't get wound up."

"My problem is, I'm not smart enough to tell Willie what the car is doing, and what it needs. I feel like a little kid, riding a tricycle. I don't know if we're going the right way or the wrong way or—"

"Easy now...listen, the hardest thing is knowin' if the problem is you, or the car. You ain't got enough experience yet to know this. So lemme give you some advice: Assume it's the car. Don't get down on yourself, or this place will run you clear out of town. You just clean all that out of your mind, and hit your marks exactly, and be smooth.

"Listen, if you get all knotted up in the head, by the time you get it sorted out it's June and we've all gone home. Know what I mean?"

"Yeah," Jimmy laughed, standing and giving the older man a smile. "You're right...boy, this is sure one intimidating race track. But thanks for the help, Lloyd."

After two more sessions they were no better. Jimmy came in and Willie signaled him to climb out.

"You know, we're kind of chasing our tail here. I've got an idea, Jimmy. I think we've completely lost the balance on the car. I want to go back to our basic setup, and I want to try something else in a different direction. It might not work, but at least let's try it."

Jimmy nodded. "I'm all for anything you want to try. I wish I knew enough to tell you exactly what the car needs, Willie. If I knew, I'd sure tell you."

Willie nodded, and waved to one of the mechanics. "Take it back to the garage...I want to put a new setup on 'er."

Jimmy followed the car back to the garage, watching as the crew and Willie worked on both ends of the car. They took a minute to wolf down a sandwich, and after nearly an hour were rolling the car back out of the garage.

Jimmy looked around to realize the garage area was nearly in chaos. Several cars were on the track, while other cars were making their way back and forth from pit lane. It was a full-blown Friday thrash, as everyone prepared for tomorrow's Pole Day runs.

As the crew prepared to fire the engine Jimmy buckled in. Willie leaned over the cockpit.

"We're back to square one, almost. I made a couple of changes that you haven't felt before, but the car should be a lot more balanced. Just give me some consistent laps, and we'll see where we are."

The phrase "night and day" wasn't strong enough to describe the situation. Jimmy was immediately able to flat-foot the car through the corners, and he could feel his momentum growing with each lap. He spotted the pit board calling him in, and he soon rolled to a stop and flipped his visor open.

"Now that's more like it," Willie grinned. "Felt a lot better, didn't it?"

"Man, it's like a new car," Jimmy praised. "Whatever you did, it was right. Where are we on speed?"

"180, right out of the gate. Listen, I'm going to trim the car out a little more, and let's see if we can gain on it some more."

The next four hours were exhilarating, as Jimmy felt like he was flying around the place. His speed climbed: 181, 182.6, 183, 184, 184.9, 185. His only heart-stopping moment came later in the afternoon when he came up on a slower car, and drifted out of the groove entering the corner, the front end pushing into the gray on the exit. He figured he might have to come in for a mandatory underwear change, but Willie kept him out a few laps more.

It was about 5:10 when Willie called him in, signaling for him to climb out.

"Listen, I want to simulate a qualifying run. It isn't so much about the speed, but I want you to concentrate on four consistent laps, just like you'll do tomorrow. And I want the car in qualifying trim; not a lot of fuel on, with a fresh set of tires. So we'll take it back to the garage and get the fuel right, and we'll be ready in about 15 minutes."

Soon Jimmy rolled out for his test run, laying down a smooth warm-up lap. The car felt good, and he concentrated on hitting the corners exactly right on his first lap. As he came around the next time a crewman held a signboard up with his speed: 188.4.

He refused to allow himself to get excited, and he focused on the task at hand. The next two laps clicked off in quick succession: 188.25, 188.18, but on his final lap he encountered a slower car entering turn three and had to lift, killing his momentum. Still, when he guided the car back to his pit, Willie and the crew were actually applauding as he rolled to a stop.

"There you go," Willie said simply. "That's all you've got to do tomorrow, just lay down four laps just like that. I think we're in pretty good shape."

"Can we get some more fuel and go back out? I'd like to see if I can go faster."

"Nope, we're done. Let's just relax, and get ready for tomorrow."

Jimmy spent the final 15 minutes sitting on the pit wall, watching a dramatic flurry of laps where the day's top speed honors changed hands at least a dozen times as the afternoon shadow darkened the entire front straightaway.

At the closing gun he grinned at the drama, hoping that one of these days he might find himself in the middle of such a battle for bragging rights.

CHAPTER 15

The small heater hummed in the garage on Gasoline Alley at the Indianapolis Motor Speedway, warming the room. Jimmy sat on the wooden workbench, gazing at the No. 51, studying how the white paint was accented by the blue striping, with the orange Meteor Foods logo splashed on the front cowling and the rear wing.

His crew nearly filled the small area, nervously puttering around the car. Willie eased onto the workbench alongside Jimmy, glancing at his watch.

"We'll roll the car out in a few minutes," he said, his voice quiet and steady. "Any questions about the format, or what we need to do?"

"Nope," Jimmy said softly. "Just stay clean in practice, and get the car qualified. Right?"

"That pretty much covers it," Willie nodded. "Just do what you've done the past week: be smooth and be smart. I'm confident you'll do a great job."

Jimmy nodded.

"Two things I want you to think about," Willie continued. "One, it rained pretty hard last night, and it washed away all the rubber from this week. It's a green race track, and it'll feel different than what you've seen so far. Just keep that in mind when we practice.

"Secondly, take this notepad, and pen," he said, handing them to Jimmy.

Jimmy grasped the items and waited for Willie to continue. The older man paused for a moment, and it seemed the entire room hung on the moment, wondering what profound thing was in Willie's mind.

"Now, write this down: 198.413. Got it? Now, study that number."

Jimmy stared at the number for a minute, then looked up. "And...?"

"That's the track record here," Willie said. "If you break that record today, I'll kiss your ass at the start/finish line and give you 20 minutes to draw a crowd."

Jimmy and the crew erupted in laughter, melting away all the tension in the room. Nobody had approached such a speed all month, certainly not a rookie like Jimmy.

"All right, let's get to pit lane," Willie commanded, watching the crew swing the garage doors open and roll the car out.

Jimmy walked outside, where a deep gray cloud cover gave the scene a surreal cast. Gasoline Alley was a madhouse of people, with yellow shirts blowing whistles and mobs of people pushing in close to get a look at the cars and drivers.

The two other Meteor cars were also being rolled out, their crews carefully navigating through the sea of people.

Johnny "Nick" Nichols emerged from his garage, waving at Jimmy, just as Ian Montgomery walked up from Jimmy's right. The three men soon began making their way toward pit lane, listening as people shouted their names and begged for autographs.

"Bloody hell, look at that mob of people," Ian said in his heavy English accent. "It's...it's amazing!"

"Try not to let it distract you," Nick cautioned. "Today and race day, this big crowd kind of plays with your head...just pretend like it's another practice day."

"Right," Jimmy said, shaking his head. "Man, how can you not be distracted by all this? It's like an ocean of people, staring at you, waiting for you to screw up."

Nick shrugged. "I know, but try," he smiled. "I've been here several times and I still get all wired up, but you've got to turn it off and really concentrate. Otherwise you're in trouble."

Jimmy followed his car to their pit location, and in a few moments began climbing inside. All the cars were now running, filling his ears with a steady roar. The air was thick with methanol fumes, making him blink his eyes a bit; at least he thought it was the fumes. The roar diminished as he pushed earplugs in place, but he could still hear the rise and fall of engines as they were gently revved, building heat.

As he prepared to slide his butt into the seat he looked around. The entire front straightaway was like a giant valley, with a wall of people on each side, making a colorful mosaic that stretched all the way around turn one, and past turn four behind him.

He could only grin and shake his head as he positioned himself in the seat, slowly buckling in. His crew cut the engine, carefully looking over the car for any leaks or other problems. An official said something to Willie, who nodded and leaned into the cockpit. His face was inches from Jimmy's, but he still had to shout to be heard over the roar around them.

"Just take it easy, and feel the car out," he cried. "There will be a lot of cars out there, so look as far ahead as you can in case somebody dumps it in front of you. Watch your board and we'll let you know how you're doing."

Willie motioned to the crewman behind the car, and he spun the Offy to life. Jimmy revved the car gently, watching the crewman standing directly in front of the car, waiting on the signal. Suddenly the crewman stepped out of the way and motioned, and Jimmy pulled the car into gear and eased out on the clutch. He foot was too quick, and he killed the engine.

He felt stupid, and he glanced at Willie, who merely gave him a confident nod. The engine was quickly restarted and Jimmy made his way down pit lane.

After a couple of slow laps the green light flicked on, and Jimmy pressed down on the throttle. He quickly built speed, carefully maintaining his distance from the car ahead. The other car seemed slower than he wanted to go, so he carefully moved alongside as they came off four, gently moving to his left when he knew he had the car cleared.

Willie was right; the track had changed completely. Gone was the heavy black "groove" he had been following all week, replaced by a much smaller and lighter trail through the corners. The first few laps Jimmy was forced to lift slightly, because the grip wasn't there to get through flat.

His practice laps clicked off and he watched his pit board each time by as the crewman posted his speed. 182.5, 182.7, 183.1; he couldn't help but feel a tinge of disappointment, as it was at least 5 mph less than he ran the previous day.

Jimmy saw the checkered flag, and he eased up on the throttle. In a few moments he was pulling to a stop in his pit, gently revving the Offy before cutting the ignition. He climbed out as the crew pored over the machine.

He and Willie followed the car back to the garage area as another group of cars began their practice session. Once inside the garage, Willie explained their strategy.

"The air's still pretty dense, and that'll slow everybody down," he said. "The forecast calls for clearing skies, and if the humidity moves out that will improve conditions quite a bit. The trick is to get out when the air's better, but before the sun warms the race track up too much.

"We drew seven, but I'm not going to put the car in line yet. Let's watch everybody else and see what develops."

The next few hours were a painful exercise in patience for Jimmy. Qualifying began with a flurry, as several cars took runs. He and Willie studied the speeds, noting how today's speeds compared to what that particular car had been running all week.

"It's getting faster," Willie noted just past noon, looking skyward. "It's clearing off pretty nice, and you can feel that the air is drying out."

He looked at Jimmy and smiled. "Let's go ahead and get in line...it will take a few minutes to get through tech, and maybe we'll get lucky with our timing."

Soon Jimmy found himself walking with the car as it went through technical inspection. One ear was glued to the PA, as the run for the pole was now in earnest. Two-time winner Joe Newton thrilled the crowd with a speed of 192.8, bringing a roar so loud it startled Jimmy.

Jimmy realized they were getting closer to the front of the qualifying line, and Willie nodded for him to climb aboard just as Ian Montgomery rolled out for his first attempt, and Jimmy listened carefully as his run unfolded. The Englishman's first lap sent the huge place into a giant, roaring spasm, as Ian's speed report was read.

"Here it is! Here it is!" came Tom Carnegie's impassioned voice, inflaming the huge crowd. "The time, forty-six-point-zero-eight seconds," came the report, "and the speed...One-hundred-

and-ninety-FIVE, point-three-one-three-miles-an-hour!"

"Yeah," Jimmy shouted. "Go get 'em, Ian!"

The next three laps fell off only slightly, and Ian now held the pole with an average of 193.8. Jimmy felt certain that would hold, but he quickly concentrated on his own place in line.

Soon the car directly ahead of him rolled away, beginning his run. Jimmy sat patiently, his stomach churning, as Willie leaned into the cockpit.

"Four good laps," Willie said confidently. "Just make 'em smooth, and we're there. I'll give you your speed on the board, but don't let it distract you. Just stay focused on running good clean laps. If you see me waving the yellow, back off and bring 'er in."

Jimmy was left with his thoughts as he waited. Suddenly the official motioned to his crew, signaling that the other car had waved off his run, and the track was now Jimmy's. The crewman lit the Offy, and Jimmy eased onto the giant race course.

All week long he had practiced in front of nearly empty stands, but today a wall of color surrounded the track. He laid down a nice warm-up lap, and felt surprisingly calm as he saw the starter showing him the green as he approached the flag stand. He sped through the south end, smoothly hitting his points, and was quickly on the backstretch. In a few moments he was back around to complete the first lap, and he wondered if he was doing all right.

As he came off four to complete his second lap he glanced to the left at his board, watching for Willie's yellow flag. Instead his sign-man held the board aloft: 186.2. He was disappointed, because he had hoped for something closer to the 188-mph range he ran yesterday. But he stayed with the run, focusing on laying down three more smooth, consistent laps.

He exhaled deeply as he saw the checkered flag, and as he rumbled into the pit area he saw a waving throng of officials guiding him toward a mass of waiting people halfway down the pit lane. Jimmy cut the engine and popped his belts as car owner Lou Warren, Willie, and several other team members applauded. As he climbed from the car his crew surrounded him, whooping and hollering, slapping his back and congratulating each other.

"Great job!" Lou grinned, giving Jimmy an emotional hug. "You looked like a veteran out there!"

"We're in the show," said Willie, pointing to his clipboard. "Look at this, Jimmy...you only dropped off a couple tenths on all four laps...your average is 185.9. That'll hold up no matter what happens!"

Jimmy grinned as he looked at his lap times. The vast crowd in the Tower Terrace grandstand cheered him as he offered a smile and a wave.

Suddenly he felt a powerful surge of emotion, and felt his hands trembling. He fought back the tears that suddenly filled his eyes. He glanced around, fearful that people might see him cry, and he wished he could run away to a private place and bawl his eyes out. He managed to regain his composure without completely losing it.

He was quickly ushered to a man holding a microphone and he realized he was being interviewed on the radio network. He remembered all those days when he listened to this broadcast, and he could suddenly picture the small picnic table behind his boyhood home in Illinois, a small radio connected to the house through an extension cord.

He stumbled through the interview, trying to keep his emotions in check, and was then shuffled to another man, who asked him to wait for a moment. The man's voice was familiar, and he suddenly realized it was one of the famous pitside PA announcers. A few moments later there was a lull in qualifying activity, and the man flicked on the microphone and leaned close.

Jimmy could hear the man's voice just a few inches away, and in the background could hear the sound echoing around the speedway. The man introduced Jimmy as the fifth-fastest qualifier so far, and Jimmy heard the crowd give him a warm ovation.

He wasn't sure if anything he said made sense; he was so overwhelmed, he wasn't sure of anything. But the man was cordial and pleasant, helping him through his stumbles. When the interview was over the man offered a handshake of congratulations before moving away.

Someone was tugging on Jimmy's sleeve, directing him back toward the car, which had been rolled into a designated position for his qualifying photograph. He stood in the cockpit, while Lou and Willie and the crew stood alongside the car.

Suddenly he realized something: He had seen this photo a hundred times before, but with other guys in the middle. Now here he was, on racing's greatest stage, and he was so excited he thought he might explode.

It was just past 3 p.m. when Jimmy was late in a 20-lap run, getting the feel for the car when it was on worn tires. He was halfway down the backstretch when he saw a sudden burst of smoke up ahead, and he instinctively glanced in his mirrors and checked up, moving lower on the track.

He had slowed considerably as he came upon the crash, and his heart sank. Nick Nichols had smashed the Meteor Foods car into the outside wall, and the car was just sliding to a stop as Jimmy drove past. The yellow light was already on, and Jimmy eased his car toward the pit lane.

His crew stepped over the wall as he rolled to a stop, cutting his engine. He knew the track would be down for a while, so he popped his belts and climbed from the machine.

Jimmy looked up at Willie, and their eyes met.

"It was Nick," Jimmy said, pulling his earplugs out. "Pretty big one."

Willie tossed his clipboard onto the wall, slumping to sit forlornly, his arms crossed. He looked at Jimmy and shook his head, swearing out loud.

Jimmy wasn't quite sure why he was so upset. At the moment all he cared about was whether Nick was okay; he didn't get why Willie was suddenly so dejected. He moved closer, sitting his backside next to Willie on the wall and looking quizzically at his crew chief.

"You know what this means, don't you?" Willie shouted as several cars moved past on pit road.

Jimmy thought for a moment, and he suddenly had an idea of what was happening, in Willie's mind at least.

"Uh…no backup car?"

"Oh, they've got a backup car, all right," Willie said, his voice now quiet. "Right there is their backup car." He pointed at Jimmy's No. 51.

Jimmy didn't speak for a few moments, his mind reeling.

"Man…we're in the third row," he finally said, his voice almost a whisper. "Would they really put Nick in our car, knowing he's got to start last?"

"Their primary driver is Nick. Then Ian, then you. They've got to have Nick in the race, because of series points and because Meteor figures him as their main guy."

The two men sat without speaking for a moment, listening for any word over the PA.

"Johnny Nichols is walking to the ambulance," boomed a voice over the loudspeakers. "Looks like he is all right. But the car appears to be heavily damaged…"

The fans in the nearby stands applauded the update on Nick. Willie stood, and told the crew to take the car back to the garage area to await some kind of directive from Lou Warren.

Willie looked at Jimmy and arched his eyebrows.

"Well, let's hope we can fix that race car," he said quietly.

Jimmy nodded, gathering up his helmet and gloves and beginning the long walk back to the garage. Suddenly the sunshine didn't seem so bright, and it was hard to smile at the fans who shouted his name, clamoring for autographs.

Damn it, he scolded himself. *I should have never got my hopes up so high…*

Chapter 16

Early the next morning Jimmy walked through the garage area at the Speedway, headed for the Meteor Foods stable. Lou Warren waved as he saw Jimmy approaching.

"Good morning," Lou called out. "Where'd you go yesterday? I was looking all over for you."

Jimmy thought about some snappy line, but he just gave Lou a direct, honest smile.

"Well, I was feeling kind of sorry for myself so I went to work on my sprint car," he admitted. "I thought that might take my mind off things."

"That's what I wanted to talk to you about," Lou continued. "You're not out just yet, Jimmy. If there is any possible way we can fix Nick's car, that's the plan. Hey, we still want three cars in the race."

Jimmy looked surprised as he shot a glance at Lou. "You mean there's a chance you can fix it? I figured it was done after such a big hit."

"We're sure gonna try. In the meantime, I want you to sit tight. We might still need to put Nick in your car, so I can't afford to let you back out on the track until we know for sure. Okay?"

"Sure," Jimmy nodded. "Where is Nick? Is he here?"

"I would bet he can't even get out of bed today," Lou said. "That was a big hit, and I suspect he's feeling it this morning."

The next few days were the most difficult Jimmy could imagine. He wandered between Gasoline Alley and the pit area, observing as the Englishman, Ian Montgomery, continued to practice in the second Meteor car.

Early Friday morning Lou asked Jimmy to step into his garage for a private conversation. The deep lines in Lou's face revealed the strain of the past few days.

"I'm not going to sugar-coat it," Lou sighed. "I don't think we're going to get everything back together in time, Jimmy. The car is repaired, but we can't locate a gearbox. I've talked to everybody I know, but they're hanging onto their stuff until this weekend's qualifying is over.

"We have no choice but to use the gearbox from your car in Nick's. I've tried every way I know, but I can't find another damned gearbox. By the time qualifying is over this weekend and guys let loose some of their spares, it would be too late to run you. You have just a few laps in race setup, and I'm not going to put you out there with so little experience on race day."

Jimmy felt a huge pain sinking in his gut.

"Now, there is still a chance, and I haven't given up completely. Maybe we can come up with something yet today. Who knows... but I wanted to be straight with you about where we are."

One of Ian's crew opened the door and looked inside. "Hey, Lou...sorry to interrupt...could you look at these setup sheets for a minute?"

Lou hurried to the other garage, and Jimmy walked outside. The sun was shining beautifully, and the sky was a pure shade of blue. But it might as well have been pouring rain, because nothing about today looked nice to Jimmy.

He was tempted to leave, and go mess with the sprint car. But the car was ready, and he figured he wouldn't feel any better hanging around by himself in the shop.

Jimmy walked up pit lane, pausing to chat with a few people he had met over the past couple of weeks. Now and then somebody in the crowd would call out his name, and he waved and offered a smile. He felt like a fraud, wondering if everybody knew he wouldn't be in this year's race after all.

As he walked further down pit lane he saw Steve Graffan sitting on the wall, watching as a group of guys rolled a tired-looking old car to their pit. Jimmy turned his head and tried to walk past his old nemesis without being noticed; the last thing he wanted to hear was any crap from Graffan.

Jimmy was amazed when Graffan offered a slight wave, and a half-smile.

"How's it going?" Jimmy said, pausing to talk.

"Not very good," Graffan sighed. "We've done everything we

can, and I can't find enough. We're about three mph short, and we're about out of time."

"Is it the handling? Or not enough power?"

"The motor is tired," Graffan said, lowering his voice. "Real, real tired. This is a low-buck deal...they've got no spares, not enough help, and this motor isn't strong enough. I'm flat all around, lap after lap, but we're just slow."

"What's your status? Are they going to get Nichols's car fixed or not?"

"Right now, it looks like they're not," Jimmy admitted. "I dunno...just wasn't meant to be, I guess."

"We're just destined to be sprint car drivers, looks like," Graffan said, a tinge of sadness in his voice.

"Yeah...maybe you're right," Jimmy nodded. "Well, anyways, good luck this weekend."

"Same to you," Graffan said, reaching for his helmet and gloves as Jimmy shuffled away.

An hour later Jimmy stood at Ian's pit, watching the crew work on race day setups and fuel runs. Ian sat patiently as the crew bolted on another set of tires. A few feet away Johnny Nichols prepared for a practice run.

"Yellow," somebody called out. They looked around, wondering if there had been a crash. In a few moments a deep voice intoned from the loudspeakers.

"Yellow flag," the smooth voice said. "Looks like a tow-in on the backstretch for the 93 car."

"Graffan," one of the crewmen said. "That ol' sled finally gave up, I'll bet."

The guy was psychic; a few minutes later Graffan's machine came rolling silently down pit road behind a safety truck, and as it passed slowly by their pit a strong odor of hot motor oil trailed behind him.

"Cooked that baby," somebody said.

"We may have some fluid on the course," the PA voice called. "A full track inspection is under way."

Jimmy looked down the way as Graffan climbed from the car. He sat dejectedly on the wall, slowly peeling off his gloves and helmet. The crew removed the rear cowling, but after a quick glance they replaced the cowling and began to gather up their tools and things, their heads hanging in defeat.

It was probably 20 minutes later when one of the Meteor crewmen ran excitedly up to Jimmy.

"Lou needs to see you back at the garage," the man panted. "Said to hurry your ass up!"

Jimmy trotted back to Gasoline Alley, where he saw several members of the crew working at the back of his car.

"Get dressed," Lou said quickly. "We found a gearbox, and we'll be ready to go out in less than an hour. That will give you about three hours of practice."

Jimmy nodded, feeling a massive leap in his spirits.

"Where did you get the gearbox?" Jimmy quizzed, as if it mattered.

"Got if from the 93 car," Lou explained. "They scattered their last engine, and they're done. What was that young guy's name in the car…Griffin?"

"Graffan," Jimmy corrected. He still felt elation; but despite himself, he couldn't help but feel bad for his rival.

Jimmy stood next to the Meteor Foods car, preparing to climb in. He tried to ignore the mass of humanity that filled the grandstands along the front straightaway, instead trying to calm himself and focus on the task at hand.

500 miles. It was really that simple. 500 miles.

His crew chief, Willie Moore, patted his back confidently. "You'll do fine," he said. "You've done a great job all month…just focus on being smart, and patient."

Jimmy tried to quell the butterflies in his belly, but they persisted. He took a long drink of water, handing the jug back to the crewman.

"Drivers, to your cars!" the PA intoned, and the crowd roared. He stepped into the car and settled himself in, buckling down and pulling on his helmet. The pre-race ceremonies were well underway, but he concentrated on getting comfortable.

Nearly all his life he had hoped and prayed he would one day be here; now that it was happening, it seemed surreal, impossible.

As he pulled his gloves in place Willie leaned into the cockpit, his face inches from Jimmy's.

"Watch your mirrors, and watch the board," he reminded him. "Take it easy on the start, and remember: You can't win this thing on the first lap, but you can sure as hell take yourself out. When you come in, remember what I told you: You've got to hit your marks to give our guys room to change tires. Don't take off until you're told. Got it? Get ready, because we're going to fire the engine here in a minute."

Jimmy sat in silence, the outside world nothing but a muted blur. In a moment he heard a faint voice over the PA, and the crowd offered a massive roar.

"Fire it up!" Willie shouted, and a crewman triggered the starter. Jimmy hit the switch as he feathered the throttle and the Offy spun to life, burbling loudly. Out of Jimmy's sight a crewman raised his arm to signal they had fired.

Just as the pace car began to pull away, Willie leaned in and patted Jimmy on the helmet. Their eyes locked, and they nodded good luck to one another. As Willie stepped away from the car Jimmy pulled the car into gear, easing out on the clutch as the car surged.

Jimmy carefully trailed the car ahead, concentrating on running a perfectly straight line as they completed the parade lap. As they rolled down the backstretch the third time he saw the bright pace car begin to pull away, and he gripped the steering wheel and focused on his right foot. The butterflies were gone; now it was all instinct, and he knew what he needed to do.

The field roared as they moved through four, and the packed grandstands on both sides of the straightaway became a colorful blur as Jimmy pressed the throttle. The cars darted and moved all around him, and he eased into line as they moved into the first turn. In an instant they were through the turn and onto the short chute, ducking back to the bottom.

Within a couple of laps he found himself racing with Johnny Cole, finally settling in behind the veteran racer to follow him for a while.

Hey, the guy won this thing a couple of years ago, he figured. Maybe I can learn something.

Jimmy fought to maintain his focus through the early stages of the race. As his fuel burned away he was faster on the straightaway, but his tires were going away as well. He knew their pit window was around 25 laps, and each time by the front straightaway he watched his sign man. Finally on the 19th lap he saw the board: "IN."

He slowed on the backstretch, crossing his fingers that he could get this right. He rolled down pit road, turning smoothly into his pit. It was a fuel-only stop under green, and he was out in 12 seconds. The pit was busy with cars making their first stop, and he glanced at his right-side mirror as he roared from his pit. He was soon back to speed, and after the first round of stops remained in eighth.

Jimmy paced himself through the next 80 laps, trying to run consistent laps and keep a clear head. He knew he was still on the lead lap, and he was encouraged. Around the halfway point he made a nice pass for seventh, and a few laps later saw the car ahead drop off the pace. He wondered if it had been a lapped car, but on the next round his signboard read, "P6."

Things soon got more complicated. He rolled in for a stop under caution for fuel and tires, and Willie was waiting. He pointed to the boost dial on the dash, and screamed at Jimmy, "Turn it down a notch until we tell you!" Jimmy nodded, and when they were clear he roared back onto the track.

Okay, he repeated. Turn it down a notch until the yellow. They must want me to conserve fuel.

It was around lap 130 when Jimmy noticed his signboard saying, "UP." Did that mean to turn the boost up? Now? Or did it mean for him to pick up the pace?

He was unsure, so he left it alone. Two laps later Jimmy was passed by two cars, and dropped back to eighth. On his next stop Willie was red-faced as Jimmy screeched to a stop for fuel and right-side tires. Willie reached into the cockpit and turned the knob back to the original setting, screaming at Jimmy, "Watch the board!"

As Jimmy headed back out, he shifted from second to third and heard a big "KLUNK!" He felt the shift lever vibrate, and realized third gear was gone. He had no choice but to go to fourth, lugging the engine badly. He was well onto the backstretch before he had returned to his normal RPM range.

Up front Ian Montgomery was showing his strength, leading much of the way. Jimmy saw his teammate coming up in his mirror on lap 150, and he was surprised how much faster he was running.

Or am I just slow? Jimmy wondered.

The last two pit stops were difficult for Jimmy. Lap 158 was for fuel and right-side tires, and he realized the clutch was getting balky as he stopped. The crew had a difficult time getting his right rear wheel off, and they were lucky the stop was under caution. After some intense hammering and prying, they slapped the new wheel in place and Jimmy was underway, but Jimmy guessed that the stop was near 30 seconds.

Immediately, he knew something was wrong. He could feel a vibration, and guessed that the one of the wheels was not tight. The caution was still out, and he decided to duck down pit road to have it checked. Sure, Willie might be furious at the extra stop, but better to be safe than wadding the car—and himself—into a little ball. As he rolled down pit road he happened to notice his signboard: "IN." They must have realized they didn't get the wheel tight.

After a quick stop Jimmy was back underway, and he made his final stop under caution on lap 175, taking only fuel. He killed the engine trying to take off; the clutch was now getting to be a real problem. After getting underway, he adjusted the boost a couple of laps later when his signboard signaled, "DOWN" and he knew they were hoping to make it the rest of the way without another stop. As the laps dwindled he saw a slower car rolling along the apron in turn four, dead stick. His heart sank as he realized it was Ian. After a brilliant race, something had broken with less than 15 laps remaining.

On lap 190 Jimmy felt a growing vibration, and his car was a handful. He slowed a bit, giving up a position, trying to hang on till the end. He scared himself at least twice a lap over the final circuits, tightly clenching the wheel and praying that he could hang on long enough to finish. He saw the white flag, and the next 50-some seconds seemed like an eternity. Coming off turn four he saw the checkered flag waving, and he breathed a huge sigh of relief as he slowed into turn one, rolling through the short chute and down the backstretch.

He followed the other cars off the track, rolling to a stop at his pit. His crew surrounded the car, applauding and slapping his helmet. He slowly climbed from the car, quickly realizing that his legs and arms were complete rubber. He eased himself onto the pit wall as someone helped him remove his helmet; the vibration had tingled his fingers completely to sleep, and he felt nothing but pinpricks.

Someone helped pour some water into his mouth, and he began to feel better. Willie grinned broadly, grasping Jimmy's limp hands, coaxing a weak smile.

"We did it, Jimmy!" he shouted. "Brought 'er home in eighth! Pretty damn good for a rookie in the third car!"

In a few moments Jimmy learned that Johnny Cole had won, and that Ian had a two-lap lead on the field when his engine expired. Nick had dropped out before the halfway point when his clutch failed.

As they celebrated, one of his crew members shouted, "Hey, you might get Rookie of the Year!"

Jimmy thought for a moment.

"No way," he said, meaning it. "Ian was on the pole, led a bunch of laps, and would have won it. You've got to give the rookie deal to him, that's all there is to it."

He sat on the wall for a few minutes, finally mustering the strength to grab his helmet and gloves and begin the long walk back to the garage area. He looked around as the huge grandstands were emptying, wondering if he might ever stand in this same position again.

Jimmy was only sure of one thing: He had raced at Indy. One of the great goals of his life had been fulfilled. But instead of feeling satisfied, or proud, he just felt…tired. Very, very tired.

Chapter 17

Jimmy hauled the sprint car deep into the corner at Franklin, feeling it bite on the heavy track. He hammered the throttle, the rear tires driving him away from the guardrail.

It was two laps into the feature, and already he knew he was in trouble. An overnight rain had left the track plenty wet, sending the track crew scrambling this morning to prepare the track. Large black heaps of dirt had been graded to the inside, leaving a treacherous no-man's land. It was fast, it was getting rough, and it was damned dangerous.

Although Jimmy had timed second-quick, he threw a big setup change at the car after his heat race. He was certain the track would dry out for the feature, but the night air had brought a new batch of moisture to the surface, much more than he had anticipated.

Now he had a car that was so tight it was a stinking handful.

Jimmy soldiered on, trying different lines. He ran in the second five throughout the race, not fast enough to make a run at anybody.

With five laps to go he got into turn three a little too hot, and bicycled wildly. His quick wrists saved him, and he landed his left-side wheels back on the track so hard it knocked the wind out of him for a moment. He chugged through the loose stuff and kept it going, although at least two cars got by.

He eased into the pits after the checkered had flown, rolling to a stop and cutting the engine. He slowly climbed out, disgusted with the outcome.

"Where were we?" he asked Mike White.

"Tenth, I guess. Man, I thought you were a goner down there in three."

"Who won?"

"Graffan. Bobby Mancini was second."

Jimmy stared at the car. He had raced here plenty of times…

how could he have guessed so wrong about what the track would do?

"Well, we missed it tonight, didn't we?" Sid Johnson smiled. "Our car wasn't much better...I think Rick was eighth."

"Boy, I was sure wrong on the track," Jimmy said glumly, shaking his head. "You know, don't take offense at this, Sid, but I sure miss having Harvey around. He's awful sharp on reading the track, especially here."

"Hey, no offense taken," Sid insisted. "Jack's about as good as it gets...remember, he's been doing this longer than almost any of us. How is he doing, by the way? Any change?"

"Gonna go home this week. He's in some kind of rehab right now, mostly on his leg. They've also got a lady that comes in and helps him with his memory, asking him all kinds of questions, kind of getting his confidence back. The head injury deal is much better...I saw him a couple of times this week and he's a lot more clear about things, and the confusion is just about gone. Their big concern is how to keep him off that leg when they let him go home. They're probably right...as soon as he gets out, I don't know how we'll keep him away from the race car."

"You know, messing with the car might do him some good," Sid mused. "Might get him fired up a little bit...listen, our deal still stands: whenever you want to put your motor back in Sonny's car, no hard feelings from me. I understand completely."

"I appreciate that. But I don't think Harvey is anywhere near ready yet. Hell, he'll be in a wheelchair for a month or so before they'll even let him use crutches. So it'll probably be later this summer."

"Whenever it is, just let me know. It'll be good to have the cranky old goat back, to tell you the truth. I kinda miss him rantin' and ravin' at everybody."

"I sure appreciate you keeping me going," Jimmy said sincerely. "Without you offering me the use of your car, I'd have been done. I just wish we'd run better, because we haven't made you much money the last three or four times out."

"Aw, don't worry about it. It's a different car, and that always takes some time. Plus, I haven't given you the attention you probably need at the race track, because I'm focused on my main car. All things considered it ain't gone that bad."

It was a quiet Sunday evening, and Jimmy was having dinner at Bobby and Sandy Mancini's. The kids and Sandy had gone into the living room to watch TV, leaving Jimmy and Bobby at the kitchen table.

"This is a nice setup," Jimmy said, looking around. "Nice little house, couple of kids, good wife...I want to settle down like this one of these days myself."

"What's stoppin' you?" Bobby smiled.

"For starters I don't have a wife," Jimmy replied. "Minor detail."

"You could probably find something pretty easily. Besides, even without a wife you could buy a house. You ought to do that."

"Nah."

"Why not?"

"I'll wait till I'm married."

"Oughta buy it now, so you can get the one you want. If you wait, you'll end up in the house *she* wants."

Jimmy smiled. "Never thought of it that way."

"No kiddin', you ought to think about buying your own place. And you need to move back here to town. Living out in the sticks isn't good for you. You need to be here where all the racing people are."

"I don't think so," Jimmy said with an earnest cast to his face. "You know, Bobby, I've got to where I really like it out in the country. I've made a lot of friends up there, and they're great people. I suppose I can't live rent-free in Gene's old trailer forever, but I wouldn't mind buying a couple of acres and putting up a house, or maybe even a trailer. I don't need to live fancy.

"I actually called about a little place up on 13. I don't know how serious I am, but I wondered how much they were asking. You know, just trying to keep my eyes open."

"And I suppose this has nothing to do with that little farm girl up there...Elaine, is that her name? You ain't kiddin' me."

"Well, maybe that's some of it. She's a really nice girl, Bobby. Totally straight-laced, down-to-earth, goes to church...just a real nice lady."

"She's got a nice butt, that's for sure," Bobby mused, noticing Jimmy's surprised stare. "Well, she *does*. I'm just sayin.'"

"Knock it off, Bobby!" Sandy's voice called from the other room.

"Quit listenin' in," Bobby countered over his shoulder, turning back to look at Jimmy. "So when are you gonna get Sonny's car back out? You ain't hit a lick in Sid's ol' car."

"You know, I don't get it," Jimmy shook his head. "It's a nice car, only a few races on it, and it's almost exactly like Sonny's chassis. Same engine, same driver…but it's been a struggle, I'll admit."

"It's Harvey," Bobby insisted. "I mean, what else can it be? As much as I hate to admit it, that mean ol' buzzard is good with the race car. Either that, or he really *was* cheating earlier this year when you won all those races."

Jimmy stiffened. "It's the same motor," he said. "If he had it cheated up, it would still be cheated up. We haven't touched it."

"Well, maybe he was, maybe he wasn't…I'm just sayin', what else could it be but you're missing Harvey? C'mon, man, just look at the results. You guys win four in a row, then he gets wiped out and you can barely crack the top-5."

Jimmy listened quietly, taking a sip of his beer. "We won at Sunset Park."

"I know, but usually you guys are consistent, more than anybody."

"You're right," Jimmy said after a moment. "When Harvey is there, I run better. I ain't ashamed to admit it. He's real sharp, everybody knows that…and we've got chemistry. We kind of click, even when we're fighting."

"So do you miss it?" Bobby grinned. "Getting your ass chewed out every time you get out of the car?"

"I don't miss *that*," Jimmy laughed. "But I do miss running better. If I have to have the ass-chewings to win, I'll take it."

The big crowd filed into the grandstand at Western Speedway, a fast 5/8-mile paved track near Central City.

Jimmy and Elaine stood in line at the pit shack, chatting with other racers as they waited. This was a new experience for the pretty young woman, making her first trip to the races with

Jimmy. Soon they signed in and moments later were unloading the race car while Sandy talked with Elaine. Jimmy hoped the two girls would hit if off, because it would give Elaine someone to sit with.

As he began jacking up the rear of the car he spotted Al Petrov walking along, writing on a clipboard.

"Hey, Al!" Jimmy waved. "Got a minute?"

"Hi Jimmy...what's up?"

"Say, about these west coast races..."

Al chuckled, and shook his head. "I know, you heard we had three races in California."

"Something like that."

"Jimmy, Jimmy, Jimmy...how does this kind of thing get started? We've only got our one swing out there. Anything else is just a silly rumor, son."

"Just one swing? You sure?"

"Absolutely. Well, unless there is something I don't know. But I haven't had any conversations about additional racing out west."

"I thought it was kind of farfetched."

"You like running out there?"

"Oh, man. I love it!"

"Long way out there."

"Yeah, but I'd probably find somebody to stay with, and spend a few weeks."

"Really? I heard you'd probably be married by the fall."

Jimmy shot a glance at Al, who had a twinkle in his eye and a mischievous smile. Al nodded toward Elaine, who was standing near the truck several yards away.

"Al, Al, Al...how do these things get started? Nothing but a silly rumor, son."

As much as Jimmy had struggled in recent weeks, tonight was the breakthrough. Sid's car was strong and comfortable, and Jimmy posted quick time and ran off and hid in his heat race.

He was in a great mood, standing on his trailer watching the fourth heat, where Bobby was battling a Chicago racer named Marty Riconti. Jimmy was impressed with how well Marty was running, trying to remember if he'd ever seen the guy win even a heat race.

In the waning laps Bobby ducked to the inside as they entered turn three, pulling alongside as they navigated the sweeping corner. Bobby's car suddenly twitched, and his right front clipped Marty's left rear.

Marty spun and bumped the outside wall, and Jimmy thought maybe he could restart. But the official waved for a wrecker, and he came in on the hook.

"The Chicago gang isn't gonna like that," Jimmy shouted to Sid. He immediately regretted saying it, because he noticed the fear that had registered in Sandy Mancini's eyes.

"It'll be okay," Jimmy assured her. "There might be some pushing and shoving, but they aren't going to hurt Bobby."

Bobby went on to win the heat, then steered toward his pit. By the time he arrived it was nearly a mob scene, as at least two dozen Chicago people were waiting, in full anger, surrounded by several dozen spectators.

As Bobby climbed from the car Marty was in his face, screaming profanities in a mixture of English and Italian. A very large guy wearing a "Sal's Towing" shirt was screaming as well, and after a moment Jimmy figured out this was Sal Galuzzo, the car owner.

It was touch and go for a few minutes, as officials tried to calm Marty and his crew. By this time Bobby had heard enough, and he was suddenly pushing back at Marty, their noses nearly touching, both men cussing at the top of their lungs, gesturing wildly at various points on the race track.

Jimmy had been right; there was some pushing and shoving, but after a few minutes everybody began to disburse. No punches, but there had been enough profanities thrown to fill Lake Michigan.

Jimmy looked over at Elaine, who wore a look of complete shock.

"I'll bet you hadn't heard some of those words before," he kidded.

She shook her head, her eyes wide. "Is...is it always like this?"

"Nah," Jimmy assured her. "Just sometimes, when people are mad. But it always blows over. You'll see."

"Have you ever talked like that?"

"No, of course not."

He knew it was a lie. But just a little white one.

It had been a while since Jimmy felt this strong. The car screamed down the straightaways, and handled like a dream in the corners. The race went without a caution, and Jimmy waded through traffic at will.

He was having a tough time getting past Sammy Caldwell, and was getting annoyed that the starter wasn't showing Sammy the move-over flag. But as he waved the white flag Jimmy wondered if maybe Sammy was running second.

He eased up on the throttle for the final lap, following Sammy to the checkered. He drove back around to the finish line, coasting to a stop as he jabbed the throttle several times before cutting off the fuel. The big crowd roared as he climbed from the car, and he gave them a wave. Sid was nearly ecstatic as he gave Jimmy a bear hug, both men laughing wildly.

Elaine seemed excited, but it was obvious she wasn't sure how to act. Jimmy gave her a kiss and hug.

"You passed everybody," she said, smiling. "Gosh, that was fun!"

Jimmy did an interview on the PA, and held the trophy aloft as he posed for the photographers. In a moment the big gate on the front straightaway swung open, and fans streamed onto the track, quickly surrounding the car.

Jimmy shook hands and signed autographs, enjoying the moment. He looked up to see something that brought a gigantic lump to his throat.

Jack Harvey was rolling toward him in a wheelchair, with Slim MacDonald pushing him along. Sonny Ellison walked alongside the two men, giving Jimmy a wave and a broad grin.

"Holy cow!" Jimmy said, his voice breaking. "Holy cow...this is better than winning the race! How are you, Harvey? You look great! Slim, you too! Boy, I miss you guys..."

His voice hung in his throat, and he was nearly lost for words.

Harvey had lost weight, and he looked pale. But his voice was strong, and when he spoke Jimmy could sense the fire returning to his voice.

"You better bring this car over to the shop this week," Harvey began. "We need to pull the motor out of it."

"We do?" Jimmy smiled.

"Yep...gonna put it back in our car. They tell me you ain't been runnin' good, and I needed to come save your season."

Jimmy laughed out loud, shaking his head. "Man, I can't believe I'm actually enjoying hearing you say that. Hey, what about tonight, Harvey? That wasn't too bad, now was it?"

"Eh," Harvey shrugged, his face a familiar scowl. "Even a dumb dog finds his way home now and then."

They all laughed, and Jimmy leaned over to pat Harvey on the shoulder.

"I guess you're right," he said, winking at Sonny. "I guess you're right."

Chapter 18

The wisp of wind coming through the open garage door offered only a slight relief from the torrid summer day, and Jimmy drew his forearm across his face, blinking the sweat from his eyes.

He examined the cut on his thumb, watching small drops of blood form then drop onto the floor.

"I need a Band-Aid, Harvey," he called, shaking his thumb. "I'm making a mess."

"On the shelf in the bathroom," Harvey grunted, nodding in that direction. "If you'd watch where you put that thumb, it wouldn't be bleedin.'"

Jimmy stepped into the bathroom, and in a moment had covered his throbbing wound.

"Yeah? Well, if you'd watch where you were goin', you wouldn't be riding in that wheelchair, would you?"

Harvey just gave him a sour look, grasping his wheels and moving himself closer to the race car. He bumped the big cast on his leg against the side of the car, bringing a grimace to his face.

"It's taking me ten times longer to get this motor in than it usually takes," he groused. "I've had enough of this wheelchair, and this damn cast. I'm halfway tempted to get a saw and take it off right now."

"You aren't that dumb," Jimmy smiled. "At least I don't think you're that dumb. When do you take your medicine again?"

"I ain't takin' any more. Makes me goofy."

"Goofy! You can't blame it on a pill!" Jimmy laughed, and then turned serious. "Listen, you need to be taking your medicine."

"Aw, it's just for pain. The other stuff I take in the evening, and it's okay. But that pain stuff, I can't think straight when I take it."

Jimmy leaned over the car, fiddling with the throttle linkage. He looked up at Harvey, studying the big man, and then he grinned and shook his head.

For a moment Harvey stared, finally speaking up. "What are you lookin' at?"

"You," Jimmy laughed. "Bumping around in that chair like a bull in a china shop, banging your leg around, cussing...man, I can see how glad you are to be back!"

"Well, it's mostly to rescue your sorry butt," Harvey retorted. "To watch you out there thrashin', like a monkey on a football, I felt sorry for you. I said to myself, 'That boy is goin' clear down the tubes without me.' So I knowed I had to get back here before you completely ruined yourself."

Jimmy rolled his eyes. "Whatever," he sniffed. "Here, give me that half-inch wrench. And by the way, I did win a couple of races without you. Just remember that."

"Well, let me tell you something, boy," Harvey said, smirking. "I've won a helluva lot more races without you than you've won without me!"

"Yeah? That's only because you've been doing this for about a hundred years. And, oh by the way, how many races did you win the season before I came along?"

Harvey stared at the engine, pretending not to hear. Finally he looked up at Jimmy, who stood with his hands on his hips.

"I don't remember," Harvey mumbled.

"I do!" Jimmy laughed. "It was, well, let me see...ZERO!"

Harvey reached for a ratchet and snugged several bolts tight. He looked at his work and wiped the sweat from his forehead and looked back at Jimmy.

"You don't know this, boy, but we had motor trouble right up until we hired you. It just so happens that right before I talked Mr. Ellison into giving you a try, I found our problem. So don't think YOU'RE the reason we're winnin' again."

Jimmy laughed out loud, wearing an expression of pure amazement. "Man, you lie like a rug! Motor trouble? What a load of crap. And YOU talked Sonny into hiring me? I don't think so! You tried to fire me two minutes after I got here. Hell, you fired me ten times that first season, until you finally realized you needed me to carry this tub of junk."

Harvey began to stare, shaking his head, and then came the smug expression that drove Jimmy crazy. Harvey smirked again, staring at Jimmy with feigned sympathy.

"Funny thing is, boy, I think you might actually have some ability...if we could get rid of that squirrely attitude, we maybe could get you right yet."

Jimmy gritted his teeth and stared back at Harvey, his eyes clenched into two slits. He felt pain in his fingers, and he realized he was grasping a screwdriver so tightly the handle was pinching his palm.

Harvey could see he was getting under his skin, and he guffawed.

"Now, I said you MIGHT have some talent. I ain't completely decided yet. So don't get the big head."

He guffawed again, leaning back over the engine and finding more bolts to tighten. Jimmy bit his lip, then began messing with the linkage again.

"You miserable dog," Jimmy seethed. "I ought to go find something else to do, except there wouldn't be anybody to help load your fat ass in the truck to take you home tonight."

Harvey laughed even louder, pitching his head back, his body shaking with laughter and a smug, satisfied grin on his face. It was the first time Jimmy had seen him really smile since the accident.

That's good, Jimmy said to himself. *Kind of.*

"I can't wait to meet everyone," Elaine said excitedly. "I'm kind of nervous, though. I mean, your team, that's kind of like your family, isn't it?"

"Aw, it's not a big deal," Jimmy smiled, his eyes on the highway ahead. "If you just kind of stay in the background, that would be better. Until everybody gets to know each other."

"Are you sure it's okay if I stay with you? In the pits, I mean."

"Of course it's okay. I want you here. But Harvey is kind of gruff, and, well...he isn't a very nice person sometimes. I'm just telling you in advance, you probably won't like him. But he's a great mechanic, and once you get to know him he's all right. In a funny kind of way."

"I'll be on my best behavior," she insisted. "I promise, I'll stay out of the way. And if he yells, I won't let it bother me. Does he... does he use bad language, like those men in the pits last time?"

Jimmy smiled knowingly. "He probably will."

"Well, then, I'll just brace myself. Oh, Jimmy, I wanted to double-check with you on your schedule. Next week you're racing, but the weekend after that, you're off, right?"

"That's right."

"Perfect! We have that family reunion I was telling you about, the one on my dad's side of the family. I'd really like you to come with me. There's like a hundred people there, and they'll be so excited to meet you. Don't forget, okay?"

"I wouldn't miss it for the world," he smiled.

Soon they turned from the state highway onto the long lane leading to Sunset Park. Jimmy felt kind of funny pulling into a track without towing the car himself.

"I hope Mr. Harvey is all right," Elaine sighed. "With a broken leg, I imagine he's in all kinds of pain. He must be a very strong man."

"Oh, yeah," Jimmy nodded. "Very strong. Let's get signed in."

Soon they were walking toward their pit, and Jimmy got a chill when he saw the Ellison 49 sitting in the morning sun. The car had never looked more appealing, at least in his eyes. The pearl white paint sparkled, with the pinstripes proudly dancing the length of the car.

"Is that your car, the number 49?" Elaine said, holding his hand. "Wow, that's a pretty car...it's the prettiest car here, I think."

"Prettiest car in the country," Jimmy corrected.

Slim gave a wave as he saw them approaching.

"Whad'ya say, Slim," Jimmy grinned. "This is my friend Elaine. Elaine, this is Slim."

"Call me Charles," Slim corrected. "If you don't mind."

"Charles??!!" Jimmy quizzed. "I didn't know that was your name. Okay, I'll call you Charles."

"Not you," he said quickly. "She can call me Charles. Sounds better from a lady."

"Oh, for cryin' out loud," Jimmy said, shaking his head. "Where's Harvey?"

Slim nodded across the way, where Harvey was chatting with Al Petrov and Sammy Caldwell. Harvey spotted Jimmy, and said something to the two men before wheeling back to their pit.

Jimmy realized he was nervous as he introduced Elaine, who offered a bright smile.

"Well, hello," Harvey beamed, holding a lingering handshake. "You know, I think...well, no, I'm sure of it."

"Sure of what?" she asked.

"Of all the different girls he's brought with him, you're the prettiest. No doubt about it."

She laughed, and Jimmy could tell from the way she shook her brown curls that she was enjoying the attention.

"Has he brought a lot of girls to the race track?"

"Well, let me put it this way, honey...if he won a race every time he brought a new girl to the races, this team would be the all-time champions!"

Everyone laughed, except Jimmy, who folded his arms across this chest.

"This sure is a pretty car," Elaine offered.

"Why, thank you," Harvey nodded. "We work hard to make it look nice, and run good. Do you know much about race cars?"

"Hardly anything."

"What??!! Why hasn't he told you about them? Here, let me tell you about a sprint car."

Jimmy watched in amazement as Harvey pointed out the finer qualities of the Ellison Special, with Elaine offering all sorts of questions and compliments. He couldn't figure Harvey out...was he just being cute, or had the big guy somehow lost it?

"Hey, are you going to the driver's meeting or not?" Harvey said, nodding toward the judge's stand.

"Uh...yeah, I'm going. You want to come with me, or stay here?" he asked Elaine.

"She's fine," Harvey insisted. "You want something to drink, honey? We've got cold drinks in the cooler..."

Jimmy soon finished qualifying, and he and Elaine walked to the small tower to watch the last few cars time. They joined Bobby and Sandy Mancini along the rail at the back of the tower.

"Where are you?" Bobby asked.

"Sixth," Jimmy grinned. "How about you?"

"I'm quick right now. Man, how do you sandbag like that? You know just how to let off and get on the front row."

"Hey, that's all it had," Jimmy insisted. "I just hope nobody else is quicker."

They paid particular attention as Steve Graffan rolled the Strong sprinter out, cutting a nice warm-up lap.

"There it is!" the PA boomed a few moments later. "Quick time!"

"How about that, killer!" Bobby teased. "Now you're in the fourth row!"

"Maybe not," Jimmy countered. "Maybe you won't make it in. Not that I'm cheering against you or anything."

They walked back toward their pit, where Slim was fueling the car. Jimmy hung around for a minute, chatting with Elaine and Sandy.

"Um...is there a rest room around here?" Elaine asked.

"Oh, not in the infield," Sandy said quickly. "That place is so bad, you don't want to even walk through the door. Let's walk over to the grandstand, at least it's tolerable."

Just as they turned away Jimmy noticed a familiar face coming toward him with a confident gait. It was Lou Moore, the Meteor Foods team owner for whom Jimmy had driven at Indy.

"Hey, Lou, great to see you," Jimmy smiled, offering a handshake. "What brings you to a sprint car race?"

"Oh, just had a weekend off, and wanted to check things out," he said. "Plus, I wanted to talk with you, if you've got a minute."

"Sure."

" We've got some Champ Dirt races coming up, and I wanted to see if you'd be interested in running for me."

"I sure would," Jimmy said eagerly. "How soon?"

"How about Missouri in two weeks?" Lou quizzed. There's no conflict with the sprint car schedule, and we'll have the car ready by then. If you can make it out there, I'd like to see what we could do with the old car. My deal is 40 percent, just like always."

"You've got a deal. I've been wanting to run the big miles for a long time...and I know I enjoy racing with you guys. Who is the crew chief?"

"Me," Lou grinned. "I'm tired of shuffling papers in the office...I'm ready to get my hands dirty."

"Then we'll have a good time," Jimmy nodded.

"I better let you get back to work," Lou chuckled. "Don't want Harvey getting after me."

"You know Harvey?"

"Oh, yeah. Back in the day we raced our sprint cars against each other just about forever. He's rough around the edges, but he's a helluva wrench. I heard about the highway crash...looks like he's getting on all right."

"Yeah, he's doing better. Probably does him some good to go racing."

Just then Harvey came rolling up, offering a nod to Lou.

"Hello, Jack," Lou smiled, offering his hand. "How's that leg getting along?"

"Ain't slowin' me down, if that's what you mean," Harvey offered. "What you been doing? Still running those prima donna cars?"

"Yeah, still hanging in there," Lou nodded, looking at Jimmy. "Harvey doesn't like rear-engine cars much, as I recall."

"I want nothing to do with those damned funny cars," Harvey insisted. "Too flimsy, too flaky, and way too political."

Lou nodded in agreement. "You're a lot more right than you realize," he said. "Especially the political part. You've got a pretty good boy in your sprint car, I see."

Jimmy felt himself flush with pride for a moment.

"What? This boy? Hell, he ain't even half educated yet," Harvey scoffed. "I got to watch him like a hawk, because he's got that squirrely attitude. But he's got some potential, I think...maybe."

Lou laughed loudly, shaking his head. "Some things never change," he said, then waved to both men. "I'll get out of your hair, and let you get ready for the feature. I'll watch from the stands... good luck to both of you."

Lou walked away, and Harvey offered a sly grin. "What's up with him hangin' around?" he asked Jimmy.

"Nothing much," Jimmy replied. "Just talking."

"Sure, just talking...are you gonna run his dirt car out in Missouri?"

Jimmy shot an annoyed look at Harvey. How did that nibby so-and-so always know what was going on?

"Maybe," Jimmy mumbled.

Harvey chortled. "Hell, that ain't no news flash!" he continued, reaching for his longest needle. "I heard Lou was getting that old box out to try and sell it. Steve Graffan already turned down the ride, as I hear it, so that makes you second choice...but you never know. I guess you can hear anything."

Jimmy just continued with the annoyed stare. "What's with you, anyways?" he quizzed Harvey. "Are you off your nut, or what?"

"Me? Hell, I'm just an old invalid trying to help a lost cause. What makes you think I'm up to something?"

"Because you're all nice and sweet to Elaine. What's up with that?"

"Can't a guy be nice without being up to something? Boy, if she's hanging around with you, she needs people to be nice to her. Out of pity, mostly. But she's a nice little gal. So is it okay if I'm nice to her, mister lost cause?"

"I don't believe you...you don't even think women should be allowed in the pits. What are you up to?"

Harvey guffawed loud enough to turn heads across the way.

"Boy, you worry too much! All I'm interested in is getting your head right to drive this race car. With that much on my mind, I ain't got time to be up to anything else!"

Jimmy lined up seventh in the feature, right behind Bobby. On the start he quickly chased his friend to second, settling in on the back bumper of the Otley sprinter. Graffan roared to an early lead, and the three cars were nose-to-tail on the exciting and dangerous banking.

Within five laps Graffan began to pull away as Jimmy searched for a way around Bobby. He could pull alongside on the outside, but couldn't get enough momentum to make the pass. Soon they were in traffic, and Jimmy tried to screen Bobby off on slower cars to no avail.

At the halfway point Rusty Fernandez spun harmlessly to the bottom of the track in turn two, and Jimmy caught his breath as they idled around the big half-mile. He saw Harvey gesturing from his wheelchair at the pit entrance, pointing to the top groove.

Jimmy nodded, and flexed his fingers as the starter gave them the furled green flag. On the restart he moved a half-width higher, and began to gain momentum.

Twice he could get alongside Bobby, but couldn't hold onto the car enough to clear him. They were wheel-to-wheel for two laps before the caution light blinked on again, and Jimmy spotted a yellow car stalled along the berm on the backstretch.

As he rumbled around under caution he looked for Harvey at his usual spot near the pit entrance. He was startled to see that Harvey had pulled himself out of his wheelchair, and was leaning tenuously against a post, one arm clutching for balance and the other arm gesturing heatedly at Jimmy.

He could almost read his lips as he rolled past, with Harvey pointing to the higher groove.

Move up, idiot! Or something to that effect, Jimmy imagined.

As they rolled toward the restart, he focused on the two cars in front of him. Just as they came through turn three, Graffan's car suddenly slowed, forcing everybody on the brakes for a split second, then back on the gas.

It turned the restart into something of a melee, and Jimmy roared past Bobby, clearing him going into one. He expected them to call the start back, but was surprised that they let it go.

He was incensed at Graffan's brake-check, and he clenched his jaw as he chased the blue car. He caught him with a big run two laps later, and got alongside.

They entered the corner, with Graffan in the middle groove and Jimmy on the high side. The Ellison car was so close to the guardrail Jimmy was certain he saw sparks on his right side. The big crowd was on their feet as they came roaring onto the front straightaway, with Jimmy seeing Graffan slowly disappear on the left.

Jimmy wasn't sure how many laps he'd clicked off after that, as the Ellison car was a rocket. He saw the white flag, then the checkered, and he slowed along the backstretch, catching his breath.

He pulled to a stop on the front straightaway, quickly surrounded by officials and photographers. He climbed from the car and acknowledged the crowd with a wave, grinning broadly.

Elaine was excited as she stood behind the photographers,

and Jimmy waved for her to come closer. He saw Harvey and Slim hurrying across the track, Slim half pushing while Harvey's hands furiously grabbed at the wheels.

"You finally listened to me!" Harvey yelled as he arrived at the car. "Damn, boy, you fiddled around all day on the bottom, what were you thinkin'? When you went to the top you blew his doors off, just like I knowed you would. Didn't you see me wavin' at you?"

"How could I miss you?" Jimmy answered quickly. "Dumbass, standing clear out of your wheelchair. You tryin' to break that leg again?"

"I wasn't gonna fall! You just get me all worked up when you're out there just riding around, playin' with yourself."

He turned quickly to Elaine and nodded. "Excuse my language, missy. But I just hate to see the boy out there flounderin' around."

An official moved them all into position for some photos, and Jimmy held the trophy aloft. He looked over at Slim and grinned.

"Smile...*Charles!*"

The track announcer moved in for an interview, arching his eyebrows.

"Jimmy, quite a bit of conversation here after the race...you won the race, but a little bit of disagreement with Jack Harvey, your crew chief?"

"Not really...just routine stuff after a race, and we kind of break down what went wrong and what went right...usually, I'm wrong and he's right."

The crowd laughed, and Harvey crossed his arms.

"Quite a big day all around, Jimmy. Jack's first day back after a long layoff, and you're in victory lane. Is that a sign of things to come?"

"I hope so," Jimmy said, nodding. "He gets after me a little bit, and usually when that happens, we get going pretty good. And right now, winning a race is probably good for his therapy."

"You're back on top of the points race, and this win should build your lead a little over Steve Graffan and Bobby Mancini. Talk about what another USAC championship would mean to you and your team."

"It's a little early to talk championship," Jimmy smiled. "But

I'll tell you right now, we're getting it together. The Ellison team, I think we're gonna make some noise."

Jimmy steered his pickup out onto the state highway, the evening sun in his eyes. He pulled down the visor, driving easily along the tidy rows of three-foot-tall cornstalks in the fields lining the highway.

"That was so exciting," Elaine chattered. "Twice I've come with you, and both times you won the race! This is really fun!"

Jimmy looked at her in amusement, shaking his head slightly.

"It's not like that every time," he cautioned.

"Oh, I know. But gosh, when you passed that blue car, I held my breath! I grabbed Sandy's arm so hard, I almost left a bruise, I was so scared! And everyone in the grandstand...gosh, Jimmy, they really like you. When you won they really clapped.

"But isn't it hard, like when you passed Bobby? He's so nice, and when you passed him, I felt really bad. And Sandy was so mad at that blue car...I kind of picked up that nobody likes that guy very much."

"Not very much," Jimmy agreed, nodding his head.

He reached over and held her hand, enjoying her beaming smile.

"You're my good luck charm," he offered. "You'd better plan on coming with me for a while."

"Oh, it isn't my good luck," she laughed. "You're pretty good at this."

She was quiet for a moment before she spoke again.

"And by the way, Jack and Charles were wonderful. Were you kidding earlier when you said Jack gets a little bit gruff sometimes? He seems like a really nice man."

He looked at her incredulously. "Now, listen," he began, shaking his head vigorously. "What you saw today, that just wasn't...real. I don't know what was up with Harvey, but that's the first time in three years I've seen him be truly nice to someone. Maybe it's the bump he took on the head, I don't know, but that's not Harvey. Not the one I've learned to hate."

"Oh, don't be silly. You don't hate him."

"Really? Well, you stick around and catch him on a bad day,

and see if he's a lovable teddy bear. More like a grizzly bear."

"If you hate him, why would you work with him?"

"Well…he helps me win races, bottom line."

"And that's the only reason?"

"Pretty much."

"Oh, I don't know about that," she smiled. "I recall a guy by the name of Jimmy sitting by Harvey's hospital bed, getting him drinks of water, helping him sit up, worrying about him. Those aren't things you do for someone you hate."

He stared through the windshield for a moment, watching the sun drop over the horizon.

"It's complicated," he finally said, shrugging his shoulders.

"Now that is right!" she laughed. "This whole business about racing is complicated! I thought it was simple, just cars going around in a circle. But, boy, it isn't like that at all! The cars, the people, it's hard to make sense of it all."

He looked over at her and smiled. "Are you having fun?"

She nodded, her eyes as pretty as the sunset that lay before them. "It's fun being with you," she said, reaching over to rub his shoulder.

"Hey, I almost forgot to tell you," he said suddenly. "I've got a chance to drive Lou Warren's Champ Dirt car! Isn't that great?"

She nodded, grinning broadly. "It sure is! What's a Champ Dirt car?"

He laughed. "It's a little bigger than a sprint car, and they only run the big tracks."

"Like Indy?"

"No, not that big…one-mile dirt tracks. It pays pretty well, and it's kind of a big deal. I've always wanted to drive one of those cars…they're long, and beautiful, and there's just something about 'em…I'm really excited."

"When's your first race?"

"Two weeks," Jimmy explained. "Out in Missouri. Hope you'll come with me."

She grinned but suddenly stopped. "Jimmy! Two weeks…what about the family reunion?"

His eyes widened. "Shoot!" he said, looking at her helplessly. "I forgot all about that!"

"Well...can you postpone driving the car, until the next race after that? Everybody in my family is excited about meeting you."

"Aw, Elaine, I don't dare do that. When somebody like Lou asks you to drive his car, you accept. Period. He's one of the best owners in the business. I can't risk losing an opportunity like this."

She frowned for a moment, and he could see the hurt in her eyes. Then she forced a smile, and patted his arm. "I understand," she said. "I know how much this means to you."

They rode in silence for a few miles, and Jimmy spoke up. "What day is the reunion...Saturday or Sunday?"

"Saturday."

"Well, let me find out something...I don't know if the race is on Saturday or Sunday. If it's Sunday, I can do the reunion, no problem."

"But don't you have to drive to Missouri?"

"Aw, that's no big deal. I could drive out in the evening, and still get some sleep. Easy."

She perked up a little, and he felt better. But he felt a little guilty at what he was thinking, and he was glad she couldn't read his mind.

He didn't care much about the reunion. But that big ol' dirt car...he wished it was tomorrow, because he wanted to feel those belts on his shoulders, and feel that long car sliding into the corners.

But why tell her? She'd never understand. Even if she tried.

Chapter 19

The summer morning was crisp outside the window of his pickup, and Jimmy could still feel the dew in the air. He rolled west, the air gently pouring through the open window. Birds flitted away as he approached, with the long shadow of his truck cast in front of him on the highway.

The evening before had been pleasant, as he enjoyed a nice visit with his family back in Illinois. The visit was both practical and enjoyable; it gave him a three-hour head-start to Missouri, and the track, for Saturday morning.

He felt a gnawing nervousness in his belly, and he grinned at the idea. This was a new adventure, something he had hoped for. A long, beautiful Champ Dirt car was waiting, a car he hoped would help him earn more respect from Lou Warren, owner of the Meteor Foods team. If he ran well enough in the dirt car, maybe Lou would give him some seat time in his championship car.

For now all he wanted was to get on the big mile track out in Shady Bluff. He tried to imagine those long straightaways, and the flat turns, and how different the car might be from the sprint cars he was accustomed to.

He looked over at the empty passenger seat.

I wish Elaine could have come along.

He imagined the scene at her family reunion later today, when she explained to everybody why he wasn't there.

No wonder she's kind of sore...but nothing I can do about it. Can't turn down Lou's offer, not for anything or anybody.

He crossed the muddy river at Hannibal, looking off the bridge to see the barges as they plied the waterway, moving so slowly they seemed to be standing still. He rolled into the historic old town and followed the marked highway through, past tourist homes and sagging wooden houses.

Wonder what Mark Twain would have thought about race cars...

The town thinned out and soon he was back among the country fields, and he glanced at his watch.

Hmmmm...hope I'm making good enough time...got to get there early, don't want to be late.

He pushed down harder on the gas pedal, his fingers clenching more tightly to the wheel with each passing mile. Shady Bluff lay out there somewhere in the distance, and he wished he was already there, wished the car was fired, wished he was under way.

"Seat feel all right?" Lou Warren asked, leaning over the roll cage.

"Yeah, it's fine," Jimmy said, smiling. "A seat's a seat. Wide enough for my butt, that's all I need."

Lou nodded, and turned to a shaggy-haired young mechanic standing at the toolbox.

"Say, Wart, did you put fuel in?"

The man nodded, and Jimmy climbed from the cockpit. Lou busied himself with the tires, and Jimmy stood around. Nothing to do now but wait for hot laps.

He looked up to see Al Petrov approaching, wearing a broad smile.

"I heard you were going to be here...are you excited?"

"Hey, Al. Yeah...just anxious to get going, I guess," Jimmy nodded, feeling a little on edge. "I didn't know you worked these races, too...I thought you just handled the sprint car deal."

"Oh, I work all of 'em I can get to," Al laughed. "Got to keep you guys straight. Have you been in one of these before?"

"Nope."

"They're a little different...heavier and slower, and you have to think ahead just a little farther. They're not as nimble as what you're used to, and on these big tracks they take a while longer to get whoa-ed up."

Jimmy listened carefully. "What about at the start, when you've got all that fuel on...does it push pretty bad?"

Al nodded. "Way bad. But this is a patient man's race car. You don't win these on the first lap, not even the first 50 laps. And don't even think about abusing the right rear when you're heavy with fuel. The car will be sucking wind before you're halfway if you do that. Say, looks like we're getting ready to warm 'em up."

"Thanks for the info. You could have ridden out with me!"

"I rode with the crew…pretty much everybody is in Central City, and we take the van. Don't your folks live along the way, over in Illinois?"

"Yeah, I stayed there last night. I'm going back home tonight, though."

Al arched his eyebrows. "That's a pretty good ride, after racing a hundred-miler."

Jimmy laughed. "I'm tough," he teased. "Just call me the iron man!"

Soon the cars were rolled into position, with Jimmy in the first group. Lou waited at the front of the car, with a big electric starter. The long shaft was shoved through a round fixture on the frame, and cables ran to a big battery pack alongside. Jimmy was tightly buckled in the car, waiting nervously.

"Let's go!" an official shouted, waving his hand in a circle over his head. Lou made eye contact with Jimmy, who nodded in reply. The whirling sound of the starter was quickly overcome by the roar of their race engine, and Lou pulled the starter away. After shoving the starter to the side Lou and Wart got behind the car and began to push it slowly forward, as Jimmy revved the engine and grabbed the clutch lever with his hand.

He winced as he revved, trying to feel the clutch engage. He moved the lever too quickly, and suddenly the car shuddered and the engine fell silent.

Damn it! Jimmy cussed inside the privacy of his helmet. He looked at Lou and shook his head, feeling small. Lou nodded confidently, offering silent encouragement, and in an instant had the starter back in place. They fired the engine again, and this time Jimmy managed to pull away without killing the engine.

He was amazed at how the car lumbered at low speed. He picked up the throttle slightly, moving slowly down the backstretch, and as he rolled through turns three and four he saw the yellow light go out.

Far in the distance he saw the starter offering the green flag, and he pressed the throttle. The car seemed to take forever to get fully up to speed, and he saw the first corner rushing toward him. He eased into the corner, feeling the tires slipping on the sandy surface, getting the feel of this big machine.

After a few laps he felt good, learning a little bit with each round and shaking away the lingering butterflies.

"Second quick, that's great!" Wart said as they leaned against the car. "For your first time, man, that's pretty good!"

"My early number helped a bunch," Jimmy offered. "That sun is hot, and the track went away pretty quickly. But I'll take it."

"You know about pacing yourself?" Lou said, wiping the sweat from his neck. "It's a hot one, and a hundred miles is a long way."

"Yeah, but I usually don't wear out too bad."

"Now, I know you want to win…I want to win, too. But on this first one, just concentrate on finishing. That's important, to show yourself that you can last to the end. We haven't had this car out for two years, and frankly, that's my goal, too. I want to see if we can finish, and then see what we need for the next one."

Jimmy nodded, swallowing mouthfuls of cold water from a tall plastic cup.

An official came hurrying past.

"Let's get the cars lined up on the front straight!" he called. "Driver introductions in five minutes!"

Jimmy felt a pang of nervousness in his gut, swallowing as much water as he could before helping the guys roll the car onto the grid. He tried to wipe the sweat from his eyes as they pushed, and he felt rolls of sweat pouring down his back.

Soon the announcer was calling out the names and numbers of the cars. Jimmy looked up into the big covered grandstand, eyeing the large crowd that applauded with each name. The names read like a who's who in racing; legendary veterans, Indy 500 racers, household names in the racing world.

"Starting second, in the white-and-blue Meteor Foods number 51, from Greensburg, Illinois, now living in Central City…he's a USAC sprint car champion, today making his rookie start in the Championship Dirt division…Jimmy Wilson!"

The crowd applauded politely, and Jimmy smiled and waved.

He climbed into the car, settling his butt into the seat and taking his helmet from Wart.

"Remember, you've got 75 gallons of fuel on," Lou explained, leaning in close. "When you get to the first corner, this thing will NOT want to turn. Just be ready for it, and stay on your toes. Get down to the inside right away, and give yourself lots of time to make that first corner. This thing is going to be terrible until some of the fuel burns off. Okay?"

Jimmy nodded, pulling his helmet in place, tugging his gloves on. A few moments later came the command to fire the engines, and soon he eased the No. 51 into motion.

They rolled slowly down the backstretch, and he glanced to his left, where Joe Newton's No. 37 lumbered along on the pole.

Joe Newton! He's twice won the Indy 500! Jimmy couldn't help but grin, amazed at where he was and what he was doing.

After a couple of pace laps the field rumbled toward the start, easing through turns three and four with growing tension. Jimmy concentrated on listening to Newton's engine, picking up the throttle in unison.

Suddenly Joe's engine roared to full song, and Jimmy answered. They screamed along the front straightaway, the sound echoing under the covered grandstand to create an immense wave that seemed to shake the steel and concrete structure to its foundation.

Lou was right; this thing did NOT want to turn. Jimmy found himself sliding to the outside, desperately pedaling the throttle and brake and hanging on, as two cars passed him on the inside. He had the same problem at the other end; it took him a couple of laps to figure out the right mark on the track to hold the car on the inside pole, but by then he had fallen back to eighth.

He settled in for the long haul, surprised at how much effort the car required. Even though it was actually a relatively small percentage larger than the sprint car, everything was different, and he found himself struggling to get a firm handle on things.

By the 40-lap mark he had finally begun to find a rhythm. He saw Sammy Caldwell's machine some 30 yards ahead, and he realized that he was reeling him in. He closed to his tail, then pulled alongside on the front straightaway, just clearing him in the drag race to the corner, both cars headed for the inside rail.

Jimmy's confidence was growing, and he set sail on the next car. He used a similar move to the outside on the straightaway, beating the car into the turn and claiming the spot.

Next was a yellow No. 80, and Jimmy could soon faintly hear the roar of his engine as he closed in. He held back slightly on the backstretch, allowing some space to open between them, and carried as much speed as he dared into the corner. Just as they came off the corner and the car moved to the outside, Jimmy used his momentum to pull alongside on the car's left, gradually pulling past as they headed for the first turn.

Now he rode in fourth, and he glanced at the wooden scoreboard along the straightaway. A kid was hanging the number four alongside a seven; 74 laps down, 26 to go.

What was that smell? In an instant Jimmy recognized the acrid scent of hot motor oil, and he looked toward the car ahead, which was easily 20 car lengths away. He saw no smoke, and he felt fairly sure that the oil might be coming from his own car. He glanced at the temperature gauge, but the needle was steady at 240. If she was sick, at least she wasn't getting hot yet.

Soon he began seeing black oil splotches on his visor, and saw a faint stream of white smoke trailing from the right side of the engine opening. He glanced again at the temperature gauge; still 240, and the oil pressure was steady.

One lap later smoke was pouring from the right side of the car. Jimmy found himself covered with oil, and he clenched tightly at the wheel to keep his hands from slipping. He used his last few tear-offs, and was soon drawing his glove across his visor to try and maintain some vision. His eyes watered amid the pungent smoke, and he blinked through a visor that was now an ugly mess of black streaks.

For a moment he thought about opening the visor a crack, but knew that would be a bad idea. So he wiped his oil-soaked glove across the visor again, but it only seemed to further smear the mess.

He felt a wave of uncertainty. *Should I pull in?* He looked for Lou along the front straightaway as he sped past, but instead saw several officials intently studying the Meteor Foods car.

As much oil as he had now lost, he wondered if the engine might scatter itself, and he hated the idea of trashing Lou's stuff. But to pull in when you're running fourth...maybe it would hold on and he could finish.

As he came off turn four to complete the next lap he saw motion in the flag stand, and saw the starter showing him the black flag. He continued on through one and two, then eased off the throttle and moved to the far inside lane, holding up his right hand to warn the drivers behind him that he was slowing.

He rolled into their pit, where Lou stood frowning, looking at the car carefully as it stopped. Jimmy was completely covered with oil, and he suddenly realized he felt a burning sensation on his neck. Some of the hot oil had apparently soaked through his uniform, and was stinging his skin. He tried to quickly undo his helmet straps, peeling off his gloves to get a better grip, but everything was so slippery he struggled.

Lou leaned in to offer help, and soon had his helmet off. Jimmy was startled when he saw his nice white helmet, totally smeared with black streaks mixed with brown dust.

"I need a rag to wipe my neck," Jimmy called to Lou, his voice hoarse and dry, straining to be heard over the roar of the cars. "Burnin' me."

Wart quickly grabbed a couple of shop cloths, handing them to Jimmy, whose hands were trembling so badly from fatigue that he could only fumble awkwardly around his neck area. Wart saw what was happening and assisted, wiping the oil from Jimmy's neck.

Jimmy slowly began climbing from the car, and when his feet hit the ground he suddenly felt faint, and the landscape appeared a little swirly. He gripped tightly to the cage, bracing himself, trying not to let on that he was winded.

"He's hot," Lou shouted to Wart. "Get him a cold drink, and get some ice on his neck. See that cooler there? Pour it down his back real quick."

Lou grabbed Jimmy's elbow, steadying him. "Lay down," he commanded. "Try and catch your breath."

"No," Jimmy wheezed, shaking his head. "Just let me sit down."

"You need to *lay* down," Lou insisted. Jimmy shook his head stubbornly, glancing around at the handful of people looking on. Lou got the message, and grabbed a nearby lawn chair, and Jimmy eased himself into the seat.

Wart handed Jimmy a tall cup of water, and Jimmy poured the cool liquid into his mouth, savoring the sensation. But the water tasted of oil, and Jimmy realized his lips and tongue were covered with a black residue. He swished the water in his mouth, spitting into the dirt, and repeated several times until the taste began to diminish.

They poured several cups of ice down Jimmy's back, and he shivered from the shock. After a few minutes he felt a little better, although he could sense a pounding headache coming along quickly.

Lou and Wart pulled the cowling from the car, and were studying the right side. Oil dripped from the length of the car, forming in dark puddles in the dirt. Jimmy heard the roar diminish, and realized the race had finished. Lou wiped his hands on a rag, shaking his head in dismay as he turned away.

"Valve cover gasket," he called to Jimmy. "Rotten luck. You feeling better?"

Jimmy nodded. A grin spread across Lou's face, and he chuckled.

"You look like a raccoon," he said, tossing a clean rag to Jimmy. "You might work on that face a little."

Jimmy wiped firmly at his face, glancing at the black streaks that appeared on the rag as he worked. After a few minutes he felt good enough to stand, although he still found himself woozy.

The area was soon crowded with people, but Jimmy had no appetite for conversation. He grabbed his bag and began straggling toward a small building behind the scoring tower, walking into a darkened room that reeked of mildew. He walked to the showers, but found the two units had the handles removed. Out of order.

He stepped over to a tiny sink, checking to see if there was water. Yes; cold only. He stripped to his shorts, and rifled through his bag for a washcloth. He shook his head in frustration as he realized he must have forgotten to pack one. There were some brown paper towels near the dingy sink, so he wet down several and tried to clean himself as well as he could.

No matter how much he cleaned, he couldn't get rid of the burning, bitter smell that seemed to hang in his nostrils, enveloping him.

"Well, that's it," said Lou, looking at the car as it rested on the trailer. Wart was cinching the straps, and Lou drew his forearm across his face, blinking to clear the sweat that was stinging his eyes.

"You did a good job, but it wasn't our day. You sure you're okay to drive home?"

"Yeah, I'm fine," Jimmy insisted. "I'm feeling a lot better." That was a lie, because the pain in his head was so powerful he was having a hard time thinking straight. But he was pretty sure once he got on the road and got some air moving, he'd feel better.

The summer heat hung in the air as the cars around them were loaded. Jimmy picked up his bag, and Lou offered a handshake.

"I'll call you, and we'll run this thing again," he promised. "I think the ol' bus can still go all right…we just need to finish a race or two."

Lou gripped Jimmy's hand tightly, and pulled him closer. He offered a grin.

"I told you this thing wouldn't want to turn, didn't I?"

Despite the pain, Jimmy managed a sheepish laugh. "Yeah, you were right about that…I could see that outside rail coming up real fast, and I figured, 'Well, Lou isn't going to like this very much, crashing in the first corner.' But next time I'll know what to expect."

He waved to the two men as he walked away, finding his pickup in the infield parking lot. He eased out onto the busy street in front of the fairgrounds, driving toward the business district where he would pick up the highway.

Soon he was back in the countryside, and the sun was only now beginning to loosen its grip on the scene. He glanced at his watch…quarter to seven, and he figured he'd get home sometime after midnight.

As he rolled along and the evening took on a golden cast from the sun's fading rays, his headache became so intense he was seeing splotches of color dancing in the distance. He felt sick, and he eased off the side of the highway, stepping out of the truck to walk around to the passenger side.

He looked at the fence lining the road, and the soybean field on the other side, the rows neat and orderly in the evening light. He put his hands against the top wire of the fence, suddenly feeling himself wretch. But there was nothing but dry heaves, and he wiped at his mouth, feeling himself wobbling as he placed his hands on his knees, bracing for another round.

After a few minutes the feeling subsided, and he stood and walked gingerly back to his truck, sliding behind the wheel.

He drove along at around 45 mph, feeling very lightheaded, glancing in his mirror and ready to move over if another car approached. But there was nothing but the countryside as the sun disappeared behind him, leaving only a reddish, fading glow.

Jimmy saw the lights of a town on the horizon, watching for the speed limit signs as he approached. He saw the small green sign, perched on two spindly posts.

"Eliza, Missouri" was neatly lettered across the top, with a handwritten, "Pop. 2,218" scrawled below the name.

Jimmy didn't remember coming through here on the way out, and for a moment he nearly panicked, thinking he might be on the wrong highway. But he saw the "U.S. 36" sign, and his confidence returned. He rolled slowly into the small business district, resting his arm on his outside mirror as the red neon sign caught his eye.

The glow from the sign cast an orange tint on the street as he eased his pickup into a parking spot out front, cutting the engine. He reached for the door handle, and walked shakily toward the front door. He studied the letters, D-R-G-S with a U in the middle, not illuminated. As he approached the store he saw the entire sign suddenly go dark. He paused for a moment, then walked the few feet to push at the front door, finding it locked.

That's when he noticed the "Closed" sign hanging on the inside of the door. He took a step back and turned away, and felt for a moment felt like he could almost sit down on the curb and cry. The pain, the nausea, the frustration, everything.

"You need something?" a voice from behind him called out. Jimmy turned to see the door of the drugstore half open, a bespectacled man with a balding pate and a salt and pepper moustache standing in the door looking at him. The man wore a white druggist's smock, and he stared intently at Jimmy.

"Well, I'm not feeling very well," Jimmy began. "I was hoping I could get something for my headache."

The man carefully studied Jimmy, then glanced at his truck, eyeing his out-of-state tags suspiciously.

"Well...the store is closed."

"I know. I'm a race driver, and I've been over at Shady Bluff today, racing. I think I'm sick from some fumes or something, and I was thinking if I could get rid of this headache I could drive on home tonight."

The man looked at Jimmy without blinking, then after a moment he eased back from the door a bit, holding it open.

"Come on inside."

Jimmy told the man of his afternoon.

"I think I breathed some of those oil fumes, or maybe swallowed some," he explained. "I sure do have a powerful headache."

"It could be the fumes, but more likely you just overheated. I can make you up something for your headache, but it's probably going to knock you out. I don't think it's a good idea to drive home."

"Is there a motel in town? I could get a room if I have to."

"No, that closed years ago. I can put you up at my house...it's not wise for you to drive on by yourself, especially if it gets late. You're going to get really sleepy from this medication."

"Oh, I can't let you do that," Jimmy insisted. "I mean, that's very kind, but I'm not going to impose on you like that."

"Nonsense. Our kids are grown and gone, and we've got plenty of room. It's no trouble at all. It's certainly better than you falling asleep at the wheel."

"No, really, I can't," Jimmy smiled. "I'm a total stranger, and I'm not going to put you out like that. I really do appreciate it, though."

"Well...if you're driving on tonight, I don't feel comfortable giving you this medication."

"How about if I lay down for a while in the back of my truck? I can sleep for a little bit, and when I wake up I'll move along."

"It's going to rain tonight," the man said, shaking his head. "But if you insist, I'll mix this up."

The man walked behind the counter, swiftly reaching for a couple of glass bottles on a nearby shelf. He mixed a small amount of medication, and in a moment came walking around the counter with two small capsules on a silver tray.

He handed Jimmy the tray, and motioned for Jimmy to follow him. They walked to the soda fountain, where the man poured some water in a paper cup and handed it to Jimmy. In a moment the capsules had disappeared.

"Thanks a lot for helping me," Jimmy said, reaching for his wallet. "What do I owe you for the capsules?"

The man smiled and shook his head. "No charge," he said. "We'll just say it's part of our town rolling out the welcome mat."

"Aw, I need to pay you," Jimmy insisted, to no avail. The two men walked toward the front of the store, where the man unlocked the door and swung it open. They stepped outside, the evening still sweltering.

"I'd certainly feel better if you didn't drive," the man said. "There's no doubt the medicine will make you sleepy."

"I'll just crawl in my truck. Really, I can sleep just about anywhere."

They were startled by a voice behind them.

"Everything all right, Marvin?"

They turned to see a young police officer walking toward them. A cruiser was parked at the curb, and the cop was eyeing Jimmy carefully, holding a large five-cell flashlight in his left hand.

"Hello, Tim," the druggist smiled. "Yes, we're fine. This gentleman is driving back to Indiana, and he's a racing driver. He was competing at Shady Bluff this afternoon. He's feeling ill, and I suspect he got himself overheated. I gave him some medication, and I'm trying to talk him into staying here in town tonight. It's not safe for him to drive, I believe."

"I'm going to sleep," Jimmy explained. "That's my truck there, and I'm going to stretch out in the back. Is there a city park here in town, where it's quiet?"

"Gonna rain here shortly," the cop said, still studying Jimmy. "You got any identification?"

Jimmy reached for his wallet, handing the man his driver's license. The cop studied the license, handing it back to Jimmy.

"The name matches the plate," the cop said to Marvin. "There was nothing on the vehicle, so I guess he's all right."

He turned back toward Jimmy. "It ain't a good idea for you to sleep in your truck," he said, his face hardened and without expression. "Kind of gives the town a bad impression, people sleeping in parks. Can he make it to Hannibal, Marvin? There's a motel there."

"I don't think he should drive at all," the druggist said, shaking his head. "Not a good idea. I've offered him a place at my home, but he's not comfortable staying with us."

"Oh, hey, nothing against your house," Jimmy said quickly. "I just feel a little funny, putting you out like that, when you don't even know my name. Just…I feel that's imposing on you and your family too much."

"Indiana…you're a race driver, eh? Don't suppose you'd know a state policeman there by the name of White, do you?"

Jimmy perked up. "Mike White? Well, yes, as a matter of fact. He's a good friend of mine!"

"Really?" the cop said, finally allowing the faintest of smiles to cross his face. "Where do you live?"

"I live in Perkinsville, just a couple of miles from him. In fact, this summer he's helped out on our race car several times. Mike and his wife Charlotte are really good people."

"Yeah, they are. I knew he was a big racing guy. That's funny, that you know him. Small world."

"Sure is…how do you know Mike?"

"We were in the Army together."

Jimmy paused. "I didn't know Mike had been in the Army. Huh…he never mentioned that."

They stood on the sidewalk for a moment.

"Are you sure you won't reconsider?" the druggist asked. "You're going to be feeling the medication fairly quickly."

"I really don't want you sleeping in your truck," the cop said, shrugging his shoulders. In the distance they saw a flicker of lightning, and a few seconds later heard a distant rumble.

"See? You can't sleep outside tonight. How about if I put you up?"

"Well…like I said, I feel pretty weird sleeping in somebody's house—"

"Not my house," the cop laughed. "Up at the jail."

Jimmy looked at him in surprise. "The jail? Are...are you serious?"

"Sure. We put people up now and again who are passing through, have car trouble or something. Don't worry, I'll leave the cell door open."

"Wow...I never heard of that. I...I guess that would be all right. I mean, I don't have much choice."

"It ain't a bad setup," the cop shrugged. "You got a nice cot, clean sheets, and we could probably even scare up something to eat."

"Well, okay then. I'll follow you." Jimmy turned to the druggist, and shook his hand.

"I really appreciate you helping me. Opening the store again and staying late, that's very kind of you."

"You'd do the same for me in similar circumstances," the man said with a gentle smile. "It's our duty to help others when they're in need. And I could certainly see that you weren't feeling well."

The man hesitated for a moment, and finally pointed toward Jimmy's face.

"Say, I hate to mention this, but you've got big black streaks behind your ears..."

Jimmy shook his head in resignation.

"Oil," he said, dabbing at his ears with a fingertip. "It's everywhere...I'm just looking forward to a shower."

"We've even got a decent shower," the cop laughed. "All the comforts of home."

In a few moments they pulled in front of a well-lit brick building. The cop unlocked the front door, and Jimmy followed him inside, carrying his bag.

"You hungry?"

"To be honest, I just want to sleep...he was right, those capsules are about to knock me out."

He followed the officer down a hallway, where a small cell awaited. Jimmy looked around at the empty cells along the way.

"We don't have any guests right now," the cop explained. "A town this size, things are pretty quiet. It's Saturday night, though...

we'll probably have a couple in here later, but they'll be in the drunk tank. You won't even hear 'em. You sure you don't want anything to eat? We've got some bologna and biscuits in the back."

"No thanks," Jimmy said, placing his gear on the floor. "Just leave that door open, okay?"

The cop laughed. "Don't worry, you're free to go whenever you want…I'll be up here doing some paperwork, and another officer comes on at eleven. Unless we get busy, somebody will be here all night. If not, and you need to leave, just let yourself out the front door."

Jimmy sat on the cot, feeling its firmness. He began taking off his shoes.

"Thanks again for everything," he said to the cop, who waved and shuffled down the hallway, the keys and gear on his wide belt rattling as he walked.

Soon there was nothing but the silence, and Jimmy was so exhausted he didn't even undress. As soon as he closed his eyes, the scene faded to the image of a screaming race car, and the bitter, pungent scent of oil.

He was grateful, regardless of the setup. But he was glad his mother wasn't here to see it.

Chapter 20

Franklin Speedway was quiet under the morning sun as Jimmy stood in the line at the pit shack. It was still early, and he and Elaine chatted with Bobby and Sandy Mancini and several others as they waited for the window to open.

"So what does a farm girl do for excitement?" Bobby teased. "Do you go out and pet the cows? Drag race the tractors?"

Elaine smiled, taking it all in stride. "What do we do for fun? We make fun of city people, mostly. Especially the loud ones, who are always trying to make a joke."

Everyone laughed, and Sandy beamed. "Boy, has she ever got you pegged," she laughed, gently elbowing Bobby's ribs.

Bobby grinned, and looked at Jimmy as he nodded admiringly. "This one here, she's got some spunk," Bobby said. "Nothing like all those other duds you bring around."

"Well, thanks," Jimmy said. "I think."

"Boy, I could tell you some stories on this guy," Bobby continued, pointing at Jimmy. "He's not the best-behaved guy in the world, that's for sure. And his temper! Man, watch out when he's mad. Mostly, though, he's trouble. T-R-O-U-B-L-E. I've seen it! When he's not around, I'll clue you in on some things."

Jimmy arched his eyebrows, smiling knowingly at his friend. "Bobby, I don't think you want us telling stories, eh?"

"Yes, let's do," Sandy said suddenly. "I'd be interested in hearing some of these stories."

Bobby's eyes widened, and he glanced nervously at his wife before offering a dismissive laugh. "Aw, I'm just kidding, killer! Just havin' some fun."

"I am impressed, though," Jimmy said seriously.

"Really? At what?"

"I can't believe you could spell a word with that many letters."

"Aw, now you're insulting me. I'm the smartest guy at this race track, you know that? You know how I can prove I'm the smartest guy here?"

"No, but you're going to tell me."

"Dang right I am...I'm the smartest guy here because I married the greatest wife," he said, draping Sandy in an embrace and schmoozing kisses on her neck.

They rolled their eyes, and laughed. Sandy giggled and squirmed. "Boy, now it's getting deep."

"You know, we were arguing on the way over here," Bobby continued. "You know why? She says I don't take her anywhere. Can you believe that? I mean, just this week we went to K-mart. Can't get much better than that."

They laughed, and by now Bobby was on a roll. "She says I don't let her do anything, either. Which, I don't understand. I let her mow the grass, I let her feed the dog, I even let her paint the kitchen last winter. And, you know, I even offered to let her change the oil in my truck. Now, a man can't love a woman much more than that."

They all laughed again, and Jimmy nodded his head.

"Man, this is great," he said, winking at Elaine. "I'm looking better by the minute, I think!"

Jimmy was in the first heat, where he scored second with a last-lap pass on Sammy Caldwell. He climbed from the car, wiping the sweat from his face and grabbing a big swallow of water from a plastic cup.

Slim checked the fuel and tires as Harvey maneuvered his wheelchair close by and looked up at Jimmy.

"Looked like you were tight," he said.

"Yeah, but it's so rough, I don't know what I'd do to it. Let's look at it after the heats...I'm going down to watch in three and four."

He trotted toward the north end of the pits, slipping past a wire fence to walk down into the turn. The second heat was just getting started, and he used his hand to shield his eyes from the bright sun.

Bobby had started sixth, and was quickly to third. Jimmy watched as his friend intensely battled the car ahead, their machines bucking and jarring on the rough, rutted surface. For several laps they sparred, and midway through the race it looked like Bobby got a good run as they entered turn three.

He pulled alongside the car, his tires churning in the loose stuff just beyond the cushion. It was a nice move, and Jimmy grinned in appreciation as Bobby screamed off the corner to take the spot.

One lap later Bobby tried the same move on the leader, and pulled alongside entering the corner. But the other car, apparently hustling to hold the lead, plowed too deeply into a big chasm midway through the corner. He bicycled wildly, then shot to the right, clipping Bobby's front end.

Bobby's car veered to the right, smacking the guardrail with a resounding bang. The car executed a quick barrel roll, then came to rest lying on the left side, the front end pointed toward the outside rail.

Jimmy instinctively looked up the track, when a yellow blur rushed past. Another car, still nearly wide-open into the turn, slammed directly into Bobby's car, launching them both through a grinding, violent series of flips. As the cars came to a stop the rest of the field either slipped past or rumbled to a quick stop, leaving an eerie quiet to the scene.

Jimmy began running toward Bobby's car, as he heard several shouts and screams. He got there at the same time as several others, gingerly leaning into the cockpit to get a read on Bobby's condition. Bobby's visor was half knocked off, and Jimmy could see that Bobby was out cold, his eyes closed and unmoving. Suddenly a couple of guys with the ambulance crew pushed their way through the tight gathering of people.

Everyone backed up to give them room, and the two men were soon joined by a younger guy. They quickly had Bobby's belts unfastened, and were trying to pull him from the wrecked car.

They would pull him from the seat a few inches, but then stop. It was obvious he was stuck, and the two older guys on the crew began shouting instructions to each other, adding more chaos to the scene. They tried another couple of times to no avail, and kept shouting as they stepped back, wide-eyed, obviously stumped on what to do.

The younger guy was yelling at the two older men, asking what they should do. All three men were yelling, and it was difficult to make out what was happening, because they had obviously lost control of the situation. A couple of racers began shouting at the crew, and Jimmy saw a dark liquid dripping steadily from under the car, forming a black blot on the dirt surface.

"Everybody shut the hell up!" Jimmy screamed, stepping toward the car. Everyone was so startled they fell silent, and Jimmy motioned them out of the way. "Get back and let me in there," he said, his voice calm and strong.

He knelt by the cockpit, squeezing so close his head was bumping Bobby's helmet. Jimmy saw that the steering unit had been wrenched from its mounts, and was pressing against the top of Bobby's legs. He pulled the gear away enough to realize that wasn't what held Bobby fast.

He slipped his hand between Bobby's right leg and the steering unit, extending his arm as he felt along the smooth surface of the white uniform. He found nothing contacting the leg, and he moved his hand to Bobby's left leg. As he moved his hand over Bobby's knee, a moment later he felt something sharp and wet. He gently touched the area, pulling his hand back.

"He's got a compound fracture on his left leg, just below the knee," he said, looking up to see Sammy Caldwell and Rusty Fernandez standing a couple of feet away. "It's caught on one of the bars...let's get that belly pan off!"

The two men quickly tugged at the pan, and in an instant somebody had a pry bar and some tools. In a moment they had pulled the pan back, and Jimmy leaned in for a closer look. One of the older ambulance guys squeezed alongside Jimmy, but when he saw the bone gaping several inches through Bobby's uniform, the man fainted dead away.

Somebody nearby caught the guy, easing him onto the ground. Jimmy leaned in close to Bobby's still form, grabbing the leg both above and below the knee, trying gently to help it clear a piece of mangled tubing.

"Can you push his butt forward? Yeah, there we go!" Jimmy carefully manipulated Bobby's leg until it cleared the bar.

"Okay, take him out real easy...there you go."

As they gently slid Bobby from the car, he suddenly began

to stir. He flailed his arms for a moment, then began screaming, almost incoherently.

"Ahhh, my leg, my leg," he cried. The men quickly had Bobby on a stretcher, where they immediately pulled a restraining belt tight across his chest, holding him in place.

"Get a tourniquet on his leg, as high as you can," Jimmy urged the older guy. "Can you give him some morphine? Hurry up, put him out."

"Can't do that," the guy said, shaking his head and climbing inside the back of the old Cadillac ambulance. "We're only a minute or two from the hospital…they'll assess him there and help him as quickly as they can, I promise. Let's go!"

The younger guy hesitated as he opened the driver's door. "What about Larry?" he said, nodding toward the guy who had fainted, now sitting groggily on the track.

"Throw him in the front seat," the older guy commanded. "C'mon, right now!"

A couple of guys grabbed the man and in an instant had him in the front passenger seat, where the guy was rubbing his head, still a pasty shade of white.

Jimmy looked up to see Elaine and Sandy pushing their way through the crowd. Sandy was ashen, her hands visibly shaking. Elaine wore an expression of complete shock, as if she were in a dream. Al Petrov quickly opened the back door of the ambulance.

"Hey, can his wife ride along?"

"No room," the man shouted. "Tell her we're going to Memorial, over on 25th Street. Just a few blocks. C'mon, dammit, let's go! NOW!"

The ambulance began rolling forward, letting go with a quick blast of the horn. In a moment it sped past the old pit shack where there had been such joking and laughter a couple of hours before.

"Elaine!" Jimmy called. "Take Sandy to their car, and follow the ambulance. You drive! I'll meet you there as soon I can…it'll probably be a couple of hours."

Elaine nodded, and she and Sandy hurried away. There was soon the wail of the old ambulance as it left the property, and the guys with the wreckers began clearing the debris, lifting the shattered remains of Bobby's car off the ground, creeping back toward the pit area.

Jimmy looked up at Sammy and Rusty and offered an strained smile.

"Never seen an ambulance guy faint before," he chuckled.

"That guy's in the wrong line of work."

The two men nodded slightly, their expression solemn. They walked back toward the pit area, and Rusty draped his big arm over Jimmy's shoulders.

"That was great," he said, nodding. "The way you jumped in there for Bobby."

"Cool under pressure," Sammy said softly. "Something tells me you had a pretty eventful previous life."

Jimmy shot him a quick glance, but Sammy just nodded, his eyes full of understanding.

Jimmy walked silently to the Ellison Special, where Harvey and Slim were waiting, staring intently at Jimmy as he approached.

"Bobby all right?" Slim asked.

"He'll make it," Jimmy answered.

They didn't speak for a moment, and Jimmy realized they were looking at him with a weird expression. He gave them a quizzical look, until Harvey rolled his wheelchair toward him, his brows knitted tightly and shaking his head slightly.

"Uh, boy..." he said, pointing at Jimmy. Jimmy didn't understand, until he lifted his hands. They were covered with a mixture of blood and dirt, and dark spots dotted the arms of his uniform.

"Must have been when I grabbed Bobby's leg," he said aloud. "Guess I better go wash off."

People would talk about the feature race for quite some time, about how Jimmy and Rick Wagner locked into an intense battle for the final ten laps. Trading the lead, racing inches apart, their tires clawing at the tortured surface as the crowd roared in approval.

On the final lap Jimmy was sure he had him, driving deep into turn one and simply out-braving Wagner. He raced on the razor's edge, hanging on, pulling ahead decisively as they hit the backstretch. He hammered the Ellison car through the ruts in three and four, and as he got back on the throttle felt the engine stumble for an instant.

It was just the break Wagner needed. He pushed Sid Johnson's machine to the inside lane, beating Jimmy to the finish by a car length. The crowd convulsed in a massive roar, and Jimmy gripped the wheel so tightly it hurt his hands.

Jimmy steered into the pit area, knocking the car out of gear and rapping the throttle repeatedly. He had too much speed as he approached, and he locked it up and slid to a stop in his pit. In a heartbeat he was up and out of the car, walking directly a few feet to pick up his bag, muttering profanities, tossing his helmet roughly inside. Slim offered him a drink, but Jimmy waved him away.

"What happened?" Harvey quizzed, his face a picture of shock. "You had him!"

"What happened? This piece of crap wouldn't run, that's what happened. Don't you even open your mouth to bitch at me, Harvey, because I ain't gonna hear it. I raced my guts out and this box died on me. That's all there is to it."

"Well, I—"

"I said shut your damn mouth!" Jimmy shouted, his voice breaking. "I ain't gonna hear it!"

Harvey clammed up, opening his eyes wide and casting an uncertain look toward Slim.

Jimmy stood for a moment, praying Harvey didn't give him a smart remark, afraid of what he might do if it came. When there was only silence and Harvey's blank stare, he turned to walk toward the old infield building to change.

The track's PR guy hurried over, trying to get his attention.

"Hey, Jimmy!" he called. "Don't run off! We need you for an interview on the front straightaway."

"Not today, Randy," Jimmy said, forging ahead.

"Hey, now wait a minute," the man said with an angry tone. "You gotta do an interview…you owe it to the fans! Hey! Hey! Listen, don't walk away when I'm talking to you!"

The guy grabbed Jimmy's sleeve, and in an instant Jimmy whirled to snatch the man's hand away, gripping it tightly and pushing him backward. They teetered there for a moment, their faces an inch apart, and Jimmy suddenly relaxed his grip and stepped away.

"I said not today."

He picked up his bag, and walked ahead.

"What a jerk!" the man called out. "I mean it! What a jerk, Wilson!"

Jimmy nodded his head, not missing a step.

"Yeah, that's me...what a jerk."

Chapter 21

The hospital corridor was quiet and cool as Jimmy looked for the waiting area. He rounded the corner to see several racing people milling about, and he knew he was headed in the right direction.

He was already sure of one thing; he had seen way more of the inside of hospitals this season than he wanted.

"Hey, Jimmy," Fred Otley called out. "Down here…Sandy is in with him right now, and she'll probably be out in a minute."

"How's he doing?"

"Aw, his leg is all busted up. They've got him knocked out, pretty much. Gonna need surgery, and he's done for a while."

"Where is Elaine? You know, the girl I brought with me…"

"She's in there with Sandy."

Jimmy leaned against the door. He studied Fred's sad eyes, and how his shoulders seemed to sag. He reached out to put his hand on the older man's shoulder.

"You okay, Fred?"

Fred looked up and managed a weak smile. "Aw, sure, I'm okay. Just feel bad for Bobby…hate to see him hurting like this. Sandy, too."

"They'll be all right…not much left of the car, I suspect."

"You know, I'll bet there ain't a straight piece of tubing more than 12 inches long on that thing," Fred said, shaking his head. "Junk. Complete junk."

"Bobby will need a car to drive next spring," Jimmy smiled.

"He'll have one. When I see him, that's what I'm gonna tell him…don't worry about my ol' car, cause I can get another one. Can't get another one of him, though."

The door at the other end of the waiting area swung open, and Elaine peered around the corner. She saw Jimmy and offered a relieved sigh, and Jimmy hurried over.

"You okay?" he asked, and she nodded.
"We were hoping you were here...Sandy wants you to come in for a minute."
"Is he awake?"
"Yes, and it's surprising how lucid he is...but he's all upset, said he needed to talk to you."
They hurried to a small room, and Jimmy's stomach tightened as he stepped inside. Bobby lay on a bed, with wires and tubes connecting him to a several humming machines. His eyes were closed, and Sandy sat in a chair scooted close to the bed, holding his hand. Sandy heard them enter, and she stood.
Jimmy hugged her close, and felt her stifle a sob. He gently held her shoulders, looking down into her eyes.
"Okay?" he whispered. She nodded.
"He's groggy, but he's been wanting to see you. He told me you'd come after the races were over."
Jimmy nodded, and swallowed hard.
She leaned over the bed, gently touching his arm.
"Honey...are you awake? Jimmy is here."
Bobby's eyes fluttered open, and he looked up at Jimmy and managed a weak smile. Jimmy eased himself into the small chair at the side of the bed.
"Killer," he said, reaching up to clasp Jimmy's hand. "Did you win?"
"Nope, second. How you feelin'?"
"I been better. Who won?"
"Wagner."
Bobby nodded. "My leg's kind of bent," he said. "They're gonna operate."
"Yeah, I heard."
"Doc said I might limp a little when they put me back together."
"Well...you already walked a little cockeyed, so maybe this will square you up."
"I need to tell you something..." he strained to raise his head off the pillow, looking around. "Sandy? Can you guys give us a minute?"
She leaned over the bed and brushed the hair from his forehead. "I'll be right outside," she whispered.

Bobby waited till the door had closed, and he and Jimmy were alone in the room.

"Listen, we're broke," he said, his voice weak and raspy. "I got no money in the bank, and I ain't gonna race for a while...I need your help, man. While I'm laid up, look in on Sandy and the kids... make sure they got something to eat, okay?"

"Quit worrying about that stuff," Jimmy scolded. "They'll be taken care of, I promise. You just concentrate on getting yourself healed up."

"I will...but I don't want them hungry. Okay?"

Jimmy laughed softly. "Man, do not worry. We know a lot of people, and they aren't going to suffer. I promise."

An hour or so later he and Elaine walked out to the parking lot, looking for his pickup. He was completely exhausted, but the beautiful summer night made him feel a little better. The evening breeze whispered across their faces as they walked hand-in-hand, and as they reached his truck he pulled her close in an embrace.

He moved his hand softly up and down her back, letting her hair tickle his face. He looked into her eyes, and smiled.

"You were great," he said. "It really made a difference, being there for Sandy. I'm proud of you...you were so strong, right when she needed you—"

Elaine suddenly burst into tears, and he held her close, smiling and gently nodding his head.

"I understand," he whispered. "Let it all out..."

She regained her composure, and dabbed at her eyes with a tissue. "Jimmy...I can't do this."

"Do what?"

"Just...*this*. Watching him get hurt, watching Sandy try to deal with everything, seeing Bobby laying there in pain...this whole racing thing, Jimmy. I can't do it. I just can't."

She began to cry again, and he embraced her even more tightly.

"Just let it out," he repeated. He felt bad for her. And for himself, too. Because this wasn't a good sign.

The small living room was cluttered with items, scattered across the floor as if the room had been stuck in a tube and shaken vigorously.

"Anybody get killed in this wreck?" Jimmy teased, stepping over a pile of racing papers leaning against an easy chair.

Sandy managed a smile, pulling a strand of hair from her eyes and trying with little success to keep it on the top of her head. She looked at him and sighed, shrugging her shoulders as she slumped into one of the chairs.

"I started reorganizing everything Saturday morning," she explained. "Then Bobby had his crash, and I've been at the hospital every day since…"

"Aw, I'm just playing with you," Jimmy laughed. "You know I'm kidding. Where are the boys?"

"Our neighbor lady is watching them for the day. She's been great, and she kept them till late last night. Gosh, this has been a blur, you know? Spending two nights in Franklin, then home, then Bobby has surgery yesterday…I feel like I'm barely hanging on."

"That's why I stopped by," Jimmy nodded. "I was up at the hospital, and Bobby said you had gone home for a few minutes. I figured I'd see how you were getting along."

"I'm doing okay…I'll just be glad when we get Bobby home in a couple of days. Then we can start to have a normal life again."

Jimmy listened, studying her. Although her hair was frazzled and she looked tired, she still had a hint of that familiar spark. Bobby wasn't an easy man to love, he guessed, with his wandering ways and free spirit. But Sandy was the balance to his nutty personality; grounded and calm, amidst almost any circumstances.

"Sandy, I need to ask you something," Jimmy began, but she immediately held up her hands as if she were trying to stop an onrushing train.

"I know what you're going to say," she interrupted. "But I don't want to go there, Jimmy. You're too good of a friend—"

"How do you know what I'm going to say?" he countered.

"Because Bobby told me he talked to you. I could strangle that guy sometimes. Asking you for money…how embarrassing!"

"Embarrassing? Well, you better get over that right now."

She seemed surprised as she returned his gaze, and fell silent.

"The next couple of months are going to be pretty difficult, Sandy. You've got to set aside your pride and understand that everybody needs help now and then. And this is your time to need a little help."

"We'll be fine," she insisted, valiantly nodding her head. "I'm sure we'll get by somehow."

"Really? Well, let me ask a couple of questions, as your friend. Okay?"

"I suppose."

"How much money is in your purse right now?"

She arched her eyebrows and shook her head. "My gosh, that's kind of personal, isn't it?"

"Yeah, it sure is. How much?"

She leaned back in the chair for a moment. She stared at him, and he watched her expression soften a bit. "About 20 dollars."

"All right, 20 dollars. You got any money stashed around the house? Beer money, bread money, gas money, stuff like that?"

"No."

"How about in the bank? How much in the bank?"

She shook her head again, a little vigorously, and rose from the chair to pace nervously across the room. "Jimmy, I'm sorry to be impolite, but that's just not any…" She stopped and glanced at him, as if she didn't want to finish her sentence.

"Not any of my damn business, right?"

She laughed, but he could hear the nervousness of her voice as it cracked slightly. "Basically."

"You're right, none of my business. How much in the bank?"

She walked to the small picture window at the front of the room, staring outside at the summer scene. A car swept past on the narrow street out front, and he could see her stifle a sob. In a moment she slowly sat back down, one hand clutching the side of the chair, another hand dabbing at her eyes.

"About forty dollars."

Jimmy nodded, and he walked over to face her, offering a reassuring smile. He reached out his hand and helped her from the chair.

"Come into the kitchen for a minute," he said, leading the way. By then she was openly sobbing, and they embraced as he held her tightly. Her body shook as she sobbed, and he felt her relax and lean against him, her face pressed against his shoulder.

"Go ahead and get it out of your system," he said softly. "You'll feel better if you have a good cry."

In a few minutes she had regained her composure somewhat, and wiped her eyes as they sat at the kitchen table.

"Now, we might have this conversation a few times in the next couple of weeks, but we can't have you crying every time," he explained, as she half-sobbed and half-laughed. "I can't take it when a girl cries…so you've got to be strong, all right?"

She nodded and smiled, continuing to wipe at the tears that poured down her cheeks.

"Listen, Sandy, you've got to understand something…I'm your friend, and I'm not going to let you and your kids—or that mutt Bobby, for that matter—go hungry.

"You need to focus on getting his leg healed up, and keeping your family going. You've got lots of friends…me, Sammy, Rusty, Al, and lots of other people. We're gonna make sure you've got what you need. But you've got to level with me on things, okay? Don't get all proud, and get yourself in deeper. You've got to let us help you."

She drew in a deep breath, and he could see the color coming back to her cheeks. She clutched the tissue in her hand, turning it into a tight, white ball.

"First thing, you need some groceries. Milk, bread…what else?"

She thought for a moment, and glanced at him once again with a pang of guilt before she looked down at the floor.

"Well…some cereal for the kids. And some eggs, maybe."

"There we go, now we're getting somewhere. Would you make me a list?"

She nodded.

"Okay. Now, how much is your rent, and when is it due?"

"It's $185…we just paid it Friday, that's why we don't have much money left. This time of year is usually not a big deal, because Bobby makes money every weekend. But now…"

She stifled another sob, and he arched his eyebrows, gently shaking his head.

"Now, you promised…no more crying, okay? Makes me feel all weird."

She nodded, but her tone was frightened. "Jimmy, what will we do this winter? We'll miss the rest of the season with no money coming in, and then have to make it through winter. I...I'm scared, Jimmy."

"I know, the timing stinks. But don't worry about winter, Sandy. We'll think about that when the time comes. Right now, let's just focus on the next couple of weeks.

"Listen, you write me up a grocery list, at least two weeks worth. Elaine is coming into town tonight, and we'll go to the grocery and bring the stuff back here. Then, figure up the bills you know are coming up, and write them down. That way we can kind of plan things, and you won't have to get yourself sick with worry. Okay?"

"But Jimmy...you can't possibly pay all this yourself. It isn't right!"

"No, no, it's not just me. I can help you out for the short term, and it won't hurt me any. But you'll have other help for a little while."

"What kind of help?"

"Well, USAC will have some money coming to you from the benevolent fund, and that will help. Plus, I know a couple of fan clubs that can help out, maybe $50 or $100 a month. It's not much but you'll be surprised how much it helps.

"Now, tell me about your folks. You and Bobby's folks, I mean. Will they be able to help you?"

She looked down at the table and shook her head. "Bobby's folks...bless their hearts, but they don't have a dime. And my folks...I don't know. I just don't know."

"What do you mean?"

"Well, it's hard to explain...my parents never liked Bobby, and to this day they're mad that we got married. To be honest, I hate to ask them for any money, because I'll get the 'I told you so' treatment."

"I get it. Well, don't worry about it. You'll have some help early on, and we'll worry about the parent thing when that starts to dry up. And think about something else, too. Could you get a job? After Bobby starts to heal up, I mean."

"I...I guess so. I hadn't even thought that far ahead. I don't have much experience, though. But I could waitress!"

He laughed. "There you go. You get your waitress job, and me and all the racing guys will come in and sit in your area and stuff dollar bills in your apron string. Wouldn't that be cool?"

She laughed, and that sparkle had returned to her eyes. "Maybe I shouldn't tell you guys where I work," she nodded. "You'd probably get me fired."

"See, you'll figure this out, Sandy. Just keep your head up, and remember that you've got lots of racing friends. We aren't gonna leave you high and dry. Meantime, you better get that grocery list together. You'll want to get back to the hospital pretty quick before the model patient starts whining."

She smiled, and reached across the table to touch the side of his face. "You're an angel, you know that? You really are."

He laughed, and shook his head. "Sandy, let me tell you...no angel would ever think some of the things I think, I'm sure of that."

Jimmy rose from his chair, saying a quick goodbye. She gave him a hug, and as he stepped toward the door he pressed $100 in her hand. She began to resist, and he raised his eyebrows.

"Don't make me get tough with you," he teased, and she managed a smile.

A few moments later he was walking toward his truck, stuffing the grocery list in the back pocket of his jeans. He slid behind the wheel, closing the door and hearing that familiar old rattle.

He stuck the keys in the ignition, then turned to look back at the house. He sat quietly for a moment, and began to shake his head in resignation.

"Two kids, a wife, and sixty bucks to his name," he muttered to himself. "This racing deal is one fine business, isn't it?"

Chapter 22

"This is one of those all-night rains," Harvey insisted, rolling his wheelchair to the edge of the porch to peer out across the parking lot. "We're done, I'm tellin' ya. We'll never get 'em off the trailers."

"I think you're right," Al Petrov sighed, looking skyward. "Poor ol' R.B.…this would have been a home run for him, I think."

"Aw, I hate these little rat-hole tracks," Harvey scoffed. "We ought not to even come to these little places. Half-mile or better, I say."

Jimmy laughed. "I love this place," he said, scuffing the toe of his shoe against a lump of mud on the concrete. "Racy little joint. Hey, you're gettin' water on your cast, Harvey. Roll back inside here."

"Eh," Harvey snorted, glaring at Jimmy. "I don't need no nursemaid. Rain ain't gonna hurt it."

Jimmy shook his head, glancing at Al and offering a hopeless shrug.

"Say, Al, could you come inside for a minute?" R.B. Stanley called from the nearby doorway. "I just talked to the weather bureau, and it doesn't look good."

Al disappeared through the old doorway, and Harvey snorted again.

"Hell, we might as well wait in the truck," he said. "C'mon, Slim. Let's get ready to go home. They're about to call this thing."

As they disappeared, Al and R.B. came walking outside.

"Tough break about the weather," Jimmy nodded. He had always liked R.B., even though there were always rumors going around about his shady business dealings. He studied the man, who wore a stained blue work shirt and pants. Deep lines creased his face, and his sad eyes made him look much older than he really was.

"Yeah, nothin' we can do about it," R.B. replied. "We'll give it a half-hour, and see if it quits. Otherwise we got no choice…track's so muddy now, we wouldn't have 'er ready till midnight."

They stood talking for a few minutes before Jimmy walked to the edge of the porch and held his hand out.

"Barely sprinkling," he said, offering an encouraging smile.

R.B. glanced at the sky. "Still awful wet," he mused, turning to walk back inside.

Jimmy strolled along the stockade fence bordering the parking lot until he came to a group of racers huddled under the overhang of a camper.

"Hey, Jimmy, come on over," Rusty Fernandez shouted. "Have a drink!"

Jimmy was amazed to see a couple of the guys drinking beer.

"Hey, what are you guys doing? We might still race!"

"Nah," Rusty laughed. "Look how wet it is! We can't possibly race tonight. You want a beer?"

"I better wait a little bit," Jimmy said, shaking his head. "Hey, what is that?"

He saw several of the guys passing around a mason jar, sipping a clear liquid.

"You ain't never had any 'shine?" Rick Wagner asked, extending the jar toward Jimmy. "Have a sip."

"Moonshine? You're kidding…who brought that?"

"Wayne had it in his camper here. He's from Kentucky, said they cook it on his daddy's farm. C'mon, try it."

Jimmy looked again at the sky, and noticed it had begun to rain again, harder than before.

"Well…there's no way we'll race now. Okay, I'll try it."

He grasped the jar carefully, bringing it slowly to his lips. He felt the cool liquid pour into his mouth, creating a curious burning sensation that was not entirely bad. He swallowed, and his eyes watered as he grinned and handed the jar back to Wagner.

"Pretty smooth," he wheezed, his voice a high pitch. They all laughed loudly, somebody reaching out to slap him on the back.

They spent the next little while passing the jar around, and Jimmy felt himself buzzing. They laughed and traded jokes, barely noticing as the rain tapered off. The jar was empty, but in a moment the lid came off another, and they began the ritual of passing the jar around anew. Jimmy had just taken a fresh swig when a voice caught his attention.

"Hey," someone said suddenly, pointing toward the west. "Is that the sun peekin' through?"

Like schoolchildren, they leaned from under the canvas and looked westward.

"Holy crap," Rusty whispered. "It sure is!"

For a moment nobody spoke, their eyes widening at the possibilities. Suddenly a fervent whisper broke from Wagner.

"Hey, it's Al!" he said sharply. "Hide the liquor!"

Jimmy looked around quickly for a place to stash the jar. With no alternatives in sight, he simply put it behind his back as Al Petrov hurried toward them.

"Just got the word, guys!" Al said cheerfully. "If we don't get any more rain, we're good to go. R.B. and his guys are going to work the track right now and see if we can get it dried out. Good news, eh?"

They all nodded cheerfully, Jimmy with his hands behind his back like a nosy principal.

"You guys might want to let your car owners know what's going on…I wouldn't unload anything yet, but probably in the next half-hour. We're getting a late start, so I'm counting on you guys to help us out and be ready for hot laps. Okay? I'll be out on the race track if anybody needs me."

They exchanged sheepish glances as Al walked away.

"Holy crap," Rusty repeated. "This ain't good!"

"Coffee!" someone called out. "Get to the concession stand!"

A few minutes later Jimmy was walking toward the Ellison Special, still parked on the trailer. Although he felt a little better, he still had a nagging buzz in his brain, mingled with a terribly conflicted conscience.

"Hey, Harvey!" he called out. "Might want to start unloading the car."

Harvey rolled down the window of his truck. "Wait a few more minutes," he said, nodding toward the track. "It's so wet, he's gonna be a little while. What's wrong with you, boy? Your face is all flushed and your eyes don't look so good!"

"I'm catching a cold," Jimmy insisted, faking a sniffle. "See?"

Harvey just grunted. "It's more than that," he said. "Looks like you seen a ghost!"

Jimmy shook his head and walked toward the back of the car. He sat on the tail of the trailer, watching as a big gray blob of clouds approached from the west, obscuring the sunset and casting a renewed darkness over the place. He cocked his head and looked toward the heavens.

"Never prayed for rain at the race track before," he whispered. "But if you don't mind…it wouldn't be a bad idea tonight."

A few minutes later the breeze picked up, and Jimmy saw the first few drops hit the ground. In a moment the rain became a steady shower, and he couldn't help but grin as he looked back up into the sky.

"Thank you," he whispered. "No kiddin'…and I promise, never, ever again!"

He rose from the trailer and walked to the door of the truck. Harvey rolled down the window.

"Yeah, they're done," the big man said, nodding toward the track. "Parkin' the tractors now. You want to go get something to eat, boy? There's a diner out on the highway…hey, where you goin'?"

"I'll see you guys at the shop this week," Jimmy called as he hurried away. "I'm gonna hang out with some of these guys for a little while before I go home."

Jimmy and the group had just reconvened under the canvas overhang, and the rain had stopped once again. Music was blaring, and they were joined by a handful of fans, drinking beer and enjoying the party.

A long, shiny Buick came tooling up, and the driver's door swung open.

"Hey, y'all got any of that 'shine left?" a young man called out in a deep southern twang.

"C'mon in, Dawson, and have a drink with us," Wagner shouted. "R.B. let you off work early?"

"Aw, ain't nothing to do till tomorrow," Dawson answered,

sauntering over to the group. "Looks like you boys got a party goin' on."

"Man, look at that Buick," Rusty admired, stepping over to have a look. "This thing is nice! R.B. must be payin' you pretty good, Dawson!"

"It's R.B.'s car," Dawson explained. "I think it's a yard unit."

"What's a yard unit?"

"It comes from his salvage yard."

"What??!!" Jimmy spoke up. "This is a junkyard car? No way! This thing is beautiful! Way nicer than anything I drive!"

"Well…sometimes the paperwork ain't exactly right on these cars, so R.B. just uses 'em here at the track, and at the yard."

"Oh, I get it," Rusty laughed. "It's probably a stolen car. A for-real hot car!"

"No, it ain't," Dawson insisted. "It ain't exactly…well, legal. But it ain't hot."

"Then why's it in a junkyard, when it's still in great shape?"

"Aw…quit askin' questions! I just work here."

Rusty slid his big frame behind the wheel. "Man, I can see myself driving down the avenue in this thing…hey, it's even got a tape player! This baby is first class…okay if we take 'er for a spin, Dawson?"

The man looked around for a moment, obviously uncomfortable with the request.

"I don't think so…R.B. would probably get sore if I let you. Better not."

"Come on, don't get all prissy on us," Rusty argued. "It's a junkyard car, for cryin' out loud. Let's take a ride!"

"Well…you ought not to. Probably ain't the right tags, and they'll pick you up. Wouldn't be good."

"It's okay," Jimmy said, sliding into the shotgun seat. "We won't leave the fairgrounds property. C'mon, guys! Crank up that stereo!"

Soon they were tooling around the fairgrounds, honking and waving to the people camping in the back nine. Everyone waved and laughed, as Wagner extended his body out the window and held two bottles of beer in the air.

Rusty steered toward an expanse of grass in the parking area.

"Let's go off-road," he laughed, gassing up the big V8 and breaking loose the rear wheels as he made a full round of the parking lot.

"Man, you're slow," Wagner complained. "Give me a try, I'll bet I could get around here faster than you."

"You're on. Anybody got a watch?"

Within a few minutes a fairly sizable crowd had gathered to watch the "time trials." A half-dozen racers, along with a handful of mechanics and onlookers, had tried their hand behind the wheel of the Buick.

Liquor and beer flowed freely, and perhaps that's why nobody seemed to notice that the sides of the beautiful car were covered with mud, and a huge, muddy rut was being cut on the perimeter of the otherwise pristine parking lot.

Steve Graffan and a couple of his pals came walking up.

"What's going on?" he asked.

"We're qualifyin'," Rusty laughed, his words a bit slurred. "You wanna take a lap?"

"Whose car is that?"

"It's R.B.'s. Just a junkyard car, don't worry."

"Who's got the best time?"

"Right now, Wagner. 38 seconds."

The car came rolling to a stop, and Wagner climbed out.

"Still 38 seconds," someone called out.

"Let me have a try," Graffan said, sliding behind the wheel.

In a few moments his run was completed, and he skidded to a stop alongside the crowd.

"36 seconds!" they yelled. "New track record!" A cheer went up from the mob.

Jimmy grabbed the door, eyeing Graffan as he climbed from the car.

"My turn," Jimmy grinned. Graffan just scoffed, stepping away as someone handed him a beer.

Jimmy mashed the gas in the big Buick, trying to finesse the barge around the tight corners. He heard the rear tires spinning on the mud, riding against the growing rut to the outside. A couple of times he noticed a light on the dash flicker for just a moment, and as he completed his lap he glanced at the dash, but the light was gone.

"35 seconds!" came the shout, and Jimmy climbed from the car and executed a bow to the crowd.

For the next few minutes it was a match race between Jimmy and Graffan, and by the time Jimmy lowered the mark to 33 seconds the Buick was panting for breath. This time the dash light stayed on long enough for Jimmy to clearly see it the small letters on the face: Oil.

As he rolled to a stop the car died, and he pulled it up in Park and climbed out.

"Why'd you turn it off?" Graffan demanded. "I still get a turn!"

"I didn't…it just died. Hey, the oil light came on. We probably ought to let it cool off some."

"Oh, sure, since you got the best time, let's quit now, right? Nothin' doin'. Let me get in there…"

Jimmy stepped aside as Graffan fired up the big machine. He pulled it into gear, and away he went. The car slid around the corners, tires screaming, and Jimmy could hear the lifters complaining as the big V8 went well past redline. Graffan came roaring around to complete the lap, and as he rushed past the crowd he banged the right side tires against the deep rut that was now clearly visible along the edge of the field.

They heard the loud report of the tires blowing out, just as Graffan wrenched the wheel to the left to make the turn. The huge machine slid awkwardly against the rut, when suddenly it rolled onto its side, then slowly tipped onto the roof with a resounding thud.

"Holy crap," Rusty wheezed. "He dumped 'er!"

They ran toward the car, slipping and sliding in the mud. The passenger door yawned open, and Graffan came toddling out on his hands and knees, just as Jimmy and Rusty reached him. They helped him to his feet, and in wide-eyed excitement he began shouting.

"What was my time? What was my time?"

"34 seconds," came the answer, and Jimmy grinned broadly and held both hands aloft.

"How about it, man! I'm the champ!"

"You okay?" Rusty asked Graffan, looking him over.

"Yeah…but there is no way that time was right. I know I was faster than that."

"Hey, she's leakin' gas," someone shouted. "Get 'er turned back over before she catches fire."

Soon the mob of people was pressed against the side of the big car, trying to get traction in the muddy mess. The car slowly came back up on its side, then back onto its wheels with a messy plop.

Just then a pickup truck came roaring up. The doors opened, and R.B. Stanley and Al Petrov piled from the cab. R.B.'s eyes grew wide as he took in the scene and began to recognize the automobile at the center of attention, now completely covered with a brown, muddy residue, all four headlights sending a beam jutting into the night in a different direction. The top was slightly caved in and the passenger side mirror hung forlornly against the middle of the door.

"What the hell is going on here?" he barked, shaking his head.

"That's what I'd like to know," Al answered, and Jimmy could see the anger in his friend's eyes.

"Uh…well…" Rusty began, but he suddenly seemed a little short on words.

"Dawson!" R.B. commanded. "Where's Dawson??!!"

"Right here, boss," Dawson answered meekly.

"You idiot…why'd you let this happen?"

"Aw, well…they took it, boss, I didn't give 'em permission!"

"I ought to break your neck…that's my wife's new car!"

Rusty and Jimmy exchanged a surprised look.

"Oops," Rusty whispered.

"I thought it was a field unit!" Dawson insisted.

R.B. looked around at nobody in particular, his face a picture of frustration.

"I am surrounded by complete jackasses," he said. He then let loose with a torrent of profanities.

Al looked around at the familiar faces and leaned close to R.B. "I don't think we'll want to get the police involved in this, do we?"

R.B. quickly shook his head and returned Al's gaze.

"No, I don't want any cops nosing around asking questions," he replied. "Bad for business."

R.B. turned to look again at the Buick, repeating some of the profanities before turning to face the crowd.

"Everybody clear out of here. The fairgrounds are closed. Go home. Party's over."

Jimmy and Rusty and the others turned to walk away, but found Al standing in front of them, boiling with anger.

"I've never been more embarrassed for our club," he seethed. "You guys…behaving like teenage boys. We turn our heads for one minute, and you get into a mess like this."

The men began to walk along the blacktop road toward the pit area, wiping huge clumps of mud from their shoes as Al continued.

"There will be fines," he said with a fierce expression. "You can count on that. This will cost you some money. If I had my way, there would be suspensions, too. Aren't you ashamed of yourselves… tearing up a man's car, and his parking lot. You could have killed someone. Why, I wouldn't take two cents for the whole bunch of you."

"Hey Al," Jimmy said softly, beginning to grin.

Al paused a moment and glared at Jimmy with a steely gaze.

"It ain't healthy for you to get so worked up," Jimmy offered. "How about if we go get something to eat, and you'll feel better. Okay?"

Al continued glaring, and Jimmy was pretty sure he could still see steam coming from the official's ears.

"Not a chance," Al barked. "It'll be a cold day in hell before I'm interested in having dinner with any of you boys."

"But I'm a little short," Rusty called out. "Could you spot me $20 till next week? You know I'm good for it."

They laughed out loud, but Al merely gritted his teeth, snorted and stalked away.

There might be hell to pay on Monday. But this was still Saturday, and Jimmy remembered the man having another one of those jars back at the campsite. Besides, it was starting to rain again.

Chapter 23

Jimmy walked across the big parking area at Clarksdale Speedway, a weathered old joint nestled in the heart of a tough Chicago suburb. He had spotted Chuck and Loretta's camper, and he wanted to say hello before he signed in. They were loyal race fans, and Chuck was the president of a prominent racing fan club in the Central City area.

"There's the man," Chuck called out, offering a wave. "Just getting here?"

Jimmy nodded, easing into a lawn chair alongside him. "I figured I'd see you guys up here. Only a hardcore fan comes to a dump like this."

The older man laughed. "Aw, it ain't so bad. We've been comin' up here since before AAA went away. You want something to drink? Soda? Got some tea in the camper there."

"Oh, I might have a glass of tea. Where's Loretta?"

"Went to get a bucket at the KFC…hey, where's that pretty girl you've been bringing with you?"

"Elaine? She's back home…had a wedding to go to tonight."

"Ohh, they don't like missing weddings…she give you a hard time about it?"

"Nope, just kind of shrugged her shoulders. She's real nice about stuff like that, but I can tell she isn't real keen on going by herself."

"Say, how's Bobby Mancini doing?"

"He's doing real good…got through surgery, and no problems. He's done for the year, though. Pretty tough deal."

"Say, listen, I got the paperwork going on having the club get him some money," Chuck explained. "Rita said they'd get him a check probably within a week or two, and after that have a little bit to him every month."

"Boy, that's great, because they could sure use it."

"Pretty good about Fred Otley getting another car together. Who's he gonna put in it?"

"Oh, I don't think Fred will be back out for a while...Bobby pretty much wiped out his whole operation at Franklin."

"Sure he'll be back," Chuck grinned.

"I don't think so," Jimmy insisted. "Not for a while."

"Look over there," Chuck pointed toward a line of vehicles across the way, leading to a dilapidated pit shack. There was the familiar Otley No. 29, riding on the trailer behind Fred's blue pickup.

"Well, I'll be," Jimmy said in amazement. "I never figured Fred could get another car together so quick."

"Must've had more spares than you figured. Say, there comes Loretta. You're gonna stick around for some chicken, right? You don't want to be eatin' track food here, that's for sure."

"Chuck, you ever known me to turn down fried chicken?" Jimmy smiled, reaching over to pat his friend on the shoulder. "Besides, I need to help eat up some of that retirement money... keep you from gettin' fat."

Jimmy signed in and headed for the Ellison car, smiling broadly when he saw Sonny Ellison standing with Harvey and Slim.

"Hey, you're a long way from home," Jimmy said, offering a handshake. "I didn't think mama let you come out on the road anymore."

"Oh, I still like to get out a little bit," he laughed. "Besides, you guys have been going pretty good, and I wanted to get in on some of the fun."

"Always glad to have you...how's business?"

"Better than I expected. I've got my full crew on for the summer, and we'll be busy till winter. So the paving business is hanging in there."

"Say, Sonny, I've been thinking about something," Jimmy began, giving Sonny a wink. "You know what this team needs? We need a team manager."

"Really?" Sonny answered, stifling a grin.

"Yeah...all the Indy car teams have a manager. And wouldn't that be a big help for Harvey? Somebody to help keep him straight, you know, and nail down all the details."

"You show me a detail I've missed in 25 years," Harvey growled.

"You don't know what you're talking about."

"Now, don't get defensive, Harvey. I'm just saying, we ought to give it some thought. You could put a time clock in the shop, and have these guys punch in and out. And they would need to do paperwork, showing what they're doing every day. And make sure the manager likes to look over people's shoulders, and he could supervise Harvey when he works on the car. Wouldn't that be great?"

Harvey's expression was granite, and his eyes were just two slits, with a nice shade of purple rising across his forehead. The others began to laugh, and when the big man realized they were messing with him he started to relax, actually offering a chuckle of his own.

"I was about to shove one of these crutches in a place you don't want it," he said. "Besides, if anybody needs a manager, it's you. That's where I come in, boy. I light a fire where it needs lit every now and then. If you didn't have me, you'd be just another never-was."

"Oh, brother," Jimmy smiled. "Here we go again."

Rusty Fernandez came walking over, and the big redhead grinned. "Are you guys giving Harvey a hard time? You ought to take it easy on him…still crippled up on these crutches."

"I ain't crippled up," Harvey bristled. "I can do anything you can do."

"That ain't true."

"The hell it ain't!"

"Okay, I'll race you to the concession stand."

"Red, that ain't important enough to even do," Harvey scoffed. "I'm talking about with the race car…these crutches ain't slowin' me down a lick."

"I'll bet I can drive better than you."

"You're wasting your time," Jimmy chimed in. "You don't want to go down this path, believe me."

"He knows what I'm gonna say," Harvey chortled, nodding at Jimmy. "Cause I've told him many times…one of these days I'm gonna try out my experiment."

"What experiment?" Rusty quizzed.

Harvey grinned and nodded at Jimmy. "Tell our slow friend here what I have in mind," Harvey said, easing himself onto the car's front tire.

"Oh, he's got this stupid idea," Jimmy said, shaking his head. "It's not even worth talking about."

"What? What idea?" Rusty was growing more curious.

"He thinks he can train a monkey to drive a race car."

"What??!! That's the dumbest thing I ever heard."

Jimmy looked at Rusty and gave him a resigned shrug.

"Are you serious, Harvey?" Rusty laughed, shaking his head in amazement. "That's just stupid, man."

"No it ain't," Harvey insisted. "I'm dead serious...think about it: all I gotta teach him is to look at the gauge, flip the switch, gas it and steer. It's so damned easy, a monkey could do it."

Rusty stared incredulously at Harvey. "He...he's serious!"

"I told you," Jimmy said, shaking his head. "Don't get him started. All he'll do is get in your head and make you mad."

"Oh, I wouldn't want to make you mad, boy," Harvey laughed. "I know how easy you get your feelings hurt! All you young boys these days, you're all the sensitive type."

"See?" Jimmy admonished Rusty. "Now you got him wound up."

"Hell, you candy-asses couldn't drive a lap without your roll cages, and nerf bars, and fancy helmets. Back when I started, racers were tough. You boys, not so much. Not a one of you could hold a candle to Mike Nazaruk or Jud Larson."

"Whatever," Rusty argued. "You don't know what you're talking about."

"You're wasting your time," Jimmy insisted to Rusty. "It's not worth arguing with him."

"Aw, you're just full of it," Rusty insisted, his voice rising.

"C'mon, I'll let you buy me a Coke," Jimmy laughed, gently pushing Rusty toward the concession stand. "Don't show us that redhead temper."

As they walked along the line of cars they saw Fred Otley rolling the No. 29 off the trailer. Jimmy spotted a muscular guy with black hair and a moustache helping Fred.

"Who is that?" Jimmy quizzed Rusty.

"That's Jack Underwood," Rusty explained. "California driver, and evidently Fred hired him to run the car."

"Underwood? Isn't he some kind of roughneck guy out there?"

"Oh, yeah. He's been in all kinds of scraps. He'd rather fight than breathe, is what I hear. But he's supposed to be pretty good in the car."

They approached the car, and Fred gave them a wave. "Got my new car together," he beamed. "Worked like a maniac, only slept two nights this week. But she looks pretty good, don't she?"

"Real good," Jimmy praised.

"Say, this is Jack Underwood…he's from California, and he'll be runnin' my car. This here is Jimmy Wilson, and Rusty Fernandez. They're good boys, and you'll like racin' with 'em, Jack."

Underwood looked them over carefully, grunting a hello. He turned to walk toward the front of the car, busying himself with his helmet bag.

Jimmy looked the car over, glancing at Fred, who must have been reading his mind.

"Now, I told Jack straight away, this is strictly until Bobby gets healed up. Bobby is my driver, and the seat's his when he's able."

Jimmy smiled. "I didn't say anything."

"I know, but he's your friend. And I don't want him feeling like I already forgot him, because that ain't so."

Jimmy nodded. "Well, good luck with the new car." They began to walk away, and Jimmy looked back toward Underwood, who glanced up at them.

"See you later," Jimmy waved. Underwood offered a curt nod.

They were a few yards away when Rusty spoke up in a lowered voice.

"If Underwood gets going good, Bobby's old news."

"Yep." Jimmy nodded, a sad frown darting across his face.

The Ellison team struggled from the outset on this night. The throttle linkage was binding up, and Harvey took it apart after qualifying and again after their heat, trying to figure out the trouble. The track turned into a one-lane affair on the bottom, and they chased the setup, trying to get the car tight enough.

Jimmy missed the transfer in his heat, and lined up on the pole of the semi. He got a nice jump at the start and led all the way to win, hurrying back to their pit and climbing from the car.

He and Harvey began talking about the setup, and Jimmy insisted they tighten the car further.

"I don't think so," Harvey objected. "We go any tighter, and you can't get off the bottom at all."

"I'm starting outside front row," Jimmy argued. "I've got to be really, really good on the bottom, because that's where we'll run."

They went back and forth, neither man wanting to yield. In the end Harvey had the stronger will, and he insisted they leave the car alone.

"If you get into traffic and need to use that second lane, you'll be okay," he explained. Jimmy had his doubts, but he just shook his head and sat on the end of the trailer to put on some tear-offs.

"Gentlemen, let's go," an official called as he hurried past. "Let's get 'em in the lineup chute!"

In a few minutes Jimmy was buckled in, waiting to be pushed. Harvey braced himself against his crutches, looking over the car. He tossed his crutches aside, hobbling a few feet to lean into the cockpit.

"Just be patient, boy," he insisted. "Big thing is, go easy on that right foot…feather it as gentle as you can, and you'll go faster. If you get into traffic, run just one car width to the outside, and I think she'll work decent there if you have to. Keep your head in it!"

Soon the field was rumbling toward the start, with Jimmy to the outside of Rusty. The field snarled as they anticipated the green, and Jimmy eased into the throttle as gently as he dared, feeling the tires spinning and searching for traction.

Rusty led him to the corner, and Jimmy tried to move down as quickly as he could. He moved in behind the leader, and felt the car slipping through the corner. The car was good, and he concentrated on being smooth and hitting his lift points.

A few laps in he saw a flash of movement from the hood of his car, but it was such a blur he wasn't even sure he had seen anything. A few moments later the caution light blinked on, and the field slowed.

Jimmy flexed his fingers as he idled around the track, looking for whatever brought the yellow. As he rolled through turn three he saw an official waiting to cross the track, and he spotted a black piece of debris lying to the outside.

When he reached the front stretch, a couple of officials had inched onto the surface, studying the Ellison Special as it passed. Suddenly they nodded and emphatically pointed toward the back of the field. Jimmy held up his hands at the starter, who pointed to the tail.

As he passed through turn three an official stepped onto the track, holding up an injector filter and pointing at Jimmy.

Must have been mine, he realized, his heart sinking. *Probably got jarred loose when we were messing with that damned throttle linkage.*

Just to be sure, he held his position as they approached the flag stand. Several officials pointed to their backside, and the starter showed him a furled black flag and pointed rearward.

He moved to the outside, allowing the field to pass.

Now you've got your work cut out for you, he mused, tightening his grip on the wheel.

If there was an upside, at least it had happened early. Jimmy would think of that later, when he had time to replay the night in his mind. When the race resumed he was surprised to find that the car worked much better in the second groove than he had anticipated. He was the only car on the track able—or perhaps desperate enough—to try the outside, and while everyone freight-trained the bottom he steadily picked his way forward.

With 10 to go he was third, dispensing with Rick Wagner and Underwood after a side-by-side duel that had the fans on their feet. Jimmy now found himself on the tail of Steve Graffan, who was on the bumper of Rusty, the leader.

By this time he had used the Ellison car up. He struggled to decide: Do I dare go to the outside again to try Graffan? If I slip, I'll go all the way to the back again.

Before he could make up his mind, he felt a firm rap from behind, sending the tail of the Ellison car to the outside. He flexed his wrists to try and save it, but the car was too far gone, and he found himself spinning. For a split second he considered gassing it up to try and do a 360 and keep it going, but with nearly the entire field scrambling to miss him, that didn't seem like a smart idea.

As he found himself backward he saw the Otley No. 29 flash past on the outside, and his face flushed with anger. Underwood had spun him out.

He pounded the steering wheel as he sat silently on the track. At least everybody had missed him; when the wrecker arrived he was good to rejoin the field.

In the handful of remaining laps he managed only to pass a few cars, and he guessed it was his most dismal finish this year.

He drove back to the pit area and the car fell silent. Harvey looked disgusted as Jimmy climbed from the car.

"Somebody spun you out!" Harvey yelled. "I ain't sure who, but you flat got took out!"

"Underwood," Jimmy said, seething. "Must have been him."

"Maybe that's how they race out there," Harvey complained bitterly. "Boy, you done a good job. I was right, wasn't I? Car worked decent up there when you had to."

Jimmy wiped his face, swishing a gulp of water and spitting it into the dirt. He looked down the way at the Otley pit, where Underwood and Fred were talking and looking at their car.

Jimmy clenched his jaw as he stared, feeling the anger rising in his gut.

"If you don't go down and put a stop to it now, he'll push you clear back to Illinois," Harvey said, shaking his head.

Jimmy nodded, and he tossed the cup toward the car. He walked briskly toward the other pit, his mind filled with anger.

I can handle this guy, he told himself. *I handled Graffan earlier this year, didn't I? I'm probably a lot tougher than I realize…besides, at the very least I'll get his attention, and we'll have no more trouble.*

Fred had knelt behind the car, and was looking at the rear end with a flashlight. Jimmy walked into their pit, and Underwood gave him something of a curious look.

"You took me out," Jimmy said flatly, rearing back to swing a roundhouse right hand.

Underwood instinctively flinched back, and Jimmy's punch caught nothing but air as it rushed past. In a blur Underwood stepped inside and drove his right fist into Jimmy's chin.

Jimmy felt the blow rock his entire body, sending rounds of

tingling electricity all the way to his ass, upon which he happened to now be sitting. Every part of him hurt, from his neck all the way down his back, and he could already feel his jaw aching.

Fred looked on in complete surprise, and Underwood stood over Jimmy, fists clenched in readiness. Jimmy sat in the dirt for a moment, trying to remember exactly where he was and what this was all about.

For a few seconds nobody said anything, and Underwood stared intently at Jimmy before finally speaking.

"You gonna get up?"

"Not right yet," Jimmy said, flexing his jaw to figure out if it was broken.

Underwood relaxed, giving Jimmy a steady gaze. He leaned over a little, extending his hand, and helped Jimmy to his feet. Jimmy was a little wobbly at first, but managed to straggle to Fred's pickup and take a seat on the tailgate, still letting the cobwebs clear out.

Underwood walked to a nearby cooler and came back with a couple of beers. He handed one to Jimmy, and opened the other and took a long draw.

"You're wrong about me taking you out," he said calmly. "I never touched your car."

At the moment Jimmy didn't really care much either way, as he gamely opened the beer and took a drink.

"Well, it sure looked like it from my seat," he said.

"I know what it looked like…but I never touched you."

"Well…either way, I shouldn't have taken a poke at you. Guess I was just pissed."

Underwood nodded. "Been there myself a time or two…you sure you're all right?"

"Yeah, I'm fine. Just moved my jaw back a foot or two. Where'd you learn to hit like that?"

"My dad was a boxer," he explained. "And our neighborhood was kinda tough."

Underwood let out a long sigh, a look of sadness on his face. "What's up with you?" Jimmy asked. "You surely don't feel that bad for knocking me on my ass."

"Aw…it's just, I've wanted to come out here and race with

USAC for a long time, and I get my break and the first night…I get set down for fighting. Kind of hoped it'd work out different than this."

Jimmy looked up to see Al Petrov and Leon Hartke hurrying over.

"What's going on here?" Al quizzed, studying the two men. "We had a report there was trouble."

Jimmy looked at Underwood and smiled. "No trouble here, Al," he said, shaking his head. "Just having a beer."

Al stared intently at Jimmy, and after a moment he relaxed. "Okay, then," he said, nodding his head slowly. "Okay."

The two officials walked away, and Jimmy looked at Underwood and shrugged. "See? No trouble."

Underwood nodded, and smiled.

Jimmy stood up, pausing for a moment to make sure his balance still worked all right. He started to walk away and Underwood spoke up.

"I was kind of hoping you'd help me," he said.

"Help you? Do what?"

"Pavement…plus, I don't know these tracks any. Thought maybe I could ask you for some pointers."

Jimmy smiled, and nodded. "We'll talk," he said, lifting his beer slightly. "Thanks for the beer."

Underwood nodded, and returned the smile.

Jimmy walked back toward the Ellison car, where Harvey was waiting with something of an amused look on his face. He studied Jimmy and grinned, and Jimmy gave him a serious look.

"That'll teach him," he said, walking past Harvey to retrieve his helmet bag. He heard someone call his name, and he turned to see Rick Wagner approaching. Rick held up his hands innocently.

"I know you're pissed, but I want to apologize," he began. "I carried too much speed into the corner down there, and got into the back of you. Totally my fault, Jimmy. I was sick when you spun out. I know you don't race me like that and I would never hit you intentionally. I think you know that."

Jimmy laughed out loud at the situation, and Rick gave him a confused look.

"Aw, we're all right," Jimmy said quickly. "I'm just laughing about how dumb I am sometimes."

Rick offered his hand, and Jimmy held the handshake for a moment.

"I'm not kidding, I'm sick about this," Rick insisted. "I feel real bad."

"Nah, we've got no problem," Jimmy replied. "I accept your apology, and this is already forgotten."

Rick nodded, and turned to walk away. Jimmy walked to the cooler, fishing out another beer. He eased himself onto the back of Harvey's truck, sipping the open beer and rolling the other cold brew across his jaw, flexing it and trying to get it to stop hurting.

Slim began to gather up their stuff, and Harvey leaned on his crutches, looking at Jimmy and suppressing a laugh.

Jimmy returned the gaze, and gave him that serious look again.

"I really am a badass," he said. Harvey laughed out loud, and Jimmy did too, wincing in the process. It had been a long night.

Chapter 24

Jimmy eased onto the busy Interstate, crossing his fingers and holding the gearshift lever firmly with his right hand. On pins and needles, he accelerated as gingerly as he dared, watching the mirror, waiting for the tractor-trailer to yield the slow lane.

He was in no mood for this, and he cursed the timing. As he pressed further on the throttle, there was a bang from under the floorboard, and his hand jumped along with the shift lever. The engine revved helplessly, and he clutched the truck and got it back into gear, glancing nervously into the rear-view mirror to see if he was about to be run over.

"You miserable piece of junk," he hissed. Why did stuff like this have to happen? One day before he was headed out west on a 10-day road trip, he can't keep this damned thing in gear.

Jimmy settled in behind a slow-moving semi going about 50, with traffic whizzing past. Every couple of miles the tranny would spit the lever upward, and Jimmy would get it back into gear as quickly as he could. Soon he flicked on his signal to exit, and in a couple of minutes steered into Al Petrov's driveway.

Nancy Petrov beamed as she answered the door.

"Well, I'll be," she said, giving him a hug. "Haven't seen you in forever. You hungry for some lunch? Let me make you a sandwich."

"Thanks, but I really need to use your phone. Is Al around?"

"He'll be back in ten minutes, just ran to the drugstore. He and the guys are leaving this afternoon. When are you leaving?"

"That depends," Jimmy smiled, opening the yellow pages. "My truck needs a transmission…if I can get one right away from the junkyard, I can leave in the morning like I planned."

"My gosh! You can replace the transmission that quickly?"

"Sure. Sonny Ellison has a lift in his maintenance shop, and it won't take me but a couple of hours."

"Are you driving all the way out there by yourself?"

"Yeah...normally Bobby and I would ride together, but with him being laid up...I kind of like riding by myself anyway. I'm not much on sharing space with people."

Jimmy began dialing junkyards, the same question every time. "How much for a three-speed transmission for a '66 GMC pickup?"

Of course everybody had one, ready and waiting, as long as he had fifty bucks. The trouble was, the $27 in his wallet wasn't quite going to get it done.

He glumly hung up the phone just as Al walked into the small kitchen.

"Truck trouble?"

"Yeah, keeps jumping out of gear. No way it could make it to California."

"Nobody's got another transmission?"

Jimmy laughed. "Oh, they've got 'em. But I need to win a couple of races first before I can pick one up."

"Tapped out, 'eh? You need some money? I can front you a little."

Jimmy stood thinking for a minute. "Ah, I don't know...I probably need my head examined, scrambling around like this. It's going to take at least a hundred bucks, because I'm sure the clutch is shot, too. Even if I borrow some money from you, I'm already gonna be close on having enough gas money to get out there."

He slumped into a chair, looking at the sandwich and glass of tea Nancy had prepared for him.

"I should have planned this better...should have arranged to ride with a couple of the guys. Rick Wagner and Rusty, something. Now I'm backed into a corner."

"You'd be welcome to ride with us, except we're full," Al explained. "We've got the van, but there are five of us riding. How about Sid Johnson?"

"They left yesterday," Jimmy said between bites.

Al slid into one of the chairs, giving Jimmy an amused look. "You could always ride with Harvey."

Jimmy groaned. "No way...I'd rather walk."

Al laughed. "In that case, you better get started right now...it's a long ways out to Ascot."

They sat for a minute while Jimmy finished his lunch. He wiped his face with a napkin, staring at Al.

"If I ride that far with Harvey, we'll kill each other. Or I'll lose what's left of my mind. Who else is driving out there…who else?"

They wracked their brains for another few minutes, Jimmy getting up to pace around the kitchen in exasperation.

"I can't think of anybody," Al said finally, rising from his chair. "I've got to finish getting ready, Nancy has to drive me over to the USAC office to meet the guys here in a little bit."

Jimmy looked helplessly at Al, shaking his head. "I'm gonna have to do it," he said, talking to himself as much as anything. "I'm actually going to have to ride with that bozo clear out west. I can't believe it…what did I do in a previous life that was so bad, Al? Why am I being punished like this?"

Al laughed. "Ah, this is nothing. You should have made this trip back in the three-A days…little narrow highways, no speed limits, that was wide-open traveling. And some of those old heaps we drove, they weren't fit to ride in. Death-traps, really. But we made it…put hair on our chest. You might be surprised…you might even have fun with 'ol Harvey. And it isn't like you've got a choice."

Jimmy looked over the traveling rig, and smiled.

"That's a pretty good setup," he nodded to Slim. "Where did the camper come from?"

"Harvey borrowed it from somebody…he had to weld up a thing where it would mount up right in the truck bed, but it's pretty nice. Has a couple of padded benches and a fold-down bed, and there's a little table and a propane cooking stove. Everything you need for living on the road."

"Ain't that the snazziest setup you ever saw?" Harvey bellowed as he came limping from the office of Ellison Paving. The wheelchair and the crutches were nothing but a memory, although he was still gimpy. "I'll bet we got the best rig in all of USAC."

"It is pretty nice…doesn't hurt that Sonny's letting us use one of his newer pickups. When are you leaving?"

"First thing in the morning."

"Got room for one more?"

Harvey raised his eyebrows, and Slim offered his goofy grin. "You mean…you?" Harvey asked. "You want to ride with us?"

"Aw, my old pickup…the tranny is shot, and it won't make it out there. Hell, it won't make it out of town, really. So I need to catch a ride with somebody."

"I guess….sure, you could ride along. Matter of fact, that ain't a bad idea. You can help with the driving…with a third driver, we can drive straight through."

Jimmy nodded. "Suits me. What time in the morning?"

"Aw, I don't know…five or six, maybe."

"Why don't we just leave tonight?" Slim asked. "If we leave tonight, we can make some stops if we want to. You know, Lone Star stops."

Harvey looked at him and grinned. "That's a damn good idea, Slim. How about it, boy? You up for leaving this evening?"

"Whenever is fine with me. Beats sitting around here."

Soon Jimmy had tossed his helmet bag and his small suitcase into the camper. It really was a nifty setup…a nice crew-cab pickup, with a tall camper bolted into the bed, the kind that extends out over the cab. Their open trailer was hitched behind the truck, the Ellison No. 49 sprinter gleaming in the bright summer sun.

Harvey made one more quick check of the fluids under the hood of the truck, while Slim double-checked the hitch and the hold-downs on the little trailer. As soon as he was finished Slim scrambled into the shotgun seat.

"C'mon, Harvey, let's get going!" he called out.

"We've got 2,000 miles to go, Slim," Jimmy laughed. "You in a hurry?"

"Just itchin' to get rolling…"

Jimmy slid into the back seat, closing the door and getting a feel of the interior. In a moment Harvey climbed behind the wheel, turning to look at the two men.

"Okay, I'll take the first shift, and I'll drive till I get tired. Then one of you guys can take over. Driver gets to choose the music. Let's get going."

They eased through the local neighborhoods, soon finding the Interstate and pointing the nose of the truck west. As they settled in, Harvey grabbed a tape from a box in the middle of the seat.

Soon there was music that seemed strangely familiar to Jimmy, and he cocked his head as he listened, trying to pin it down.

"Is that...*Lawrence Welk??!!*" he quizzed in amazement.

Harvey turned and beamed, bumping the volume a couple of notches. "Yeah! You like Lawrence?"

"Aw, my folks loved him," Jimmy moaned. "But...*Lawrence Welk*, for 2,000 miles...c'mon, Harvey, that's cruel."

"Quit your whinin'," Harvey sniffed. "Better than listening to some faggot in skin-tight clothes, with hair down to his ass, screaming into a microphone...don't even think of listening to that crap when it's your turn, boy...I can't stomach that music."

"You don't like the Beatles?"

"Bunch of fags."

"How about Grand Funk Railroad?"

"Never heard of 'em."

"But Lawrence Welk is okay...is that how it is?"

"Hell, yeah. You ever watch Lawrence on TV? Best show on television. And that broad he's got playing the piano, what's her name? Castor? She's great."

"Castle. Jo Ann Castle."

Harvey roared with laughter, looking at Jimmy in the rear-view mirror. "You DO watch Lawrence on TV!"

"I said my folks watched him," Jimmy corrected. "I had no choice."

"Yeah, Jo Ann, that's her name...you ever see the rack on that broad? She gets to poundin' that piano, boy, that's somethin' to see!"

"He scoots his chair up close to the TV set," Slim interjected, grinning.

"Damn right! Hey, here's my favorite Lawrence song...*You're The Cream in my Coffee*...ah, ain't that great?" He reached over to give the volume another bump.

Jimmy sagged back into the seat, shaking his head in disbelief as the clarinet and organ melded together, with an accordion mixed in for good measure.

This was going to be a long, long ride.

Jimmy felt the truck rocking slightly, and he awoke and looked around. Harvey was steering into a truck stop, the bright lights cutting through the summer night. The truck eased along the gas pumps, and soon the engine fell silent.

The doors yawned open, and the men slowly emerged, stretching off the effects of the miles.

"Where are we?" Jimmy asked, glancing at his watch.

"Missouri," Harvey answered, rubbing his eyes. "Somebody's got to take a turn, I'm just about wore out."

"I'll drive," Jimmy offered. "But I'm hungry. Want to eat something here?"

Harvey paused a moment, before nodding. "Yeah, might as well. Slim, check the cooler up there, and see how the ice is holding up. I could do for a hot dinner, myself. We'll save the sandwiches for tomorrow."

"I got some good shut-eye," Jimmy smiled. "I slept right through St. Louis."

They were soon seated at a table where they could keep an eye on the car. An attractive waitress brought over a pot of coffee, and they stared admiringly as she walked away.

"Hey, Harvey," Jimmy teased in a whisper. "You know what? She looks like Jo Ann Castle."

The big man glanced at Jimmy, and shook his head. "Don't start with it," he groused. "Hurry up and order, so we can keep rollin.'"

Jimmy guided the truck through the night, the white lines of the highway flashing past in steady rhythm. The night air was cool, and he rode alone in the truck, with Harvey and Slim sleeping soundly in the camper. He shivered, and cranked up the window.

He listened to the radio for a while, then clicked it off, enjoying the solitude of the miles.

Wonder how Bobby is doing with his busted leg, he mused. *I miss traveling with him. Even if he is a pack of trouble, he's fun. Hope he's not feeling blue.*

Jimmy glanced at a station wagon as it swept past, hurrying along. When would they get to California? Not today, but sometime tomorrow, pretty sure. He felt un-tethered, and free. But free, he knew that was just a proud way to be lonely.

That race car trailing behind him, it was a powerful thing, real powerful. Enough power to win, enough power to kill, enough power to take him to another world. But it was greedy, too. It couldn't share him, no matter how much he studied and tried to find a way.

Elaine told him so, in so many words. They could be together, but every time she inched closer, off he'd go on another trip, another weekend, another day chasing…chasing something, but he didn't know what.

It damn sure wasn't money. His life could be added up pretty distinctly, and you didn't even need a comma in the total. A tired old pickup truck and $27 pretty much summed it up at this point. Not much to offer a classy girl like Elaine.

But he shook off the dark thoughts, and stared into the inky blackness of the night, following the taillights in the distance.

The miles rolled along as he crossed into Oklahoma, and soon he realized it was growing light. He felt surprisingly fresh, rubbing his face and wondering about a shave. Soon he turned his mirror to keep the bright morning sun from his eyes, and spotted the sign for the rest area coming up.

He wheeled the truck off the highway, easing to a stop and cutting the engine. He stepped outside, feeling the sweet morning air envelope him as he stretched. The camper door creaked open and Harvey and Slim emerged, straightening out the kinks as they tottered toward him.

"Bathroom stop," Jimmy said.

"You made good time," Harvey nodded, looking around and getting his bearings. "I slept like a baby…felt good. There's a campground about 20 miles up the road, we can swing in there and get a shower. I'll cook us some breakfast."

A half-hour later they were parked at the campground, and already Jimmy could feel the summer heat building. They each paid a buck for a shower, and when Jimmy returned to the truck Harvey had the Coleman stove going, rustling up a mix of potatoes, eggs and sausage, and the three men ate heartily at a picnic table.

"I've got to admit, Harvey, this is great," Jimmy praised. "Cooking like this, you'd make somebody a good little wife."

Harvey muttered a profanity, and Jimmy and Slim laughed.

"You can sleep a while up in the camper," Harvey offered. "At least until lunchtime, unless it gets too hot in there."

They finished eating and gathered up their things, packing them away in the camper. Jimmy climbed into the bunk over the cab, clasping his hands behind his head and relaxing. He heard the doors of the pickup slam closed, and he laughed out loud in anticipation.

He had found an Alice Cooper tape in the glove box, probably left by some of Sonny's paving crew. He popped the tape in the player, and after shutting off the ignition, had turned the volume knob wide open. As soon as Harvey keyed the starter…BINGO!

The first several notes of "School's Out" screamed from the speakers before suddenly falling silent. Jimmy howled with laughter, wishing he could see Harvey's face. He looked out the camper window to see the tape go sailing into the weeds alongside the driveway.

The truck eased forward, but at about 10 mph Harvey stood on the brakes, causing Jimmy to roll hard into the front wall of the camper, banging his head. He still laughed as he rubbed his scalp, enjoying Harvey's ire.

"You hear me, boy??!!" Harvey yelled, pounding on the side of the truck door. "They're gonna find your dried-up carcass alongside the road somewhere!"

Jimmy blinked his eyes open, feeling the gentle shudder of the truck as they rolled along. He guessed it was around noontime, reaching under the pillow to find his watch. Yep, just before noon.

Air streamed through the open windows of the camper, and he laid his head against the pillow, enjoying the comfortable ride. They were probably somewhere in Texas, but he had no idea where. He reached over to retrieve the little paperback western he had brought along, but after a couple of paragraphs found he wasn't in the mood to read.

He realized they were rolling onto an exit ramp, and he studied the landscape through the window. He could see homes and businesses lining the streets, but he had no idea what city it was. After stopping at the top of the ramp the truck moved slowly down the street, and Jimmy's curiosity rose as they traveled farther from the highway. Where were they going?

Soon the truck eased into a parking lot in an older neighborhood, and Jimmy heard the engine fall silent. He pulled on his shoes and stepped out into the hot summer day.

"What's up?" he asked Harvey, who just grinned.

"Just takin' a short stop," he said. "We need a break, boy. Gotta get off the road for a few minutes."

"C'mon, Harvey, let's go," Slim said eagerly.

Jimmy looked at the two men, trying to figure it out. He looked up at the large white home when he saw the sign, bright yellow with bold black lettering hanging over a huge pillared porch.

"Hey," Jimmy laughed out loud. "This is a *massage parlor!* You guys are going to a *massage parlor!*"

"What's wrong with that?" Harvey countered. "This is a nice place!"

Jimmy laughed again. "I'm sure it is, Harvey, I'm sure it is. How'd you know it was here?"

"There ain't a racer travelin' along 66 that ain't been here," he explained. "This place is a landmark."

"Let's go," Slim said again, impatiently. "What are we waitin' for?"

The two men turned to go in, and Jimmy stared and laughed, shaking his head in amazement. Harvey turned back toward him.

"Well…ain't you comin' in, boy?"

"No, thanks," Jimmy smiled.

"C'mon…I'll even stake you, if you're tight on cash. It's good for the disposition."

"I appreciate that Harvey, I really do…but when I was in the army, every time I went to a place like this I ended up in sick bay or in the stockade, or both. So if it's all the same to you, I'll pass."

Harvey shrugged. "Suit yourself," he said. "But I'm tellin' you… it's a nice place."

With that the big man hurried to catch up to Slim as he took the front steps two at a time. Jimmy couldn't help but laugh at how quickly they disappeared through the front door.

He stretched his legs a little, looking around. On the corner up the way was a small bar, and he thought about having a sandwich, because he suddenly felt a rumbling in his belly.

Jimmy took a step in that direction when he realized that the van parked a few yards away looked awfully familiar. He stepped around back and looked at the tags, then laughed heartily.

He began to walk toward the bar, and felt his back pocket. He quickly turned and climbed into the camper, retrieving his wallet from inside. Suddenly he paused, wondering if he ought to stay and keep an eye on their rig. The neighborhood was kind of seedy, and the car was sitting right here in the open...yeah, better stay here. He dug into the cooler and made himself a sandwich, pouring some tea into a plastic cup. He sat on the fender of the trailer, placing the paper plate on his lap as he looked up into the huge trees surrounding the place.

The front door of the house creaked open, and Jimmy glanced toward the porch to see a cast of familiar faces coming down the front steps, grinning like schoolboys. The five men headed for the van, and Jimmy took another bite of his sandwich and smiled.

Al Petrov saw him first, smiling sheepishly as Jimmy laughed out loud.

"Hi-ya, Jimmy," Al called out, offering a wave. "Interesting place to bump into you. Hooked up with Harvey and Slim for the ride out, I see."

"Yep...how you boys doing? Have a good...uh...massage?"

The men laughed nervously. "It was great," Al nodded. "You ought to go inside and check it out."

"You know, they say recreation is good for the soul," Jimmy continued. "And if there's a breed of cat that ought to have a good soul, it's race officials. It's good to see you boys so...*happy!* You should be in a great mood when we get to Ascot."

The other men quickly climbed into the van, but Al took his time, now laughing openly at the situation.

"Oh, we'll be in good spirits...but how about you, Jimmy? Looks awfully lonely out here by yourself."

Jimmy nodded. "Yeah...well, I'll probably be in a bad mood. But just take it easy on me, okay? I'm just a poor ol' racer, trying to get to California."

The early morning sun streamed through the windows of the truck as they rolled across Arizona, mountains looming on the distant horizon. It had been a long night, with a delay of several hours near Gallup for an upended semi. Nothing to do but sit unmoving on the Interstate, trying to catch some sleep, waiting for the side-by-side parking lot to move forward.

Jimmy steered the truck along, glancing over at Slim. The tall, angular man slept with his head against the door pillar, arms crossed and mouth open. Harvey was asleep in the back seat, head tilted on his shoulder, snoring loudly.

Suddenly the engine sputtered, and Jimmy tensed and looked at the fuel gauge. The needle was slightly below E, and he sagged in dismay.

How could this happen? How could he let the thing run out of gas?

He eased off the road, the engine silent. Harvey and Slim quickly awoke, looking around.

"What's the matter?" Harvey asked, his words slurred. "She quit?"

They rolled to a stop as Jimmy pointed to the gauge. "Looks like we're out of gas."

Harvey shook his head in disgust.

"Aw, for cryin' out loud! I told you, keep an eye on the gauge. I knew this would happen, because you don't take care of details. Well, you know the rules…you gotta hoof it to the station. I got a gas can on the trailer."

They climbed out of the truck. Thankfully it was still early morning, and the sun hadn't yet reached a punishing stage. Jimmy stared down the highway as Harvey unlashed the red 5-gallon can.

"Wonder what the nearest exit is," he mused. "Any idea how far?"

Harvey studied him for a moment, then looked around.

"Actually, boy, you're in luck. See that big foothill to our right? Directly on the other side of the hill is a gas station. It's way shorter to walk across country than to take the highway. That's what I'd do."

"You're kidding…walk across there? Up that giant hill? Geez, that's a steep hike…are you sure?"

"I've made this trip 50 times, and I know right where we are," Harvey insisted. "When you get to the station, see if the man will give you a ride back. Well, that hill ain't gettin' any smaller...better get goin.'"

Jimmy grimaced as he looked up the steep hillside, littered with dried brush and rocks. He stepped over the guardrail, watching his footing as he started up the hill.

"Hey, boy, one more thing," Harvey called out. "They've got some big-ass rattlesnakes out here...watch yourself."

"Great," Jimmy moaned. "I hate snakes!"

Jimmy carefully made his way up the hill, stepping carefully. Every sound nearly stopped him in his tracks, as he was certain he heard the ominous rattle that came before the strike. But he pushed on, panting, sweat running down his back, lifting his t-shirt to wipe his face every so often.

He wished he had thought to bring a canteen. As much as he walked, it seemed the peak of the hill was still far away, but he finally reached the apex and began making his way down the other side.

Harvey was right about the station, and Jimmy could see it off in the distance at the base of the hill. He continued to plod along, squinting in the searing sun, the handle of the gas can pressing hard into the flesh of his hand.

He guessed the station was now about three-quarters of a mile away, and he could just make out a vehicle parked off to the side with a race car in tow. *Wonder who that is...one of the other teams make a stop?* He watched his step for the next little while, and when he looked back at the station he suddenly realized something.

"That's *our* rig!" he shouted. "Our truck, our camper, our race car...what the hell is going on??!!"

He finished the last stretch between him and the station, his feet finding the smooth ground surrounding the property. He walked quickly toward their rig, parked in the shade alongside the main building. The doors were open, and Harvey and Slim sat leisurely in the front seat, Harvey propping his feet up on the door sill.

Jimmy's eyes were angry slits, staring at Harvey as he approached.

"Hey, boy, how was your walk?" the big man chortled. "Say, I plumb forgot to tell you...this thing has an auxiliary fuel tank!

Ain't that great? Just flip this little switch under the dash, and she fired right up! Amazing, ain't it?"

Jimmy walked to the trailer and placed the gas can back in its location, pulling the rubber strap across the top and hooking it to the trailer frame. He pulled off his t-shirt, wiping the sweat from his face and neck, climbing into the back seat as Harvey and Slim closed their doors, laughing hysterically.

"You bums…you better watch yourself the rest of the trip. You got one helluva payback coming."

The sprawling outskirts of Los Angeles enveloped the landscape as Harvey steered the truck off the highway, easing to a stop at a small filling station. The men climbed from the vehicle and looked around, grinning at each other among the palm trees that swayed in the afternoon breeze.

Harvey fueled the truck as Jimmy fished a single out of his pocket to buy some Cokes. He walked inside the tired old station, where an attendent stood behind the counter. Jimmy asked for some change as the young man studied him, unable to suppress a grin.

"You're Jimmy Wilson," he said excitedly, nodding.

"Yes," Jimmy replied. "You a race fan?"

"I never miss a race at Ascot…boy, I've been looking forward to this weekend! Two nights, with the USAC guys coming in! What a great setup!"

"I've been looking forward to it myself," Jimmy smiled as he walked toward the machine. "I've ran here a couple of times, and I like it. Fast place. Suits me."

The young man walked through the door into the service area, calling to two men working under a yellow Plymouth.

"Hey guys, look who's here…Jimmy Wilson, and the Ellison car! Check it out!"

The men immediately set aside their tools and hurried outside, beaming as they looked over the sprint car.

"Wow…that's a sweet race car," the tall one praised. "Our cars are sharp, but this one is awful nice. I gotta admit."

Jimmy could see Harvey's chest feathers popping out as the men admired the car.

"You guys coming out to Ascot tomorrow night?" Jimmy asked.

"Wouldn't miss it," the dark man with the Spanish accent grinned. "This is the showdown! Two nights to see who's better, our guys or the USAC guys."

"No offense, but you boys got your work cut out for you," the tall one interjected. "Mac the Knife is on fire right now…won four in a row, just dominating. Said in this morning's paper that he's gonna send you boys back east with your tail between your legs."

Jimmy swallowed some of the cold liquid from the can, feeling it tingle his throat. He looked over at Harvey, seeing in his eyes some of the same fire that Jimmy suddenly felt in his belly. The two men held the glance and Harvey's jaw stiffened, a tiny smile working its way to his lips as he turned back to hang the fuel nozzle back on the pump.

"I don't think we brought our tail out with us, did we Harvey?" Jimmy said calmly. "We'll just have to take the edge right off ol' Mac's knife, won't we?"

Chapter 25

The evening sun blazed across the pit area, and Jimmy squinted as he sat in the Ellison sprint car, the engine rumbling as it warmed. A big crowd of onlookers had already gathered, ringing the white-and-blue car, keeping their distance yet pushing in as close as possible. Harvey limped around the machine, oblivious to the crowd, his mind absorbed with the race car. Slim lingered in the background, waiting on Harvey to tell him what was needed.

It seemed that everybody in Los Angeles had come out to Ascot tonight, flushed with anticipation as USAC's best had arrived to do battle with the west coast boys. And they seemed particularly interested in the Ellison car, with Jimmy leading the USAC points and enjoying a strong season thus far.

Jimmy glanced at the people ringing their pit, trying to pretend they weren't there. A few people had small cameras and were snapping away, while a couple of serious photographers jostled among the crowd, their long lenses pointed right at Jimmy.

The sound of the idling car filled the air, and Jimmy blinked at the heavy fumes as they floated past him. Glancing at the temperature gauge, he eased his foot down ever so slightly, the car shaking as the engine picked up revs.

Harvey leaned into the cockpit, studying the gauges, apparently satisfied with what he saw. He brought his finger across his throat in a slashing motion, and in a moment the engine rose in pitch then fell silent.

Climbing from the car, Jimmy unzipped his uniform and pulled it from his shoulders, tying the sleeves around his waist. It was a warm evening, and he stepped through the big crowd and made his way along the line of cars. It had been quite some time since Jimmy had raced here, and he nodded hello to some of his old friends.

He found himself drawn toward a familiar blue car, his eyes

scanning the people standing nearby. He saw the brawny guy in a shop apron, his meaty arms crossed as he studied the machine. The man happened to look toward Jimmy, a slight smile softening his rugged features.

"Fats Donovan," Jimmy said as he approached, extending a hand. "How the heck are you?"

"I see you're still racin' with those clod-hoppers back east," Donovan needled. "Ready to get your ass kicked?"

Jimmy laughed. "By who? You guys? I doubt it."

Jimmy noticed the name on the side of one of the blue cars: Todd Carmack. On the hood was a colorful image of a shark, with "Mack the Knife" lettered across the surface.

"Hey, look at this," Donovan grinned. "Check out the artwork."

Donovan leaned over the hood and pointed to the shark image, which featured a tiny sprint car being crushed amid a row of menacing teeth. As Donovan laughed, Jimmy could see that the car being devoured was a miniature likeness of the Ellison car.

"Hey, that's funny," Jimmy smiled. "You guys did that for us? That's nice, Fats. I'm flattered."

Jimmy saw a young guy with a slight build wearing a white uniform approaching, and the kid looked vaguely familiar.

"You don't remember me, do you?" the kid asked.

Jimmy studied him for a moment, then slowly smiled as it came back to him. "Todd…you worked on the car when I drove it a couple of years ago," he said. "I guess I never made the connection…so you're Todd Carmack! Geez, you were still in high school then. How old are you?"

"I'm 19."

"Mack the Knife," Jimmy grinned, nodding his head. "Looks like you're going real good."

Jimmy studied the young driver, amazed at the transformation. Jimmy remembered him as a shy, stumbling kid, but now the boy reeked of confidence, his jaw set with a cocky air and his pale blue eyes steely and emotionless.

"When you quit Fats, that next spring he gave me a try," Carmack explained, then gave Jimmy a quizzical look. "How come you went back east? They said you ran real good here…I'm glad you left, though. Lucky break for me."

"Oh…I had a domestic situation," Jimmy smiled, remembering the raucous relationship he endured with a live-in girlfriend at the time. "I was homesick, too. But it worked out, didn't it? Things happen like they're supposed to."

"Yeah, you dog, I was ready to wring your neck when you quit me," Donovan chimed in. "I've had to wait all this time to get you back out here so we can spank you properly and send you home."

Jimmy realized that several photographers had gathered a few feet away and were furiously snapping pictures of him and Carmack. Jimmy gave Fats and Carmack a wave and turned to walk away, when a couple of the photographers called out.

"Just a minute, Jimmy! Let's get a couple of pictures!"

Jimmy and Carmack stood side-by-side for a few moments, and one of the photographers lowered his camera.

"How about you put up your dukes with each other! That would be a great publicity shot."

Carmack looked uncertain for a moment, and Jimmy shook his head.

"Nah," he smiled. "Just take your pictures, guys."

Jimmy timed in fifth, and he was amazed to discover that he was the only USAC guy among the top 10 qualifiers. These CRA guys were tough, that much was certain.

Soon they were rolling out for the feature, and never had Jimmy been more grateful for a front-row starting spot. He flexed his fingers as the Ellison sprinter idled around the famed half-mile as the field began to form up behind him.

He tensed as they rolled toward the start, listening carefully for the pole car to take off. The rumble of their engines began to increase, and he felt his right foot tremble as he clenched the muscles in his leg, waiting, waiting, waiting…NOW!

The cars screamed down the front straightaway side-by-side, pitching for the corner just past the flag stand. Jimmy hammered the throttle as he felt the Ellison car grip the black, tacky surface, racing along the cushion through the turn. He had the momentum coming off the corner, and hit the backstretch as the race leader.

He was flawless for 28 laps, listening constantly for a challenger from behind but hearing only his own screaming powerplant. The laps clicked off without interruption, but with two to go Jimmy saw a white car stalled along the backstretch, and a moment later the caution light blinked on.

Jimmy idled around, moving his head back and forth to relieve the stiffness in his neck. He felt sweat running down his chest, and he listened intently to the car at idle, hoping he could hold on for two more laps.

Harvey had made his way to the edge of the track, leaning out as Jimmy rolled past. The big man clapped his hands in encouragement, then pointed to his head, staring intently as Jimmy nodded.

A moment later Jimmy saw the starter displaying the furled green flag, and he gripped the wheel tightly. His eyes locked forward and he led the field down the backstretch at a steady speed, feeling the car bump across the uneven surface.

A good 20 yards before they reached the restart point Jimmy heard the roar of a car on his left. Carmack was alongside the Ellison car before Jimmy had begun to accelerate, and had already rushed past before they hit the front straightaway. Jimmy shook his head at the obvious jump, knowing there was no way it would stand.

They raced down the backstretch, and Jimmy anticipated the return of the caution light. But the green light remained on, and Jimmy felt rage rising in his throat as he realized they were going to let it go. He gave chase, but Carmack's momentum was simply too great. Two laps later they flashed under the checkered flag, Jimmy a car length behind.

Jimmy was so angry he thought he might pop a gasket. As they rumbled down the front straightaway on the cool-down lap he saw Carmack stop at the finish line, where Donovan and his crew rushed toward the car, arms raised in jubilation. The hometown crowd roared in approval, and Jimmy kept his eyes straight ahead as he headed for his pit.

The Ellison car rolled to a stop, and Jimmy cut the engine. He unbuckled slowly, thinking for a minute about going to see the officials. But what good would it do? He'd be just another racer bitching because he was unhappy with the outcome. He raised himself from the seat, stepping out of the car as he tugged the gloves from his hands. He removed his helmet, feeling the rush of cool night air on his sweaty face and hair.

He looked around, surprised to see that the area around his car had already filled with onlookers, studying his every move, holding their breath to see what he might do next. Thick tension hung in the air as he gently dropped his gear into the seat.

Jimmy glanced about, trying to keep his cool, a hundred people staring at his misery, nobody saying anything. It was as if he were a mad dog; fascinating, dangerous, but don't get too close… he might bite. An invisible wall formed a few yards around him, everyone staying outside the imaginary barrier.

Just then he saw a small boy of maybe eight years old emerge from the crowd, taking tentative steps toward him, clutching a pen and a racing program. The kid wore a racing hat that was pulled so low it made his ears stick out, and his eyes filled with apprehension as he inched forward, then stopped. Jimmy stepped over to the kid, reaching down to take the program and pen, signing his name on the cover.

The boy stared wide-eyed as Jimmy handed the items back. He put his hand on the boy's head, giving him an affectionate jostle and a smile he hoped didn't look phony. Suddenly Jimmy heard a stream of profanity over his left shoulder, and he turned to see Harvey storming into their pit, the veins in his neck bulging.

Well, here it comes, Jimmy figured. *Getting my guts ripped out for falling asleep…why argue with him? Won't make any difference.*

"Robbers!" Harvey screamed, his voice hoarse. "They stole it from us! That was the dirtiest jump I've ever seen, boy! Those crooked, dirty SOBs…why, they ought to be in jail, the whole damned bunch!"

"You say anything to the officials?"

"Hell yes, but it won't do any good! They rigged it so the local car would win and they'd get a bigger crowd tomorrow night…I had to leave before I broke Petrov's neck, the crook. He wouldn't even look at me, because he knows we got robbed."

Harvey let loose with another torrent of profanity, pausing to pick up an empty fuel jug. He flung it violently against the back of the camper, the jug making a big bang as it bounced off the camper and caromed harmlessly across the ground.

Jimmy arched his eyebrows, wondering if he'd ever seen Harvey so exercised. One thing was sure, though. He was glad the big man wasn't mad at him.

The following afternoon Jimmy waited for the driver's meeting to begin. He mingled with some of the USAC guys, as well as some of his old west coast friends.

The officials began the meeting by going over the particulars of tonight's program. The starter warned them about jumping, saying anybody who started early would be set back.

"Do you mean that?" Jimmy called out, and everyone turned to look at him.

"Of course I mean it," the starter replied.

"Just checking," Jimmy said. "'Cause you sure didn't mean it last night."

The starter frowned, and a hint of tension hung in the air for a moment. Jimmy saw Carmack out of the corner of his eye, wearing a faint smile.

The officials continued with the meeting and it soon concluded.

"One more thing, after tonight's race I need the top three finishers on the front straightaway," Al Petrov said as the meeting finished. "That's all, gentlemen. Best of luck to all of you."

Jimmy began to walk back toward their pit when he heard someone call his name. He turned to see Al approaching.

"Harvey was pretty rough on me last night," the steward began, studying Jimmy. "You need to be aware, I'm not going to allow him to chew me out like that again. Next time there's going to be a fine, and we'll set him down for a couple of races. You've got to keep him under control."

Jimmy laughed. "Give me a break, Al. Do you honestly think I'm going to control Harvey in any way, shape or form? Besides, if you've ever had an ass-chewing coming, it was last night."

Al raised his eyebrows in surprise, and crossed his arms. "Explain, please."

"C'mon…that kid jumped the start by 20 yards. You've put me back before for jumping, and my deal wasn't half as bad as his. For some reason you guys looked the other way last night, and we got gypped. Simple as that."

"It's not that simple," Al insisted. "We look at every situation, and make a judgment—"

"Stop," Jimmy interrupted, holding up his hand. "Don't give me that party line, because it's insulting. We've been friends for a long time, Al, and I respect you and your position. But let's face it, you guys made a mistake. No big deal; I make 'em myself sometimes. Just don't stand here and tell me it's a tough call, because it's not. You guys have nailed my ass several times in the past for jumping, and you didn't say anything then about it being a tough call."

"Listen, I've been sitting exactly where you were last night, and I know it doesn't feel good," Al countered. "But from my vantage point, it looked like a fair start."

Jimmy began to walk away. "Then you need to get a new vantage point."

"You talk to Harvey," Al called out, unsmiling. "I'm not kidding, Jimmy. He isn't going to yell at me or my officials like that again."

"I need you up on the wheel," Harvey said as Jimmy zipped up his uniform. "Tonight is the big money night. The car is going to be real tight, but it'll be fast. We can show these guys how it's done, but you gotta gas it up."

"Don't worry about me," Jimmy nodded. "Listen, you've got to lay off the officials for a while. Al says next time you go off on him, they'll park you."

"Hmmph," Harvey retorted. "They had it coming."

"I know they did, but it won't do us any good if you're suspended. You're the only reason I can go fast, remember?"

"That's right, boy," Harvey grinned. "All right, I'll take it easy."

They looked over to see Fats Donovan and his crew rolling their car forward. Carmack walked alongside, carrying his helmet, preparing to climb in. With his small stature and fuzzy-faced complexion, he looked more like a carry-out boy at the grocery than a blood-and-guts race driver.

"That's him??!!" Harvey said, incredulously. "Why, he's a little bitty shit!"

"He stands on the button pretty good," Jimmy offered.

Harvey leaned in close.

"Listen, boy…a young kid like that, might not be a bad idea to lean on him some. Just to see what he's all about, I mean. Maybe he don't like getting crowded. Might shake him up a little."

Jimmy shrugged. "I'll race him hard…but my gut says he isn't the type who rattles easily."

Soon they were watching the cars roll out to qualify, and Jimmy listened carefully to their times. He would follow Carmack in the order, and Jimmy slid into the seat and buckled in. Harvey studied the others as they timed, and suddenly leaned over the Ellison car with his wrench, making final adjustments.

As Carmack rolled out to qualify, Harvey finished and stuck the wrenches in his back pocket. He looked straight at Jimmy.

"I tightened it some more," he said. "You're either going to be dead fast, or maybe just…dead."

Jimmy nodded, grinning inside his helmet. He heard the crowd roar as the PA announcer screamed that Carmack's lap was the quickest of the night. A moment later the truck sent Jimmy onto the hallowed surface, the Ellison car blasting toward their first lap.

He was sure he had laid down a better lap sometime in his career, but he couldn't remember when. They were on the razor's edge, and twice Jimmy felt the car begin to bicycle, his left-side tires barely kissing the black clay. He knew he was an eyelash away from disaster, but his right foot refused to yield, somehow pushing his fears to the background.

As he slowed he heard the ovation from the crowd, and idled toward the pit area. An official smiled and held up his index finger, and Jimmy knew he had bested Carmack's lap.

He rolled to a stop, with Harvey and Slim both grinning like monkeys. Jimmy climbed from the car, tugging off his helmet.

He gave Harvey a satisfied smile. "Well, I ain't dead…guess I did all right, 'eh?"

A full field of sprint cars took the green flag in the feature that night, but the eyes of the vast crowd locked on the two cars in the third row and never looked away. Jimmy flogged the Ellison car as he chased the blue Donovan machine, the two cars surging to the front.

It was bare-knuckle racing, with Jimmy pressuring the kid with everything he had. He slid Carmack on the inside, allowing the Ellison car to move within inches of his foe, daring the kid to stay in the gas. But the young racer held his own, forcing Jimmy to lift.

Within a few laps they caught traffic, and it was as if the slower cars weren't there at all. The two men maintained their breathtaking pace, slicing through with moves that looked impossible, sending the big crowd into spasms of excitement.

Twice Jimmy was sure he had the kid boxed in behind a slower car, but each time the Donovan machine slipped past by the most narrow margin.

As the laps clicked off Jimmy felt the Ellison car growing even stronger. He figured to have an advantage in traffic, but Carmack was marvelous in his own right, picking the right lanes, making daring moves and forcing Jimmy to chase.

Jimmy guessed there were maybe a dozen laps remaining when they found a long gap between lapped cars. Now it was mano a mano; just the two of them on an open track, ready to settle this thing.

The Ellison car made a run to the inside along the front straight, and they set for the corner. But instead of falling back, Jimmy kept his right front wheel a foot off the inside hubs of the Donovan car.

It was a daring move, one that could spell disaster if either man bobbled. The cars snarled as they came off the corner, still side-by-side, with Jimmy gaining a couple of feet by the time they hit the next corner.

As Jimmy lifted, he heard the engine in the Donovan machine scream a millisecond longer. Jimmy grinned, because now he knew he had the advantage.

The Donovan car had too much speed as they entered the corner. Carmack was forced to brake for an instant, fighting for control, and the tiny stumble allowed Jimmy to rocket off the corner into the lead. As they passed the flag stand Jimmy stuck his right hand outside the cage, giving the kid a big wave as they headed for turn one.

Something in Jimmy's head told him to be ready for

Carmack to come back on the inside, and that's exactly how it played. The Donovan car came roaring to Jimmy's left, coming off the bottom, sliding, sliding, playing a desperate game of brinksmanship. Jimmy locked his eyes straight ahead, pressing his right foot to the belly pan, clenching his teeth and preparing for the worse.

At the last possible instant the kid lifted, and in another moment the roar of his car had disappeared from Jimmy's ears. For the remaining laps Jimmy listened for the kid to try again, but there was only the scream of the Ellison car as Jimmy took the checkered flag.

His heart was pounding, and he felt a wave of joy welling up in his throat. He slowed for his insurance lap, and the Donovan car rumbled alongside, pausing for a moment before it fell back again.

Jimmy rolled to a stop on the front straightaway, hearing the engine fall silent, beginning to remove his gloves. He paused for a moment, nodding slightly, reaching up to gently touch the dash.

"Helluva car," he said softly, his voice muffled. "Helluva car."

He lifted himself from the seat, swinging his feet onto the black surface, nearly exhausted, operating only on adrenaline. Harvey and Slim came hurrying toward the car, Harvey bellowing his satisfaction and Slim yelping for joy. Jimmy had to laugh at Harvey's gangly, limping gait. In a moment Harvey grabbed him in a bear hug, lifting his feet off the ground.

They were immediately surrounded by a mass of people, photographers blazing away. Harvey draped his big arm around Jimmy, and the PA man moved in for an interview. Before the guy could ask a question Harvey grabbed the microphone.

"How's it feel to get your ass kicked by a bunch of Indiana hillbillies?" he crowed. The crowd responded with a mixture of cheers and jeers, and Jimmy craned his neck to look at Harvey.

"Hey," he grinned. "I'm from Illinois!"

"Not tonight you ain't!" Harvey chortled.

They finished the interview, and Jimmy stepped in front of the car for more photographs. A few yards away he spotted a dejected Todd Carmack. The kid lifted his head and gave Jimmy a wave.

"By God, that kid can race," Harvey said, lowering his voice.

Jimmy nodded, surprised at the rare words of praise from the big man.

They saw Fats Donovan approaching, wearing a grudging grin and extending his hand.

"Helluva race," Donovan said, nodding his head. "See you boys next week at Manzy."

Chapter 26

Jimmy was up early on Saturday morning, climbing from their camper to walk toward the bunkhouse at the Simmons ranch. Old man Simmons owned a restaurant in Phoenix, and his ranch a few miles east served as a home base for several of the teams.

It was a fun atmosphere, racers and crews hanging around at desert's edge, with beer and hot dogs served around a campfire each night. The ranch hands were warm hosts, along with One-Eyed Louie, a huge mongrel dog that somehow took a liking to Jimmy. Everywhere he went the dog followed right behind, wagging his tail and begging for affection.

The night before had been a bit of an anti-climax, as Jimmy won without much trouble. Todd Carmack never once gave him a challenge; maybe they missed the setup on the Donovan car, or maybe the kid hadn't yet figured out the Phoenix oval.

Jimmy carried his uniform into the house, tossing it into the washing machine located in the back room. He had neglected to bring a spare, and racing in the desert heat had turned the garment into a sweaty, stinking mess. As soon as the wash cycle finished he carried it outside to drape over a clothesline, Louie trailing behind.

Jimmy sat on the steps of the wooden porch, feeling the gentle morning touch his face. The sun was now a soft and warm friend, but by afternoon it would find a harsh edge that baked and punished. He leaned back, breathing the crisp air and marveling at the brilliant blue sky, while the dog eagerly pressed close, eyes pleading for attention. Jimmy laughed as he jostled with the big mutt, glancing up to see a white pickup rolling slowly up the driveway. The truck rolled to a stop and fell silent, with ranch foreman Hector and another hand climbing out.

"Señor Jimmy, the dog likes you very much, yes," Hector called out, his bright smile contrasting against his deeply-tanned and lined face. "You will take him home with you, I hope…he is nothing but trouble for us. The smelling, he is very bad."

"Aw, he's just a good 'ol dog," Jimmy smiled.

"Si, good for nothing at all. The race, they tell me you won. Your big friend, Señor Harvey, he was very happy, yes?"

"Yes, pretty happy. That's Harvey…when you win he's the teddy bear, when you lose he's the grizzly bear."

The other man reached into the back of the pickup, using a wooden stick to lift the enormous carcass of a rattlesnake, turning to present the specimen for Jimmy's review.

"Holy cow, look at that thing!" Jimmy marveled. "Where'd you get him?"

"The pistol, she comes in handy," Hector laughed, patting his back pocket. "Our friend the snake was sunning himself along the road this morning, but—BANG-BANG!—he is not sunning anymore."

"What do you do with him now?"

"Toss him into the field and let him rot," the other man laughed. "We do not like snakes…they make trouble with our cattle, yes. One less snake is a good thing, I think."

"Before you get rid of him, I've got an idea," Jimmy smiled.

The barn doors swung open just before noon, and the cook spread out a Mexican lunch feast for all the guests. The racers and mechanics sat along a row of picnic tables in the center of the barn, and laughter and lies rolled about in equal proportions.

Jimmy saw Hector hurrying into the barn, a serious expression on his face. "Señor Jimmy, there is a very bad problem," he said. "Come quickly!"

Jimmy glanced at the others with a curious expression, rising to follow with Sammy Caldwell and Rusty Fernandez coming along. They rounded the front of the ranch house and passed the steps, and Jimmy's gut tightened as his eyes fell upon the scene.

Louie the dog was lying in the dirt, chewing away at Jimmy's uniform. One of the sleeves was already separated from the garment, and as they approached the dog raised his head to look at them, wagging his tail cheerfully.

"This one, he is no good with the manners," Hector anguished.

"Such a dog…the devil is in his heart, I think."

Jimmy picked up the remains of his uniform, feeling the wet clumps where the dog had been chewing. Rusty and Sammy began to laugh, and the dog rose to sniff at the cloth in Jimmy's hands.

"Ah, go away, dog!" Hector commanded, waving his hand. A torrent of Spanish words followed, and Jimmy could see that Hector was angry and embarrassed. "My pistol, the dog will be feeling if he doesn't go away! I tell you, Señor, he is a very bad dog. I have much apologies."

Jimmy smiled in spite of himself, reaching down to rub the dog's head.

"Don't be too mad at him," Jimmy urged Hector. "He doesn't know any better. And keep that pistol in your pocket…I can get another uniform, but there's only one Louie. Ain't that right, boy?"

Manzanita Speedway was bursting at the seams, the Saturday night crowd arriving early. Cars streamed through the nearby intersection of 35th and Broadway, the cluttered Phoenix neighborhood boasting an array of junk yards and various heavy industries. Large foothills rose from the southern horizon, dotted with red lights from the various communcations towers installed at the peaks.

The infield pit area was filled to overflowing, with colorful race cars scattered throughout. Jimmy solved his uniform dilemma by borrowing a spare from Rick Wagner, who jokingly demanded 40 percent of whatever Jimmy made that night.

"It's the only way I'll make any money on this trip," Wagner kidded. "I haven't run worth a crap out here."

The officials called for the driver's meeting to convene around a small platform where lineups were posted, and soon the area was crowded with racers and onlookers. Al Petrov and his crew soon stepped onto the platform, where they discovered a cardboard box bearing a sign in big block letters, "Official USAC Business."

"What's this?" Al quizzed the others. "Were we expecting a package?" They looked at him with an expression of surprise and mystery, shaking their head. The racers watched carefully as Al bent to examine the box.

"It's taped shut," he said, turning to Leon Hartke. "Probably somebody's idea of a joke. Just set it over there, I'll open it when we're finished."

Leon grabbed the box and lifted, allowing the unsealed bottom flaps to yawn open. An instant later the giant rattlesnake fell with a plop onto his feet.

Al must have jumped four feet in the air, and Hartke let out a surprised screech as he plunged wide-eyed toward the steps, nearly knocking over the other officials. It was quickly obvious the snake was dead, and the entire scene roared with laughter as the hapless officials tried to catch their breath.

For a good five minutes the place convulsed with laughter. Each time Al had just about got everyone quieted down, somebody would giggle, sparking a renewed spasm of hysterical laughter.

Finally order began to come, and Al looked at Jimmy with a piercing stare.

"What are you looking at me for?" Jimmy protested, mustering up his most innocent expression. "I hate snakes, man. I won't even touch 'em."

"Just get up on the wheel and drive, like you did last night," Harvey said as Jimmy prepared for his heat race. He almost wanted to pinch himself, things were going so well. They had been fast both weekends of this trip, winning two features and finishing second in another. The car was loving these big tracks, and Jimmy loved them as well.

He was confident he could make the transfer, and as the race got underway he quickly made his way forward. Within two laps he was on the back bumper of a red California car that was leading, and after riding there a couple of laps decided to give the guy a try.

He moved to the high groove and pulled alongside. But the track was just a bit too slick up there, and he spun his tires in the middle of the corner, falling back. He moved down a few feet on the track for his next try, giving the guy room but searching for traction.

Suddenly the engine began to vibrate heavily, nearly shaking the wheel from his hands. He immediately waved his right hand as a warning to the cars behind, steering toward the infield. He got the car out of gear and hit the kill switch, rolling to a stop.

He popped his belts and climbed from the car, pulling off his gloves and kneeling to study the engine. There were no visible signs of anything amiss, and as the race concluded a push truck approached.

"Will she roll?" the guy called out, and Jimmy nodded, climbing back in the cockpit. In a moment the Ellison car glided to a silent stop in their pit.

"What happened?" Harvey demanded.

"Started to vibrate real bad, and I shut it off."

"What kind of vibration?"

"I don't know…like a piston, or even the crank."

"Did it clatter?"

"No, I don't think so. I was in the middle of the corner and stepped on the gas and it just broke."

Harvey spent the next few minutes studying the situation, looking down into the injectors and crawling all over the engine. After a few minutes he wiped his hands with a rag before tossing it aside with a disgusted sigh.

"I don't know, until I tear it down. Sounds like maybe we broke a piston. But we're done for tonight."

Jimmy nodded dejectedly. He sat glumly on the rear tire, wiping the sweat from his face with his forearm.

"I knew this was gonna happen," Harvey began, tossing his hands up and glaring at Jimmy. "You guys ran this motor this spring in Sid's car, and you didn't know what you were doing. Probably hurt it somewhere along the line. I knew I should have gone through it."

Jimmy looked at him with a mixture of amazement and disgust. "Are you serious? How can you even think that, Harvey…you've been back for almost two months and this thing hasn't missed a beat."

"Well, you don't know it wasn't broke, do you? When I'm not around, things aren't done right. We should have never let you run this. Now look where we are."

Jimmy jumped to his feet, his cheeks flushed with color and feeling his ears turn hot.

"Don't even try to make this my fault," he charged, his voice rising. "We did nothing that would hurt this engine. I raced it exactly as if you were here with me."

Harvey just rolled his eyes. "Whatever you say," he sniffed.

Jimmy found himself almost trembling with anger. He wanted to lash out at Harvey and tell him exactly what a miserable, negative so-and-so he was, but he just shook his head and walked quickly away from their pit. He headed down into the corner, where he stood by himself, trying to cool his temper. A few fans approached him to say hello, and he tried to be cordial before moving away to another area as he sought some solitude.

After a little while he ambled back toward the pit area, just as the semi-feature was forming on the race track. Jimmy watched the race from their pit, along with Harvey and Slim, nobody saying anything.

The semi had soon finished, and Jimmy decided he might as well change clothes. He walked toward their camper when he heard someone call his name. He turned to see Tommy Fields approaching, a west coast racer Jimmy had gotten to know when he spent a winter here a couple of seasons ago.

"You guys hurt your motor?" Fields asked.

"Yeah, looks like it. We're done, that's all I know."

"You want to run my car in the feature? We're not running for points, and I know you are. You're welcome if you want to give it a try."

Jimmy immediately perked up. "Hey, that's pretty good of you. Yeah, I'd love to. Points wise that would help us, for sure."

"It's a good car, but not great," Fields admitted. "You'll be on the tail, but you can probably pass a few cars and maybe get a decent finish."

As they began to walk away Jimmy saw Harvey looking at him.

"I'm going to run Tommy's car in the feature," he explained, trying not to engage in any further conversation. Harvey just nodded absently, turning to walk toward their car.

Jimmy and Fields hurried to a brown No. 16. Jimmy was about the same size as Fields, so the seat and belts fit him all right. The crew had already fueled the car, and Jimmy prepared to climb aboard when he looked up to see Sammy Caldwell smiling from the next pit over.

"Well, you borrowed a uniform and you borrowed a car,"

Sammy teased. "Next thing you know, you'll ask if you can borrow my wife!"

Jimmy looked at him thoughtfully, and smiled. "Is she here?"

Sammy shook his head, and they laughed.

Jimmy slid into the seat and buckled in. Fields leaned in to explain a couple of details on the car before Jimmy tugged his helmet in place. Soon he was in the starting chute, pulling his belts tight one more time.

Tommy was right; it was a good car, but not a great car. The Ellison engine was much more crisp, and this car didn't feel as comfortable to Jimmy. But it was certainly a capable machine, and after a couple of laps to find his rhythm Jimmy began to steadily pick off cars at each end of the track.

The car liked the bottom groove, and Jimmy plied along, seeing the crossed flags of the half-way point. He found himself racing with Rusty Fernandez and a white car, a machine that was probably a CRA regular based on the good-looking paint and chrome bars.

Jimmy watched the two men race inches apart in front of him, and he elected to move to the outside. He thought he might do a two-for-one pass at the other end, and he hammered the throttle as they came off turn four, hoping to build some momentum.

Suddenly the two cars banged wheels, and the white car turned sharply right. Jimmy was on top of the guy before he had time to blink, and he felt his car jump violently into the air.

The next few moments passed in a blur. The car pointed skyward for an instant before the tail dug into the track, sending him through a vicious series of end-over-end flips before executing several hard barrel rolls. Each time the car contacted the track Jimmy felt sharp pain where his belts dug into this shoulders, and heard the engine screaming.

Suddenly everything was silent, and Jimmy was disoriented and confused. He began to realize that the car was on its wheels, and he could hear the hiss of the busted radiator and the sound of approaching voices.

In a moment the steaming wreck was surrounded by people. Jimmy looked at them through his visor, trying to sort out where he was. He recognized Tommy Fields and the guy who owned the car. They were all talking to him, but he couldn't make out what they were saying.

Suddenly he heard a medic asking, "Where are you hurting?"

Jimmy managed to lift his hand from the steering wheel and flip his visor up. "I want my helmet off."

Tommy helped Jimmy with the straps, and gingerly lifted the helmet from his head. They pulled away his head sock, and Jimmy felt a wave of fresh night air in his face. He breathed deeply, feeling pain in his neck and upper back. There was a warm, familiar taste in his mouth, and he slowly brought his hand to his lips, looking down to see blood all over his finger.

The medic leaned in close, shining a light in Jimmy's eyes.

"Were you unconscious?" the man asked.

"I…I don't think so."

"Did you bite your lip?" Tommy asked gently. Jimmy ran his tongue across the inside of his mouth, feeling a deep cut. He nodded slowly at Tommy.

"Where do you feel pain?" the medic asked again.

"Everywhere," Jimmy answered slowly. He began to gently turn his head back and forth.

"Does your neck hurt?" the man asked. Jimmy nodded, and the man pressed further. "Is it like an ache, or a very sharp pain?"

"Ache," Jimmy answered.

The man felt carefully down Jimmy's back, and his neck.

"Do you think you can get out of the car?"

"Give me a minute," Jimmy answered.

"Take your time," the man said. "We're in no hurry, son. Whenever you're ready."

His head was clearing a bit, but, oh, that neck. It hurt. And he felt pain in his knees, particularly his kneecaps and the area below the knee toward the inside of his legs.

"All right," he said, and he reached to push himself up from the seat. The other guys gently grasped his arms and helped him along, and in a moment Jimmy was coming out of the top of the cage. He heard a huge ovation from the crowd, and he managed to bring his right hand up to offer a weak wave.

He walked shakily toward a nearby ambulance, with Rusty on one side and Tommy on the other. They helped him inside, and he lay on the gurney as the medic examined him more carefully.

"You need to go in for x-rays," the medic said, but Jimmy shook his head. He was much more lucid now, and he was beginning to feel anger and aggravation that he had crashed, particularly feeling bad for the guy who owned the car.

"No, I'm all right," he insisted. "Let me go change my clothes…I want to go home and go to bed."

Jimmy sat up and rubbed his neck, getting his bearings and assessing things. The medic shook his head.

"Listen, that neck could be trouble if it's broken. It's not something you should mess around with."

Jimmy shook his head again.

Al Petrov peered in from the back of the ambulance, flanked by Rusty Fernandez and Tommy.

"How you feeling?" Al quizzed.

"I'm all right," Jimmy insisted. "I wish everybody would leave me alone. I want to go home."

"You need to get checked out," Tommy said quietly. "It's just an x-ray, Jimmy, and that won't hurt anything. Probably some good-looking nurse will rub your neck before they take your picture. You were 20 feet in the air, two or three times, and I know you hit hard. Can't hurt to get it looked at."

"Nah," Jimmy said, scooting himself off the back of the gurney and preparing to climb from the ambulance. He looked at the medic. "Really, I'll be okay. Can I go now?"

The medic looked helplessly at Jimmy, then at Al.

"I can't make him go to the hospital," he said. "But I'd sure feel better if he did."

Al leaned in close to Jimmy, reaching up to place his arm on Jimmy's shoulder.

"Would you humor me and go get checked out?" Al asked softly. "Do it for me, okay? Please?"

Jimmy frowned, irritated by the whole thing. He looked into Al's eyes, finally resigning himself to his fate.

"Okay, let's go."

Jimmy lay quietly on the examination table, feeling a powerful ache settling throughout his body. The door swung open, and a cadre of his friends filed through. Rusty Fernandez, Sammy Caldwell, Jack Underwood, and Rick Wagner approached him wearing a look of concern.

"What's up," Jimmy said, not even trying to smile.

"How you feeling?" Sammy quizzed.

"Junk," Jimmy answered.

"Anything broken?"

"I don't know…the doc hasn't come back in yet. Who won?"

"Graffan," Wagner answered. "I ran second, and Carmack was third."

Jimmy managed a smile for Wagner. "You ran better. Listen, I got blood on the front of your uniform. Sorry."

"Ah," Wagner scoffed. "It'll wash."

"I destroyed that guy's race car," Jimmy groaned. "God, I feel bad about that. I don't even know his name."

"Murphy," Sammy said. "He's from San Diego. Listen, it happens. Just be glad you weren't beat up even worse."

"It wasn't your fault," Jack insisted. "I was right behind you, and you had nowhere to go. It happened so fast, there was nothing you were gonna do."

"They going to keep you overnight?" Wagner asked.

"Not if I can help it," Jimmy insisted. "Harvey will probably want to get an early start home tomorrow, so I better be ready."

The others exchanged glances.

"He, uh…he left the track early. I think he might've already headed home," Sammy said.

"He did? That figures."

"You can ride home with us," Rusty offered. "We're not in a big hurry."

The door suddenly swung open, and an attractive and petite brunette wearing a white medical outfit and a stethoscope around her neck entered the room with a burst of energy.

"No broken bones," she announced with an unsmiling stare. "You said you have a lot of neck pain, and I suspect you've got some strained muscles, maybe even a sprain. But no broken vertebra.

"You have some very serious bruising on your legs, particularly around your knees. Keep some ice on those for the next day or so. Try to stay off your feet as much as possible."

He realized she was staring intently at his eyes.

"Look at me for a moment," she said, moving in close, holding his eyelids open and pointing a small lighted device into his eyes.

"You've got some bleeding," she said.

"That happens sometimes," Jimmy explained. The other men agreed and nodded.

She looked at them with a wry smile. "Then I suggest you gentlemen find a new line of work. That isn't good."

They chuckled sheepishly, and she turned her attention back to Jimmy.

"If your eyes don't clear up in two days, I want you to see a specialist back home. Agreed?"

Jimmy nodded.

"All right, you may go. I don't want you driving an automobile for a couple of days because of those eyes. And let me give you something for pain, because you're definitely going to need it."

A few minutes later they rolled in the drive at the Simmons ranch, and Jimmy was surprised to see the Ellison rig parked near the barn. Sammy dropped Jimmy off at the back of the camper, and Jimmy quietly swung the door open and wobbled into the darkened interior.

He managed to get himself into the top bunk, where he collapsed in a sweaty heap. Despite the pain, sleep came quickly, although it was troubled. He kept seeing the white car spinning right in his lap, and heard the scream of the engine and the ominous sounds of destruction each time his car bounced on the track.

"Boy! You all right? Wake up for a minute!"

Jimmy blinked open his eyes to see Harvey and Slim standing alongside the bunk.

"Man, your eyes," Slim winced, looking away. Jimmy didn't need a mirror to know he had a big dose of red-eye, because he could feel the pressure in his eyeballs.

"We're gonna get on the road," Harvey explained. "Just lay here and ride, and relax. I'm gonna stop out here by the highway and get you some doughnuts or something, and some bread. You'll need something in your belly if you're takin' those pain pills."

Jimmy nodded, and tried to raise himself off the bunk. A searing pain shot through his body, and his arms hurt so badly he could hardly lift them from his side.

"You need a pill?" Slim asked quickly. "Here, I'll get you some water."

"Yeah, take a pill and go back to sleep," Harvey nodded. "I got a bucket here in case you need to whiz, or if you toss your stomach. We'll fill the cooler when we stop, and fix you up some ice for your legs. They look pretty rough."

Jimmy managed to lift his head from the pillow, aghast at the sight of his legs. Streaks of purple and black ran from midway up his shin to above his knees; must have been banging on the driveline. He laid his head back and closed his eyes.

In a moment he felt the truck rocking in motion, and he looked through the front window as they made their way down the lane and onto the road. A couple of minutes later Harvey stopped to fuel the truck, and Slim filled the cooler with ice, pouring a couple of handfuls into some empty bread sacks and wrapping them in a shirt. Jimmy placed them on his knees, then tried to eat a couple of pieces of bread.

They turned onto the wide Interstate, quiet on a Sunday morning. In front of them lay 1,800 miles; it was going to be a long ride home.

Chapter 27

The pickup fell silent as Jimmy turned the key, gingerly lifting the door handle with his left hand and sliding from the cab. He grasped a metal lever, listening to the hiss of the hydraulic system as it began raising the truck toward the shop ceiling. After setting the safety latch he grabbed a trouble light and moved under the vehicle.

He gasped with pain as he lifted his arm to hang the light on the cross-member. For a moment he felt woozy; those over-the-counter pills weren't strong enough for this kind of pain, but he didn't like how the serious stuff made him groggy. So he sucked it up, knowing he had to get this tranny replaced to get back on the road again.

What a trip out west it had been…a lot of fun on the road, some great racing, and he even came home with some dough. A little over $1,200, thank you very much, and finally he wasn't broke. For now, anyway.

But he also came home beat to pieces, his neck and upper back still so sore he could hardly breathe. The nasty purplish bruises all over his legs were just starting to lighten up. The red-eye was also getting better, although he could still feel the pressure in his eyes.

Now, as he looked at the replacement transmission sitting on the floor, he wondered how he was going to pull this off. When he lifted his arms higher than his shoulder the pain was intense, and he began to think about how he might finagle something to get through the chore.

"How's it looking?" a voice called out from the doorway.

Jimmy looked up to see Wilt, the guy who took care of equipment maintenance here at Ellison Paving. The man's real name was Edgar, but everybody called him Wilt because he was a dead ringer for Wilt Chamberlain, goatee and all, only about a foot shorter.

"Not looking good," Jimmy smiled, shaking his head. "Unfortunately."

"I thought you race drivers were rich, and you paid for this kind of work," Wilt said, winking.

"Yeah, rich," Jimmy replied. "When you're a racer, you've got money for about two hours after the race, then you're broke the rest of the week. If you're lucky."

Wilt nodded. "That's a mechanic's life, too," he grinned.

The two men looked closely at the transmission, and Jimmy reached up to unhook the speedometer cable. He grasped a set of pliers, but couldn't make his arms work right to loosen the fitting.

Wilt gently took the pliers from his hand. "You're hurting," he admonished.

"I just need to get loosened up," Jimmy insisted. "Then I'll be all right."

"Well, I can't bear to watch. So I'm gonna help you."

"But it's your quitting time," Jimmy objected. "You've worked all day, and I'm not gonna ask you to stay late just to help me."

"That's right," Wilt nodded, smiling. "You ain't gonna ask me."

Jimmy sighed. This was a losing battle, and the fact is, he wasn't going to get this done by himself. Even if he got everything loose, he wasn't confident he could manipulate the tranny in and out.

"Okay," he said, reluctantly. "You can help."

The two men chatted as Wilt deftly worked, Jimmy pitching in here and there but mostly staying out of his way. Wilt had done this drill countless times, and in a matter of minutes had the transmission out, quickly replacing the clutch and pressure plate before hoisting the replacement tranny into place. The air wrench barked as he bolted things back together, and Jimmy was amazed that the entire process had taken less than an hour.

"Dang, this would have taken me all night, even if I was 100 percent healthy," Jimmy laughed.

"Practice," Wilt smiled. "These little three-speeds are simple… I've done a few of 'em."

Wilt walked over to clean up while Jimmy lowered the lift. In a moment Jimmy too was leaning over the basin, scrubbing his hands, while Wilt studied him.

"You still staying in the camper?" Wilt asked, nodding toward the rig parked alongside the race shop across the way.

"Just for tonight…I'm going home tomorrow. Had to get my truck going first, so I'd have some wheels."

"What you gonna do about dinner?"

"Aw, I'll just grab a hamburger someplace."

"Come on home with me and get a decent meal," Wilt urged. "We got plenty, and we'd be glad to have you."

"Aw, I don't want to be any trouble," Jimmy said, but a home-cooked meal sounded pretty good.

"You ain't any trouble. Looks to me like you could use a good meal, and some company."

Jimmy smiled. "Do I look that bad?"

"You look like the race car ran over you."

"I *feel* like it ran over me," Jimmy nodded, grimacing. "Twice."

Wilt chuckled, reaching to grab a black lunchbox at the end of the workbench.

"Well, fire your truck up, and follow me."

Jimmy steered the pickup off the main highway, turning north. The farm fields were a deep midsummer green, and the insects hummed as he rolled easily along the country road. The dinner at Wilt's the night before had been just what he needed to feel better, Wilt's young kids making them laugh with their silly jokes and tricks. Wilt's wife fried up a mess of catfish, and afterwards Jimmy and Wilt sat on their porch and had a couple of beers while the kids played in the yard.

Jimmy slowed and turned into the familiar driveway, where the small brick ranch home was surrounded by perfectly-maintained landscaping. He noticed the Lincoln parked near the garage, and as he rolled to a stop he had a pang of hesitation.

"I should have called first," he said aloud. He considered turning around to leave, but he spotted Elaine through the picture window, glancing to see who had driven up.

Jimmy walked toward the front door, where she stepped outside to meet him. She gave him a subdued hug, then looked at him somewhat aghast.

"Your eyes are all red," she said, studying him. "Gene said you had a big crash…is that what caused the redness?"

"Yeah, but it's almost gone," Jimmy assured her. "I'm feeling a lot better."

She stared at him for a moment, and smiled weakly.

"I'm sorry I didn't call you," he explained quickly. "I...I guess I'm not much for using the pay phone."

"It's okay," she said, glancing nervously through the door. "I understand."

Jimmy could see the back patio through the hallway, where a dark-haired man sat at the table, a pitcher of lemonade surrounded by a plate of sandwiches and fruit.

"I'm sorry I interrupted your lunch," Jimmy said. "I...I just thought I'd stop by and say hello. I should have called first."

"It's okay," she assured him. "But I do have a guest, and I really ought to...let's talk later, okay? I'd like to catch up on some things."

"Sure," he agreed. He wanted to tell her how beautiful she looked, how her hair and makeup and the touch of her hand, and her sweet perfume, made him feel good inside. But he just nodded and turned to walk back toward the driveway. He paused for a moment and studied her, and they exchanged smiles.

Then she was back through the front door and Jimmy walked to his truck and climbed inside, slowly turning around and easing back out onto the country road. The buzz of happiness he had felt a few minutes ago had evaporated, and now he felt only emptiness in his belly and a powerful ache in his neck and back. And a big headache, growing stronger by the minute.

The weather turned unseasonably cool for the Saturday night event at Western Speedway, a sweeping half-mile paved track just outside Central City. The chilly evening did little to hurt the crowd, as the old wooden bleachers were nearly packed as the field prepared for the first heat race.

Bobby and Sandy Mancini had been warmly welcomed by their friends and competitors as they made their way along the pit lane, with Bobby clearly enjoying seeing his pals. Bobby did an interview on the front straightaway after qualifying had concluded, leaning on his crutches, and he beamed as the crowd gave him a loud ovation.

Fred Otley arranged for a big lawn chair to be placed near his pit, which was adjacent to the Ellison pit. Bobby held court with a gallery of people, and Jimmy spent a few minutes cutting up with Bobby and several other guys before walking back toward the Ellison car.

"Bobby looks like he's doing great," Rusty Fernandez nodded. "I've been worried about him, being out of the loop and all. It's pretty tough to sit at home, wondering if the world has forgot about you."

"Yeah, he's doing fine," Jimmy agreed. "I think he's going to be all right."

"You think Fred will put him back in the car when he's healed up?"

Jimmy looked across the way, where Fred laughed and smiled with Bobby and others while Jack Underwood stood a few feet away.

"It's hard to say…Fred's a good guy, but car owners, they're always looking out for themselves. Just have to wait and see."

"We look out for ourselves, too," Rusty said wistfully. "Drivers, I mean…we'd leave a car in a heartbeat if a better ride came along. Not much loyalty in this deal."

"Not much," Jimmy agreed. "Kind of every man for himself. I guess I'm lucky…I've been with Sonny and these guys a long time, it seems like. It's been a pretty good deal."

Harvey stood up from examining the front suspension to glare at Jimmy.

"You gonna drive this sumbitch tonight, or is it still social hour?" he bellowed. "Maybe you boys ought to go hold Mancini's hand, in case his leg hurts."

Jimmy and Rusty looked at each other with an amused glance.

"Never seen such a bunch of girls in my life," Harvey rambled on. "Guy busts his leg, and everybody is a nursemaid. Better keep movin' around, or you'll get ants all over your candy ass."

Jimmy smiled at Rusty, offering a shrug.

"See what I mean? I'm lucky, man. Real lucky."

Jimmy wiggled the Ellison car as they rumbled along the front straightaway, getting some heat in his tires. They had been chasing the car tonight, and he wasn't sure what to expect in this 30-lap feature. He and Harvey messed with the stagger and shocks before he rolled out, choosing a setup that was a great departure from what they normally ran here.

"Let's just throw on something new and see what happens," Harvey had said. "I don't know if it's the cool weather or what, but I just can't believe the track hasn't tightened up like it usually does."

Jimmy was surprised to hear the big man admit that the track had bamboozled them. And, to their defense, it had been a tough night for everybody. Sammy Caldwell, whose smooth style usually allowed him to shine here at Western, squeaked into the feature lineup by taking the last transfer in the semi, and didn't get that until the last corner.

Jimmy found his starting spot; second row, outside. The field formed up, taking a parade lap before preparing for the start. They were nose-to-tail as they rolled through three and four, all eyes on the starter.

The green flag waved and the place shuddered from the roar, and Jimmy deftly steered the Ellison car as the rear tires spun from the acceleration. Experience told him to take it easy on his tires, and he fell into line in fourth place, roaring down the backstretch, intensely studying the cars ahead.

Underwood sped past on the outside in the Otley sprinter, with Rick Wagner following him. Jimmy saw them wiggle as he trailed them into three, and they slipped their right rear again as they came off the corner.

Yeah, go for it, he mused. *Use it all up...*

The Ellison car was decent, but not great. Somehow that didn't worry Jimmy, because his instincts told him the car would get better as the laps clicked away. That's exactly what happened, and just past the halfway point Jimmy picked up his rhythm.

A couple of timely cautions had kept the leaders from getting away, and on the second restart Jimmy dispensed with Underwood and Wagner, both fading fast. He set his sights on Sammy, powering past on the inside as they navigated three and four.

Two laps later he was squarely on the tail of race leader Graffan in the Strong sprinter. Jimmy watched Graffan as they rolled through three and four, and he could see that his rival was a bit loose. Jimmy charged alongside on the frontstretch, then eased out of the throttle as they entered turn one.

His move had the desired effect, as he watched Graffan lean on the right rear as he fought to stay in front. Twice more Jimmy showed him his nose and backed off, and on the third time powered past on the inside as Graffan's right rear tire grew hotter.

As he rolled through three and four he spotted Harvey standing in the grassy area to the inside of the guardrail, waving his arm in jubilation.

He guessed there were five laps to go, holding the car steady through one and two, trying to maintain his momentum without using too much rubber. As he came off the corner he saw the safety light blink yellow, and he quickly eased out of the throttle.

A second later Graffan roared past on his right, and Jimmy suddenly realized the light was once again green. He pressed the throttle of the Ellison car, trying to regain his momentum as Sammy Caldwell pulled alongside.

The two cars were side-by-side through three and four, and Jimmy managed to pull ahead as they exited the corner. He saw the white flag waving, and he desperately tried to catch Graffan.

He drew up to the tail of the Strong machine as they rolled the corner, and moved to the inside as they exited. But Graffan crowded him toward the bottom, trying to run Jimmy out of racetrack. Jimmy clenched his teeth as he refused to yield real estate, and their tires actually rubbed midway through the straightaway.

Jimmy thought he had enough momentum through the corner, and he picked up the throttle smoothly as they came off, staring at an approaching checkered flag. But Graffan somehow found enough traction to lead them, beating Jimmy to the line by inches.

He could hear the roar of the crowd over their engines, and he cussed out loud. Graffan was pumping his fist excitedly, reveling in joy, while Jimmy shook his head in anger.

As Jimmy rumbled along the front straightaway he looked into the flag stand, holding up his hands at starter Mike Rydman as he rolled past. He picked up the throttle and drove back around, steering the car into the Ellison pit as a crowd quickly gathered.

He was climbing out as Harvey and Slim came rushing up, out of breath from their jog from the fourth turn.

"What the hell happened?" Harvey demanded. "Did it quit?"

"Yellow light came on," Jimmy said, his voice muffled inside his helmet.

"Light came on? On the dash? What the hell you talkin' about??!!"

Jimmy pulled his helmet off, sweat dripping from his face.

"No, not the dash," he tried to explain. "The caution light... the light down in the corner. The yellow came on, and I let up, and then it was green again. When I let up Graffan got past me, and Sammy, almost."

Harvey and Slim looked at each other in surprise.

"I didn't see no yellow light," Harvey insisted.

"I'm telling you, the light was yellow!"

"Then how come Graffan was on the hammer? And everybody else?"

"I don't know...damn it, the light was yellow. Don't you think I can tell the difference between yellow and green?"

Harvey shook his head, and he began to mutter. "Why can't you just admit you screwed up, boy? You didn't see no yellow light."

By now Jimmy thought he might explode. He shook his head vigorously, trying to control his temper as he glanced at the crowd ringing their pit.

He tossed his helmet and gear into the seat and stalked toward the front straightaway. Graffan and his crew were celebrating alongside their car, and Jimmy saw Rydman walking through the fence opening under the flag stand, the pouch containing his flags slung across his shoulder.

Jimmy headed him off, staring intently as Rydman offered a curious gaze. Al quickly approached, along with Leon Hartke.

"What's your beef?" Rydman asked.

Smirking, Jimmy thought to himself. *Always smirking...that's why I don't like this guy.*

"Yellow light came on," Jimmy said flatly.

"What? What are you talking about?"

"Right there at the end, when I was coming off two, the yellow light came on. I let off, and Graffan passed me."

Rydman laughed, but Al studied Jimmy carefully.

"Are you nuts?" Rydman asked.

"The yellow light was on."

"Listen, what is this," Rydman said, his voice rising. "You got a lot of nerve, saying the light came on. You think I don't know where the switch is? Why don't you just admit you got beat."

"The light came on," Jimmy insisted. "You think I'd let off just for the hell of it?"

"Aw, this is crazy," Rydman said, growing more animated. "Al, did you see a yellow light? Or you, Leon? Anybody?"

Both men slowly shook their head, and Al spoke in a soft, firm voice.

"Jimmy, are you positive? You saw the yellow light come on?"

"Absolutely," he said. "It was only on for a moment…as soon as Graffan passed me, I realized the green was back on. It was just for one second, maybe two. Not long. But it was on. I swear it."

"This is stupid," Rydman said, his face reddening. "There is no way I turned the yellow light on, then turned it off. No way!"

Al looked at Jimmy, using his most diplomatic voice.

"Jimmy…I don't know what you want me to say, but there isn't anything I can do. The race is over. Whatever you saw, I'm sure you believe you saw it, but I just don't have anything to go on."

Jimmy could sense that this was a lost cause, and there wasn't anything more to gain from the discussion. Despite his frustration, he turned to walk away when he saw Jerry Gillespie—a guy from Michigan who ran with them now and then—approaching, wearing a deep frown.

"What's the story on the yellow light?" Gillespie demanded, studying the officials. "I let up and two cars passed me. Then the damn green is back on!"

"Thank you," Jimmy said, nodding his head, glaring at Rydman. "Now who is nuts?"

"Don't give me that," Rydman said, returning Jimmy's glare. "You put him up to this!"

"Nobody puts me up to anything," Gillespie growled. "The yellow light came on, and I saw it. You calling me a liar?"

"All right, everybody calm down," Al insisted, holding his hands up for quiet. He turned to face Rydman, studying him carefully.

"Mike, tell me about the switch setup up there…is it possible you could hit the switch without realizing it?"

"There is no way," Rydman insisted, vigorously shaking his head. "I tell you, these guys are playing a game with us. No way I turned on the yellow light!"

Jimmy looked over to see a slender guy in a Western Speedway official's shirt standing nearby, and he could see that the guy was trying to figure out if he should say something. The guy looked familiar, and suddenly Jimmy realized it was the track's regular flagman.

As the other men argued, Jimmy watched as the slender guy studied the scene, and Jimmy stepped in the middle and raised his hands for quiet. He nodded at the guy.

"I think this man might know something about all this."

The man hesitated, but slowly nodded.

"I meant to tell you about this," he said sheepishly to Rydman. "That switch up there…it's real sensitive like, and if you lean against it, it will trigger the light for just a second, and then when you get off it, it goes back to what it was before."

"I tell you you're crazy," Rydman said angrily. "I did no such thing."

"Sure you did," Jimmy said quietly. "Think about it…you reached for the white flag, and you leaned up against the switch. Then when you stood up, the green is back on."

The others began to nod, but Rydman only turned more crimson.

"It's happened to me before, just like that," the slender man admitted. "I've been aiming to have it looked at…guess we need to do that."

Al looked at Jimmy and Gillespie, offering a look that was sympathetic but firm.

"Guys, this doesn't change anything," he said quietly. "The race is over, and there will be no adjustments. It's an unfortunate situation, but I can't offer you anything more than that. We will definitely look at this before we run here again, I promise you that much."

Rydman nearly hissed as he spoke up.

"It's their word against mine," he said angrily. "I didn't hit the yellow light, Al. No way. Only two cars saw it, out of the whole field? Ask Steve Graffan if the yellow came on. These guys are yanking our chain."

By now Jimmy had heard enough of Rydman to last him a while. They exchanged heated retorts for a moment as Al tried to restore calm, and Jimmy finally turned to walk away.

"I'll just tell you one more thing, mister," he said, pointing his finger and staring intently at Rydman as he felt the anger boiling inside him. "One of these days you won't have that uniform on, and I'm gonna knock you on your ass. And it won't have anything to do with you being an official."

"You don't have the guts," Rydman glared, sticking out his chin.

"That's enough!!"Al said sharply, finally losing his patience. "Jimmy, get out of here. Mike, get your things loaded and go home."

"I'll show you some guts," Jimmy answered angrily, stepping back toward Rydman.

"I said *NOW!*" Al tugged firmly at Jimmy's uniform, pulling him in the other direction. Jimmy followed along, trying to calm himself down. They walked a few yards away, and Al was still glaring at Jimmy.

"You know I'm right," Jimmy insisted loudly. "The light—"

"Never mind the light," Al said, cutting him off. "Can't you just let it go? Is it that important to be right, every time?"

"Well…yeah," Jimmy nodded. "The guy called me a liar—"

"You're not listening," Al said in frustration. "Why can't you be mature enough to let it go, instead of having to have the last word. You won the argument, okay? We believe the light was on. But that isn't enough for you…you try to pick a fight with a guy who outweighs you probably 40 pounds. What's the matter with you? Why do you have to be such a hothead?"

"Aw…he's a jerk," Jimmy said, beginning to realize that he had probably looked pretty silly.

"And what are you, when you act like that?" Al said, his voice growing quiet, but still very firm. "You let yourself get mad, and then you act just as bad as the other guy."

"The other guy is your official," Jimmy countered. "He shouldn't—"

"And that's MY problem," Al nodded. "Let me handle my problem, okay? But you picking a fight isn't very helpful, is it?"

They walked slowly toward the Ellison pit, and Al placed his hand on Jimmy's shoulder.

"You have so much ability, but you've got a lot to learn, Jimmy. You and that temper…when it gets the best of you, it overshadows all the good things about you. You're a better person than that. And you know it."

Jimmy frowned as he listened to Al. He knew his friend was right…exactly right. Why did he get so hot about things? And when it was somebody he didn't like—Rydman was a prime example—it took almost nothing to get him fired up, and out of control.

He swallowed hard to keep his emotions in check, and realized how much he was still sweating. He unzipped his uniform to his belly, and drew his arm across his face, looking toward his pit.

Al reached up with his fist and gently clipped the bottom of Jimmy's chin.

"Don't hang that head," Al smiled. "You just need a little work, that's all. Like the rest of us."

Chapter 28

The deck behind his mobile home was a perfect setting for the lazy Sunday afternoon, with the sun gently chasing away the cool temperatures of the night before. Jimmy enjoyed the welcome respite from the summer heat, knowing that within a few days it would once again be simmering.

He leaned back in the lawn chair, drifting off a couple of times for a nap. For the first time since his crash a few weeks earlier, his neck wasn't hurting. The absence of pain made the day feel even more beautiful, and he watched the birds as they darted along the tree line behind his house.

The world of race cars, and yellow lights, and Mike Rydman was far, far away. Nothing was going to make him stop smiling today.

The only thing that would be better was if Elaine was here. He had driven over to her place twice today, hoping to catch her at home. But she didn't answer the door, and he figured maybe she went to visit relatives up in Fort Wayne.

Jimmy wished he had a phone, so he could try her house to see if she was home yet. He was in the mood for a nice dinner; maybe they could go to the restaurant where they first went out, all those months ago.

He didn't have much travel coming up, and he figured they could finally spend more time together. She had been plenty patient, he knew. Never complained, just gave him that pretty smile.

Al's words from the night before kept ringing through his head, making him think about things. Al was right, Jimmy decided. He was through being a hothead. He was going to do a better job of staying calm, and not letting stuff get him all upset.

Life is too short, he figured, to spend it with your guts all churned up inside.

He leaned his head against the back of the chair, feeling the breeze and sunshine on his face. There was nothing but the sound of the birds, but he paused for a moment, listening, wondering if he had heard something. He rose from the chair to look around, stepping through the back door of his place.

He smiled broadly as he saw Elaine at the front door, and she offered a gentle wave as he swung the door open.

"There you are," he said, opening the screen as she stepped inside. "I went down to your place earlier, but missed you."

They embraced, and he gave her a kiss.

"C'mon, I'm sitting on the porch. Isn't it a beautiful day? How about a glass of tea?"

"Nothing for me, thanks," she said, settling into a chair on the deck.

They sat for a moment, and Jimmy could only smile at her. It drove him crazy how the wind made her hair dance, and her dark eyes twinkled as she reached up to brush the hair from her face.

"I've missed you," he said softly.

"Thanks…"

"Do you have dinner plans? I thought maybe we could go over to Madison, to that place we went the first time. Remember?"

She nodded.

"Listen, I can't stay but a minute," she began.

"How is your dad?" he asked. "I haven't seen him in forever."

"He's fine. You know, Jimmy, I've been thinking—"

"Well, that's no good," he teased. "Thinking, that gets you in trouble."

She gave him a look that made him pause. "No, let me finish," she said, a little curt. Then she smiled.

"Sorry, didn't mean to bite your head off."

He studied her, now completely off balance with what was happening.

"Jimmy, you are a great guy," she began, a catch in her voice. "You've been the most exciting guy I've ever known. It's just that…"

"Wait a minute," he said softly. "Is this the, 'You're a nice guy, BUT…' speech?"

She looked at him, and brought her hand up to brush a tear from her cheek.

She stopped, struggling with her composure.

"I said it wasn't going to be like this," she sighed deeply, almost talking to herself before looking back at him.

"These last few months have been wonderful. But I've kind of figured out that our worlds are too different, too far apart."

"How? How are they different?"

She looked off into the trees, then turned back toward him.

"We want different things. I'm a farm girl, and I don't need to go far from home. I want little children, and to live quietly out here in the middle of nowhere.

"You…you have a whole different life. Racing is…racing is everything to you. It's not just your job, it's…it's your LIFE. I could never be happy, knowing I'm in second place. And you could never be happy, stuck here on the farm. It's just not meant to be.

"When we're together, it's wonderful. But then off you go, sometimes for weeks at a time. My roots are too deep…and you have no roots. It's just…it's just never going to work."

"Just be patient," he insisted. "I can work on staying home more, and—"

"No," she countered. "I could never ask you to stop racing so much, because you can't stop. And I can't give up my life as a farm girl to follow you. I can't do it..that's not who I am.

"Don't you see, Jimmy? We're just…stuck."

They sat for a moment, his mind reeling, trying to think of something to say. Finally he spoke up, his voice so soft she could barely hear him.

"I don't want you to go," he said.

"I know," she nodded, brushing another tear from her cheek.

They sat quietly for another moment, when she rose suddenly from her chair. Jimmy slowly got to his feet.

"I do love you," she said, her voice breaking. "You need to know that."

They walked through the back door, crossing the dingy living room and out the front door, across the rickety porch and along the driveway to her car. She turned and looked at him, tears welling in her eyes.

He drew his arms around her and pulled her close. They held the embrace for a moment, and he stepped back. He brushed his hand through her soft brown hair and smiled, touching his finger on the tip of her nose.

"Just one thing," he said softly. "This is only goodbye for now… maybe someday, it will be hello again. Okay?"

She nodded, and he leaned over to kiss her forehead. She quickly opened the car door, the gravel rippling as she backed out onto the road. In a moment she sped away, and he stood looking to the west, watching her car at it grew tiny in the distance, hearing the sound trailing off until there was nothing but the wind blowing across the landscape.

He stood there, expressionless, feeling the sun on his face. The wind rustled his hair, and he stuck his hands in his pockets.

He was back where he was before, back to a place he feared he might be stuck forever. Alone. Again.

Chapter 29

The Ellison sprint car rumbled easily down the pit area, slowing to a stop and falling silent. Jimmy crawled from the car as Harvey and Slim moved close to prepare the car for qualifying.

"Looks a little greasy," Harvey called out, not looking up from the tape measure winding around the rear tire.

"Yeah, a little," Jimmy agreed. "Still pretty hot…it'll tighten up when that sun goes down."

"Where are we in the order?"

"Second," Jimmy called, taking a long drink of water from the jug. The heat was almost unbearable, and the humidity so heavy you could nearly wring it out of the air. "You sure we got the right gear? I almost think we could go a few points more."

"Dammit, I know what gear to run," Harvey bristled. "I raced up here before you were old enough to stand upright to pee."

"Yeah, but you haven't been here for at least 10 years," Jimmy countered.

"What difference does that make? Track ain't grown or shrunk, has it? Gear is gear, and it don't matter how much time passes. Listen, I'll do the thinkin' here…you just drive this thing."

Jimmy shrugged, walking to Fred Otley's pit a few cars down the line.

"Hey, Fred, what gear are you running?"

Fred was crouched at the right rear, adjusting tire pressure. He gave Jimmy a grin and shook his head.

"You mean you want me to tell you my speed secrets?"

"Speed secrets??!! Whatever…what gear?"

"I run a 4:88, but Harvey's probably got a 5:04 in your car. He likes to turn his motor more than I do."

"Really? You think he'd run more gear than average?"

"Oh, he always does. But I can't afford to turn my motor that tight."

Jimmy contemplated his answer, and shrugged.

"Gee, I was thinking we should put some more gear in it, to help it off the corner."

"You drivers always want more gear, because you don't have to rebuild these motors. You'd turn 'em 9,500 if we'd hold still for it."

"They sound good at 9,500," Jimmy teased.

"Oh, yeah, they do," Fred laughed. "But it's that sound they make at, say, 9,501...that big 'CLUNK' noise. That's a pretty doggone expensive sound, Jimmy."

"We just had one go clunk, out in Arizona," Jimmy nodded. "It doesn't sound good no matter who is paying."

"No, it doesn't. But hey, if you can get Harvey to give you more gear, I'll listen to you go by. Might wince a little, though. I hate to hear anybody turnin' one too tight."

Jimmy saw Jack Underwood, walking toward them from turn four.

"How's it been, racing with your new guy?"

"It's been real good...course, it's different. Bobby is about like my son, and we've always clicked. But this fellow, he's been easy. Doesn't say much, good or bad. Just shows up ready to race."

"He told me he's not so sure about the pavement."

"You know, he told me that, too, but he's caught on pretty good. He can't help me much with feedback, but if I give him a good setup he'll sure drive 'er. I can't complain about that, the man does try hard."

"Did you know Bobby's up and around again? Got the cast off this week, and even got a job. Drives a small truck back and forth to Cincinnati."

"Yeah, he told me. He calls me every week, I think he's worried about not getting back in the seat. But I told him the ride is his, and it is. And I also told him he can't get back in the car until his doctor releases him. I don't want him hurting himself by coming back too soon."

Jimmy nodded, and Underwood drew his forearm across his face as he approached. He grinned at Jimmy, and shook his head.

"Boy, this humidity is about to kill me...we don't have this out in California."

"This? Oh, this is nothing. When I was a kid, it would get so humid my old man would row a canoe to work, four feet off the ground."

Underwood laughed. "Yeah, right."

"You figuring out this pavement deal?"

"A little...but this track here, it's got me scratching my head."

"Me too...I've never been here before, but Harvey ran here a long time ago. It's a different place, isn't it? Kind of a big circle, and the banking and radius is different on each end. I guess you set up for one corner and suffer on the other."

They saw an official making his way down the pit area, and Jimmy began to walk toward the Ellison sprinter.

"Must be getting ready to start qualifying...see you later."

Jimmy rolled to a stop from his heat race, shaking his head. Harvey and Slim approached the car with a look of concern, and Jimmy quickly pulled his helmet off.

"Something's wrong," he said. "It's cutting out, like it's starving for fuel or something."

"I heard it," Harvey said, reaching for the screwdriver in his pocket. In a moment he and Slim had the hood off, and Harvey was poking around.

"It's the mag," Harvey insisted, his weathered hands quickly checking the plug wires and electrical connections. "It ain't got anything to do with the fuel."

Jimmy leaned against the cage, watching Harvey.

"Maybe you're right. Just felt...funny, I guess. Usually I can hear if she's missing or laying down, but this was different."

Harvey cussed, wiping his hand across the back of his neck.

"Damn mosquitoes are about to eat me alive...ain't bad enough to sweat to death, but the bugs gotta make you even more miserable."

He stepped back, grimly walking toward the toolbox. "Let's swap that mag," he said to Slim. "But first make sure you fuel the car so we don't forget."

Slim nodded, reaching for a jug of fuel. Jimmy walked to the pickup, pouring some cold water into a cup. He took a swig, then poured some water into a clean rag, wiping the sweat and grime from his face and neck.

A few minutes later Jimmy was climbing into the car for the feature. The magneto had been swapped, and Harvey assured him the car was fine.

"Remember what I told you," he said, leaning against the cage as Jimmy buckled in. "Best place to pass is coming off two…don't turn in too early into one, or it'll kill you coming off. Just use your momentum and be smooth…these other yahoos got no idea how to drive this track, so you should win it easy."

Jimmy nodded, pulling his helmet on. He guessed it was still nearly 90, and sweat was pouring down his back. Harvey and Slim rolled the car forward, and Jimmy stared at Harvey as they waited for a truck. The lines were deep in the big man's face, and it looked like his eyes were sagging.

This heat's worn everybody out…I'm already tired, and we haven't even started the race.

The Ellison sprinter was soon fired, and Jimmy took his place in row four, outside. The Strong sprinter of Steve Graffan was ahead, and Underwood was to Jimmy's left.

The field rumbled into position, and the starter held a furled green flag aloft. Jimmy tensed his body as they rolled down the backstretch, clenching the wheel and focusing on the cars ahead. The collective growl began to increase in pitch, and thousands of horsepower prepared to be unleashed.

The front row stood on the gas, and everyone followed. Jimmy felt the Ellison car wiggle as the back tires slipped slightly on the pavement, and he flicked his wrists to keep the car in line. He got a great start, and squirted past Graffan on the outside as they rolled into turn one.

The car liked the outside groove, and Jimmy passed another car as they came off. He looked ahead and realized he was already fifth, and he focused on keeping the car freed up on the outside, keeping his momentum.

In five laps he was second, pressing Sammy Caldwell for the lead. Jimmy gave chase for several laps until Sammy missed slightly getting into one, doing exactly what Harvey had seen earlier: turning in just a hair too soon. The Ellison machine moved alongside, and simply drove away coming off.

Jimmy was leading, and the car felt good. That mag must have done the trick, because he felt the car pulling strongly down the straightaway.

He saw the crossed flags, and concentrated on hitting his marks. No mistakes, and this one is in the bag.

As he raced down the backstretch he felt a slight hesitation to the car, and his stomach knotted. It was doing it again...not exactly missing, but not running right, either. By losing just the slightest edge, the car was now an easy mark for the guys behind.

Jimmy heard a car to his inside, and saw it was Underwood. Jimmy's foot was on the floor, but he was helpless as he watched Jack pull away easily, and just as quickly another car was inside. This time it was Graffan, followed by Rusty and Sammy. Then Rick Wagner, and a Pennsylvania car that he had noticed earlier.

He clicked off the laps, and guessed he had fallen to ninth or tenth. He caught a glance at the temperature gauge, and realized the car was getting hot. Should he pull in? He guessed only a handful of laps remained, and he agonized; he hated the thought of hurting this engine, particularly since Harvey had just gone through it after breaking a piston out west. But it wasn't yet critically hot, so he soldiered on.

Jimmy saw the white flag, and in a final insult two more cars passed him in the last corner. He limped toward their pit, disgusted and tired and soaked with sweat.

The engine burbled as he rolled to a stop, picking up in pitch before it fell silent. He crawled from the seat, his trembling fingers fiddling for the straps on his helmet, realizing they too were soaked. Harvey stood with his hands on his hips, his body language revealing his frustration and fatigue.

Jimmy placed his helmet on the tailgate of the truck, turning to offer a shrug.

"Ran good till just past halfway, then it laid down, like it did before," he explained. "Man, I'm sure it's something with the fuel...started to get a little hot."

Harvey said nothing, his face knitted in concentration, finally shaking his head.

"I still think it's electrical," he insisted. "I'll find it...well, let's get this thing loaded and get outta here. Might get home before sunup."

Jimmy wished there was a shower here at the track, and he settled for washing himself off when he changed clothes in a ratty old room off the concession stand. He walked to Fred Otley's pit, where Jack was receiving congratulations from various drivers and mechanics.

"You're a pavement ace," Jimmy teased as he shook Underwood's hand. "I'll bet if somebody told you your first USAC win would come on the blacktop, you wouldn't have believed 'em!"

Underwood laughed easily, beaming. "Listen, I followed you, and started to figure this place out," he said. "What happened to your car? I was chasing you and all of a sudden here you come, back to me."

"I don't know what it is...fuel, electrical, something. But I was a dead duck when it started acting up. Well, I'm gonna head back home. You ride up with Fred?"

"Yeah, how about you? Ride with your guys?"

"No, Rusty came by and picked me up. I don't ride with Harvey much, we kind of wear on each other a little bit as it is. Need a little space."

Underwood laughed. "I get the impression Harvey's a hardcore guy."

"Kind of? Yeah, he's pretty much ate up with it, and he definitely lets you know when he doesn't agree with something. We've sort of figured out how to co-exist."

"He was on crutches when I first came out here, and Fred said he was in a real bad car wreck. Guess he's all healed up, eh?"

"Yeah, it's kind of amazing. He's hardly missed a beat, and I'm surprised. I figured it would take him a lot longer to bounce back, because he really got beat up in the crash. But you've got to give this much to Harvey, he's a tough ol' dude."

Jimmy wheeled the semi-truck around the bend at the grain elevator, easing into position below the large gray loading tube. He climbed from the cab, tugging back the black tarp that covered his trailer, feeling the morning sun on his face. He stepped down from the trailer and headed for the office, fishing in his pocket for some change.

Although the sun was still low in the sky, it was already a hot one. The dust in the driveway hung in the air, and the cicadas buzzed, giving a sleepy tone to the summer morning.

He glanced across the way at the maroon car parked near the office, admiring the chrome wheels and the shiny finish. He spotted the red "For Sale" sign in the windshield, and changed course to head that way. He had long admired the Pontiac from a distance, and as he approached he saw a few nicks and flaws but it appeared to be in solid condition.

After a quick glance he walked into the office, quickly closing the door behind him, feeling himself enveloped in the cool air.

"Hot out there, ain't it?" a tall young man called from behind the counter. "What's goin' on, Jimmy? Been winnin' all those races?"

"Hi Lonnie," Jimmy replied, walking toward the soda machine. "No, not for a while. Feels nice in here."

"I'll bet you're about to wear out the A/C in that semi."

"Oh, sure. Gene has 2-WD-60 air conditioning in that truck."

Lonnie gave him a confused look. "2-WD-60? What's that?"

"Two windows down at 60 mph," Jimmy replied, dropping the coins into the soft drink machine. "Hey, is that your GTO for sale?"

"Yeah," the boy said glumly.

"You love that car," Jimmy said, setting the cold can on the counter and taking off his cap, wiping the sweat from his face. "Why you selling it?"

"Aw, can't get insurance," Lonnie said with a sigh. "Got a couple of speeding tickets, and my policy got cancelled. I just got married this spring, and the wife says I gotta get something more responsible. Probably ain't a bad idea, since we got a kid on the way."

"How much you asking?"

"Well…I was hoping to get $900. It's in real good shape, but it needs tires."

Jimmy took a swig of his drink, nodding as he listened.

"It's pretty fast, isn't it?"

Lonnie beamed with pride.

"I ain't never been beat yet," he said.

"Is that a four-barrel, or Tri-Power?"

"Tri-Power."

Jimmy smiled. "Well, I better get loaded. Another load of wheat for Early and Daniels in Central City…write me up a ticket, and I'll get 'er started."

Lonnie began writing on a pad of paper, and Jimmy finished his drink before turning to head outside.

"You interested in the car?" Lonnie said hopefully. "I'd make you a deal."

"Oh, I don't know," Jimmy said, pausing at the door. "Might be kind of fun, at that. How would you trade me for my truck?"

"Hmmm," Lonnie mused. "What year is it?"

"It's a '66."

"Same as my car," Lonnie replied, thinking carefully. "Run pretty good?"

"Runs real good…just replaced the tranny, and the tires are real good. Radio even works."

Lonnie rubbed his chin with his fingers. "Bring your truck over, and we'll have a look," he said. Jimmy did his best to look disinterested, but he couldn't help but smile at the idea.

Chapter 30

Traffic moved smoothly along the wide boulevard, and Jimmy shifted gears as they picked up speed. He was still getting the hang of his new car, and was loving it.

"Man, this is a nice set of wheels," Bobby Mancini grinned from the front passenger seat. "Lots more fun than your ol' truck, eh?"

Jimmy nodded, smiling at his friend. "Sets you back in the seat a little, too," he said, jabbing the throttle, feeling the car surge before settling back to an easy cruising speed.

"A GTO...now you've got style, killer. But even with this car, I don't think you'll have any luck picking up women. Chrome wheels ain't gonna make up for that ugly mug!"

"Whatever. Hey, Al was telling me about a job opening at the machine shop down the street from you. Know anything about it?"

"Nope...then again, I'm usually not interested in job stuff. Only till my leg heals up, then I'm back racing again. No need for a job then."

"I'm thinking about going to see the guy," Jimmy continued.

"You don't like driving Gene's truck?"

"I like it all right. But I...well, I'm thinking about moving back to town. Living in that little trailer out the middle of nowhere, I'm kind of tired of that. And if I move back here, it's too far to Gene's every morning."

"Does this have anything to do with the fact that your farm girl isn't in the picture anymore?"

"No," Jimmy insisted, wondering if he was telling a lie. "I'm just ready for something a little bigger, and closer to all my friends."

"Hi guys!"

The shout surprised Jimmy, and he looked to his left. A red Mustang convertible had pulled alongside, with two blonde girls wearing bright smiles looking them over.

"There we go," Bobby said under his breath, giving them a wave. Jimmy looked over and smiled, resting his arm on the door.

"Hello, ladies," he said, studying them closely. The driver was the prettiest, but both were fine. He guessed them to be just a little younger than him, maybe even 20 or so. Music blared from their stereo, and the wind made their hair float like ribbons.

"Wanna race?" the driver called out, laughing.

"Why not?" Jimmy replied, glancing ahead.

The girl gassed it, and he could hear the little six-banger rattle in protest. He prodded the Goat, easily keeping up. After a moment the girl eased off the throttle, and they slowed.

"I think you're faster," she laughed. "Where you guys going?"

"Wherever you're going," Bobby shouted.

"Okay, pull into the Big Boy on the corner," and she shot ahead of them, moving into their lane. Her signal flickered, and in a moment they rolled to a stop, side by side, in a couple of the spots at the popular drive-in restaurant.

"You look familiar," the girl in the passenger seat said, looking intently at Jimmy. "Do I know you?"

"I don't think so," Jimmy replied. "What's your name?"

"Connie," she said, nodding to her friend. "This is Teresa. Do you live around here?"

"I live out in the country, a few miles from here. How about you?"

"We're from the south side," Teresa said, eyeing Bobby with a teasing smile. "Just two little girls out looking for trouble."

"You found it," Bobby said, returning her gaze.

"My name is Jimmy, and this is Bobby. Great night for a convertible, isn't it?"

They chatted for a while, and a carhop approached, balancing a couple of trays in each hand.

"Are you guys going to order anything?"

"Here in a little bit," Jimmy replied, noticing the young girl's frown. "Okay if we hang out for a few minutes while we decide?"

"Hmmph," she grumped, hurrying away.

"You deadbeat," Bobby teased. "I swear, killer, you cause trouble everywhere we go."

Jimmy was soon perched on a fender of the Mustang, enjoying

that Connie was so openly flirting with him. The carhop's frown was growing deeper each time she passed, and Jimmy figured they were going to ask them to leave if they didn't order something.

"We probably ought to get going," he told the others. "I think little Miss Friendly is about to give us the boot. You guys want to ride with us for a while?"

"Sure!" Connie spoke quickly. "I want to ride in that sharp car."

"I want a convertible ride," Bobby said, trying to look cool while he balanced himself on his crutches. "How about if we split up for a little while?"

The girls exchanged glances for a moment, then agreed.

"Let me drive," Bobby insisted, hurrying around the front of the Mustang, and Jimmy chuckled at how quickly he could move on those crutches.

Teresa opened the door as he slumped into the driver's seat. "Exactly what happened to your leg, anyways?"

"Long story," Bobby said, sticking his crutches in the back seat.

"Can you drive?" Teresa asked. "With those crutches, I mean."

"Sure I can drive…this little automatic is no problem at all."

Connie hurried around to climb into the Pontiac, and Jimmy started the engine.

"Meet back here in a little while," Connie called out to the others, who nodded. In a flash the Mustang was out into the street, quickly disappearing into traffic.

Jimmy pulled the car into gear, easing off the corner and pointing the car toward the outskirts of town. He looked over at the girl, admiring her short-shorts and her long, tanned legs.

"How are you?" she smiled.

"Getting better by the minute," he replied, arching his eyebrows and making her laugh.

They cruised along for several minutes, making small talk, when Jimmy noticed a white Dodge Charger approaching from behind. The car trailed him for a couple of blocks, then pulled alongside on their left.

Jimmy looked over, and the guy behind the wheel gave him a nod.

"Wanna have a go?" the guy called out. Jimmy shrugged, his grip on the shifter tightening.

Connie's eyes widened, and Jimmy quietly said, "Put your lap belt on." She quickly snapped the belt into place, wearing an excited expression.

"Let's go from 20," the guy shouted, and Jimmy nodded. The street was deserted, and Jimmy pushed the shifter into first as he slowed. He gripped the wheel, staring straight ahead, letting the other guy make the move. They continued to slow, when the Charger suddenly screamed.

Jimmy flattened his right foot to the floor, feeling his three carburetors send a jolt of power through the car. They were even for an instant, with Jimmy banging second gear and beginning to pull ahead. He hit third and the Dodge was no longer alongside, and a moment later hit fourth, feeling the power continuing to surge through his machine, seeing the Charger's headlights in his mirror.

He stayed on the gas for several moments, watching his tach, nervously looking for cops. It was obvious he had won, and he eased off the throttle and watched the speedometer needle drop south of 100, then 90, 80, 70, settling in at 60. They approached the final stoplight at the edge of the city.

"Wow," Connie said, so excited she could hardly talk. "That was amazing!"

The Charger rolled alongside, and the guy offered a frown.

"I missed a shift," he said, although Jimmy had his doubts. "Gimme another try...how about straight up here at the light for 20 bucks? We'll go to the red barn."

"No, too far," Jimmy said, figuring the Dodge had a taller gear. "We'll go to the speed limit sign. Just for fun, no money."

The guy nodded, and they both focused on the light, seeing the cross traffic lanes turn yellow. A roar filled the air, and as the light blinked green the scene was engulfed in a mingled fog of exhaust, burned tires, and a hint of clutch.

Jimmy pulled him out of the hole, and there was never any doubt. At the mile crossroads Jimmy flicked on his signal, easing onto the crossroad then backing out to head back toward town. The Dodge drew to a stop, and Jimmy paused alongside.

"Pretty quick Pontiac," the guy said, wearing a disappointed expression. "I'll tune mine up some, and find you some other night."

"Fair enough," Jimmy smiled. "See you later."

"Yeah."

The whine of the transmission rose and fell three times before settling in at a steady pitch as they headed east.

"My gosh," Connie squealed. "That was the most exciting thing I've ever felt in my life! I'm just…tingling!"

Jimmy laughed. "Didn't know you'd have an adventure, did you?"

"No…" she studied him carefully, and suddenly shouted in recognition. "Jimmy…I know who you are! You're a race driver! I saw your picture in the paper!"

"Could be," Jimmy nodded.

"Wow, a real race driver. That is very cool!"

"I'm hungry," he said. "How about we go back and get something to eat?"

"Sure."

They were soon back among the busy city traffic, and she quizzed him excitedly about sprint car racing. Jimmy eased off the street into an open spot at the drive-in, where the carhop gave him a doubtful stare as she approached.

"Okay, okay, we're ready to order," he laughed. "Just took a while to make up our mind."

He looked over at Connie. "Know what you want?"

"I'm not really hungry…just some French fries and a Coke is okay."

The carhop took their order and walked away, and Jimmy turned up the radio as he heard a favorite song come on. They spent the next few minutes talking about music when Jimmy noticed a gray Buick driving slowly into the drive-in, the man behind the wheel studying the cars intently. For a moment he thought it might be a cop, but dismissed the idea and turned his attention back to the pretty girl sitting a couple of feet away.

Connie was smiling as she described some songs she liked, when the color suddenly drained from her face and her expression turned to near panic.

"Oh, crap," she whispered, sagging back like she wanted to disappear into the upholstery. Jimmy realized the Buick had stopped, and was backing up a few feet in front of their parking spot.

Jimmy was alarmed at her reaction, and looked again at the Buick. The door swung open and a strapping young guy stepped out, walking around the front of the car, all the while giving Connie a withering stare.

Jimmy watched him carefully, trying to figure out what was happening. By her reaction, this wasn't anything good.

"What's up?" he asked. "Who is that guy?"

"It's my husband," she wheezed.

"For cryin' out loud!" Jimmy said in an exasperated tone, immediately recalling the episode after the River Ridge race a few months ago. "What's the deal with you married women? Why do you have to pick on me?"

He turned to look at Connie, who began to open her door with a trembling hand. She slid those long legs out of the car, and Jimmy spoke up.

"You know, you really ought to wear your ring."

She gave him an empty stare and walked toward the Buick, her husband glowering. In a moment the guy screeched his tires as they swept out of sight.

Jimmy sat for a moment, reaching up to turn off the radio. "Why does this stuff always happen to me?" he asked, shaking his head. "Why are girls always trouble?"

He saw the carhop approaching with a tray of food, and he raised his window a few inches and reached for his wallet. He tossed a couple of bucks on the tray, and the young girl grinned.

"Looks like Mr. GTO got shut down," she teased.

"Oh, that? Listen, that girl is an escaped convict. I was just holding her until her parole officer came by. Lucky thing, too…she's a serial killer, and you'll never guess who most of her victims are."

The girl gave him an amused look.

"Carhops?" she finally guessed.

Jimmy nodded ominously, slowly peeling the paper back from his cheeseburger.

"Sure," the girl said, stuffing the money in her pocket and stepping away from the car. "Honk when you're finished, and I'll come back over."

"Better keep your eye on me," he insisted. "I'm a notorious tray thief."

She wrinkled her nose and headed back inside. Jimmy began eating his French fries when he saw Bobby and the red Mustang wheeling into the next spot over.

"What'd you do, scare your passenger away?" Bobby said, hobbling onto his crutches as he made his way to Jimmy's car, Teresa walking alongside.

"A slight complication," Jimmy explained. "Her husband insisted she go away with him."

Bobby's eyes widened, and he couldn't help but laugh. "Wow... you're a magnet for trouble, killer. How about that!"

Teresa seemed only mildly surprised. "Oh, her husband is a stick-in-the-mud," she insisted. "He doesn't want to have any fun, and doesn't want her to have any fun either."

Jimmy looked at Teresa and shook his head. "Some fun," he said.

She laughed breezily. "Oh, girls just like to have a good time. She thought you were cute, that's all. No harm done."

Bobby leaned back into the passenger seat, finagling the crutches at his side and turning to tsk-tsk at Jimmy.

"Well, you're up to your old tricks," he admonished, stifling a smile. "You almost got me into trouble again. What am I gonna do with you, killer?"

Jimmy shook his head and shrugged helplessly. He took a sip from his drink, then turned to retrieve the other drink from the tray.

"The good news is, the husband didn't take the extra Coke! Anybody thirsty?"

They began to laugh, and Jimmy turned the radio back on. He was kind of liking this new car thing.

Chapter 31

The September breeze carried a hint of autumn, rustling the nearby trees as Jimmy leaned from the cab of the truck. He studied the stream of golden grain as it trickled into the semi-trailer, trailing a plume of dust into the air.

Satisfied that he wouldn't need to pull forward for another couple of minutes, he turned his attention back to the racing paper in his hand. Jimmy felt a tinge of pride as he saw an action shot of the Ellison Special on the cover, with a rundown of the most recent event.

He contemplated the remaining schedule, and turned the page to look at the point standings. Steve Graffan had a pretty decent lead, with Jimmy less than a dozen points behind Sammy Caldwell in third. But if they won the next couple races, he figured he might narrow the margin on Graffan and at least have a shot.

Another truck rolled into the parking lot, swinging around to pull in behind Jimmy's rig. Gene Morrison climbed from the cab, walking through the dust as he approached Jimmy's truck.

"Sure loads slow, doesn't it?" Gene called out. "I believe we could fill it faster with a shovel."

"My union card doesn't allow me to use a shovel," Jimmy teased. "The boss is supposed to load it, and I go inside and drink coffee."

"I wouldn't be surprised," Gene grimaced. "Just another one of the perks of being the ramrod of this outfit. And you'd never be in the union; you're too cheap to pay the dues. What's that you're reading?"

"Speed Sport," Jimmy explained. "Just looking over the points, trying to figure out if I can catch Graffan."

"I doubt it," Gene needled. "He's a helluva racer, that Graffan. People talk about him all over the country…best driver in USAC, that's what they say. Course, you can't believe everything you hear."

"You sure can't," Jimmy said, shaking his head at Gene. "Hey, gotta pull up, hang on."

Jimmy eased the truck forward a few feet, allowing the stream of grain to cascade farther back in the trailer. He set the brake and swung the door open again.

"I figure if we win the next two races, and he struggles some, we've got a shot."

"Has he been struggling?"

"Nope…they've been charmed all year, and haven't had any trouble."

"Well, there you go," Gene laughed. "Just ask him to cooperate, and you're in business."

"Nobody stays lucky forever," Jimmy insisted. "He's bound to have a bad night or two. Overdue, as a matter of fact."

Jimmy sat quietly in the booth at Pop's restaurant, listening as Bobby vented his frustration.

"The whole thing stinks," Bobby said, his fingers tightening around the amber bottle in his hand. "I'm pretty much all healed up, and the stupid doctor still won't let me race. What's he waiting for? Hell, I'm up and around all right, and my leg ain't hurtin' at all."

Jimmy said nothing, leaning against the side of the booth, eyeing his friend patiently.

"If I don't get goin' real soon, Fred's gonna stiff me on my ride, I know it! Jack Underwood finishes out the year, Fred will forget all about me…it ain't fair, I'm telling you. He said the ride was mine, but look at what's happened…he and Underwood hanging out together, havin' a good time, like I don't even exist anymore."

Bobby stewed, squirming in his chair. His hands spoke along with his voice, moving in swift, jerky motions, revealing his anxiety. After he fell silent, Jimmy spoke up.

"If Fred's car got bent and he quit for while, would you sit at home or would you go racing with somebody else?"

Bobby shot him an aggravated glance. "That ain't the same thing," he said. "A driver does this to make a living…Fred just runs the car for fun, kind of like a hobby."

"Fred told me the car has made money every year he's raced."

"Yeah, but...listen, whose side are you on? Don't you think the doctor should let me race? And ain't it only right that Fred keep the seat open for me? After all, I got hurt in his car. He owes me that much."

"Well, I *am* on your side. I'm not a doctor, so I can't say whether you're ready to race. And no matter whose car you got hurt in, nobody owes you anything. You get hurt, you get hurt. Part of the deal...you heal up and go back racing and hope somebody hires you. But there aren't any guarantees. Not in this business."

"Aw, I know that. But damn it, I want to race! I'm tired of driving that old truck every week. Getting up early, slogging down the highway, that ain't for me. I'm a racer, and that's all I want to do. You have no idea, Jimmy, what a drag it is to have to get up in the morning and go to some crappy job."

Jimmy glanced up from his bottle of beer, offering a patient smile. Bobby stared for a moment, then rattled on.

"Well, what I mean is, you don't have to work that hard. I mean, your job is easy, just driving around the countryside hauling corn. Ain't that right?"

Jimmy smiled and shrugged.

"Well...you don't get up early do you? I mean, why would you have to? There's no hurry getting stuff hauled to market...is there?"

"Usually we start at seven," Jimmy explained. "Sometimes earlier."

Bobby stared in amazement. "*Seven??!!* Why would anybody start that early? That's insane...I don't get goin' till nine, and even that's too early."

Jimmy shrugged again, drawing a slug from the bottle.

"Well, why do you do it, then?" Bobby quizzed. "You don't have kids at home or anything like that, so why do you need a job?"

Jimmy laughed. "Because I have to work, man. In the winter, I run out of money...don't you?"

"Nah...Sandy works at the library in the winter, so we have some money coming in."

"There you go," Jimmy nodded. "I don't have anybody else, so it's all on me. And I don't mind...it would drive me nuts to sit around the house. I like getting out and doing something."

Bobby leaned across the table, his brows knotted with

curiosity. "If you don't mind me asking, what do you do with your money?" he quizzed. "You're a single guy with no kids, and with the dough you make racing, plus your job, you've surely got all kinds of money. Plus, livin' rent-free in that trailer, you ought to be flush."

"I sure ain't flush," Jimmy said. "You know how it is with money…it comes in and it goes out. I got a little put back, but not near what I should have."

"Do you still help your folks out? It ain't none of my business, but I just wondered. I guess I'm bein' nibby."

"It's no big secret. Yeah, I was sending money to my mom, but not since June. It was mostly to help my sister get through her last year of college. She's the first one in our family to get a college degree, and that's a big deal. She wanted to drop out and get a job when my dad got hurt last year, but it would have been too bad to get that close without finishing.

"So I paid her tuition and stuff last year, and now she's all finished up. So hopefully my money will stick around a little longer now."

"I didn't know that," Bobby marveled. "You paid for your sister's college education? You're all right, killer. That's a swell thing to do."

"She's a swell kid," Jimmy explained. "I kind of owed her that. When I was in the Army I sent money home and figured out pretty quick that wasn't gonna work. My dad was still drinking, and he'd bully my mom for the money and go off on a binge.

"So I sent it to my sister, and didn't tell anybody. I kind of figured, you know, she's a kid and she'd keep a little bit back and spend the rest. When I got home from Vietnam, I didn't have 10 cents in my pocket…then I walk into the house and here's this money I'd sent home, right down to the penny. She was 16 years old, and she didn't use one dollar for herself. Pretty cool, if you ask me."

"Why were you so broke when you got home? Didn't you have some separation pay?"

Jimmy offered a wistful smile.

"Yeah, it got separated from me in a dice game the day after I got it."

Bobby laughed. "You ought to know better than throw the bones. Ain't good for your health."

"I know that…now."

They both laughed.

"So tell me again exactly what Fred told you," Jimmy said, steering the conversation back to Bobby's situation. "He told you this morning that you're still in the car when you get cleared, right?"

"Yes. But I gotta have a doctor's release. I saw the doc last week and he said no way. Not until the bone is healed a little more. But I'm walking just fine now, I'm all healed up. Pretty much."

"Then what's that cane you're using?"

"Huh? Oh, that. Just to kind of lean on. But my leg is strong as ever, man. No kiddin'."

"Yeah, I know. Just to lean on. So the doc won't release you, but Fred says you're still good when he does. Right?"

"Yeah, but—"

"All you can do is wait," Jimmy insisted. "Even if you have to drive the delivery truck all winter, it's not the end of the world. If Fred says you're still in the seat, I'll bet you are."

"It's all I can do to keep from bawling him out for making me have a release," Bobby ranted. "That's stupid…what's he care if I got a release? I can press down on the gas, can't I?"

Jimmy stared at his friend and smiled, slowly shaking his head.

"Maybe it's because he's your friend, and he doesn't want to see you get hurt. Ever think of that?"

Bobby made a face. "Nah," he barked. "He's just using it as an excuse to not hire me back. I know what's up."

"You're hopeless," Jimmy offered. "Stop worrying like an old lady and drink your beer. It's getting warm."

The old PA system echoed across the countryside surrounding Bluegrass Speedway, with the Saturday evening haze draped softly across the rolling hills. Jimmy watched carefully as Harvey looked over the car.

"You were slow, boy," Harvey began, shaking his head. "You timed 18th!"

"That's what happens when you draw such a late pill," Jimmy

explained. "Track slowed down a bunch."

Harvey looked at his driver and then at the track, offering only a skeptical shake of his head.

"Well, we better look at the setup," the big man said. "If it's already that dry...this place don't come back much after sundown, so we better work on it."

"No, don't change it," Jimmy insisted. "Just take it easy for a minute or two. We'll be all right."

"It's gotta be tighter," Harvey scoffed. "If I don't tighten it up you ain't goin' anyplace."

"Nah. It's perfect. Let's run the heat and see where we are."

Jimmy soon rolled out for his heat, where he lined up on the outside of row two. The field rumbled to the start, and Jimmy tiptoed on the cushion as he navigated through the first corner. He worked his way to the inside and spent several laps fighting side-by-side with Rick Wagner until the Johnson machine prevailed and began to pull away.

As Jimmy fought the car through turns one and two he caught a glimpse of Harvey, vigorously pointing for him to move up on the track. He ignored the instructions, fighting to hold the car on the inside through the remainder of the heat race.

He parked at their pit and climbed out. A few moments later Harvey hurried to the side of his car, wearing a look of agitation.

"What are you doin'?" he demanded. "Why you puttering around on the bottom? You were sixth, and we're in the semi!"

"There wasn't much left on the cushion," Jimmy argued. "I tried it early and it didn't work."

"You didn't try crap! You ran up there that first corner and then you got to the bottom like your car was on fire! What's the matter with you, boy? It ain't like you to fool around with the bottom!"

"Just take it easy," Jimmy insisted. "The bottom is going to come in, you'll see. I think the car is good, so we're all right."

Harvey snorted and waved his hands dismissively, turning his attention to the car.

"Might not need to fuel it, Slim," he mocked, looking at Jimmy. "Probably didn't even use a gallon, idling around on the bottom like that."

Jimmy headed down to the corner to watch the last couple of

heats. The next heat was a romp for Graffan, while the final heat got off to a rough start when Rusty Fernandez tangled with a local car, sending the local over the fourth turn guardrail. They dragged the two cars back to the pit area and the race resumed, with Sammy Caldwell winning.

Jimmy walked back to the pit area, where Virgil Moore and Rusty and a couple of helpers thrashed to repair their orange No. 55. Could they make the call for the B? It was going to be close…it took a front axle and a radiator and some new bodywork, and the men worked frantically.

"B main cars, let's go!" an official barked as he hurried past. "Get 'em to the lineup chute!"

Jimmy turned to the Ellison sprinter, reaching into the seat for his helmet. He climbed into the cockpit, buckling down as Slim checked the wheels one final time. Harvey checked the fuel level, then helped Slim as they rolled the car toward the chute.

Jimmy felt the truck engage his rear bumper, and they waited for the signal from the nearby official.

"Try to pass some cars, willya?" Harvey called out as Jimmy nodded. A moment later the official nodded and pointed, and the truck surged forward, bringing the Ellison car to rumbling life.

The field began to form up, and Jimmy found his starting spot in the fifth row. Transferring was going to be tough, but he felt confident they could get it done. As they raced off turn four to the start, Jimmy goosed the throttle and headed down the straightaway.

Another local car was on the pole, and as he entered turn one his car swapped ends, backing across the racing groove. Cars scattered everywhere, with nearly all the outside cars piling into one another and blocking the track. Jimmy first hit the brakes, but saw a tiny opening and shot through with a burst of acceleration.

As he rolled the backstretch the red light blinked on, and officials hurried to sort out the pileup. Jimmy waited patiently for several minutes, wondering how many cars would restart. Soon an official approached his car, glancing at a clipboard.

"Inside row two," the man called, and Jimmy nodded. This was a stroke of luck…now a transfer wasn't nearly so difficult.

They lined up the depleted field and tried again, this time without drama. Jimmy flirted with the outside groove, discovering a big cushion and some moisture. But his car felt tippy, so he moved back to the inside.

He rode third, then heard a car to his outside. Rusty worked the cushion to perfection and easily took the spot, but Jimmy doggedly stayed on the bottom. He hoped the race was about over, listening for a challenge from behind. It came from a dingy yellow car with a handful of laps remaining, the car working the middle groove just inches from Jimmy's right rear. The yellow car pulled even on the backstretch, carrying more momentum into the corner. Jimmy watched as the car pulled ahead, then dropped down a half-width to steal his line.

Jimmy's right foot released more of the Ellison's ponies as they came off the corner, pulling back alongside on the outside. They were side by side as they passed the white flag but Jimmy beat him into the corner, finessing the car in the middle groove. The Ellison car worked perfectly when it needed to, and Jimmy had the edge as they hit the last turn.

His foot felt for traction as they raced to the checkered flag, and he could hear the diminishing sound of the guy's engine and knew he had fourth.

Whew. We're in. By the skin of our teeth.

Harvey was nearly beside himself as Jimmy rolled to a stop in their pit. It wasn't often that the big man was speechless, but at the moment he seemed lost for words.

Jimmy climbed from the car and shrugged, tugging off his gloves and helmet. He tossed his stuff in the seat and wiped his face with a rag.

"I'll go check the lineup board while you fuel 'er up, Slim," he said.

As he began to step away he looked at Harvey, who stared at Jimmy as though he didn't know him.

"What's the matter with you?" Harvey finally said, extending his arms in a shrug.

"Nothing," Jimmy argued. "I'm doing the best I can. You think we need to change the setup?"

Harvey offered an ironic, sad laugh. "You ain't drivin' it hard enough for it to matter," he insisted, shaking his head. "What's up with you…why you actin' so weird?"

"I'm not acting anything," Jimmy retorted. "Let me check the lineup…I'll be right back."

He walked quickly to the board tacked up on the side of the infield concession stand. He found the number 49, counting the rows; inside of row eight, 15th starting spot. He looked at the car number in front of him, committing it to memory before he walked back to their pit.

Thirty laps would probably go by quickly, and he figured if he could keep the car in one piece maybe he could get into the top 10. Maybe Graffan and Sammy would have trouble and drop out; that sure wouldn't hurt.

Harvey had sensed Jimmy's mood; for the first time, Jimmy felt discouraged about their chances at the title. The long season was wearing on everybody, and Jimmy felt like he was running out of gas.

He hurried to add some tear-offs to his visor, and walked to the car. The pit area was bustling as cars began moving toward the lineup chute, and Jimmy climbed into the Ellison machine. He buckled down and grabbed his helmet, when suddenly Harvey's big paw reached inside the cockpit and pulled the helmet from his hands.

Jimmy looked up in surprise, and Harvey leaned so far into the cockpit Jimmy thought he might strap in with him. Their noses were three inches apart, and Harvey's blazing eyes bored directly into Jimmy's soul.

"Listen, boy, I don't know what's up with you, but you've got to wake your ass up," Harvey insisted.

"Nothing's wrong," Jimmy argued. "I just couldn't get my rhythm earlier."

"Rhythm…don't give me that. You were strokin' it, drivin' like you're scared. Listen, if you're scared for ANY reason, you need to get out. 'Cause you'll hurt yourself or somebody else."

"You're crazy," Jimmy said indignantly. "I told you—"

"ENOUGH!" Harvey said, his voice growing more powerful. He grasped Jimmy's chin, leaning even closer. "Wake the hell up! After I got busted up this spring, I didn't heal up just to come watch you run in the back."

Harvey stepped back, thrusting the helmet firmly into Jimmy's chest. "You either get serious and make this thing go, or I'll find somebody who will. And that's after I personally drag you out and stomp your candy ass!"

Jimmy felt a rush of anger welling up inside him, mixed with a liberating sense of excitement. His chest hurt from where Harvey had rammed the helmet, and Jimmy realized he was trembling with emotion. A fire rose from his belly, roaring up through his throat and turning his ears a deep shade of crimson.

His eyes blazed as he swore an epithet at Harvey. "Listen you fat sumbitch, you want this thing to go fast? You just watch."

Jimmy yanked his helmet into place, waving for them to roll him forward. A truck moved in behind him, and in a moment the Ellison car was alive, rolling onto the track. He realized he was out of breath, still trembling, and he tried to calm himself.

Take it easy, collect your thoughts, and focus on what you need to do here. Concentrate.

He couldn't see back in the pit area, where Harvey slowly smiled, nodding slightly. Had he lit the fire? The next 30 laps would provide the answer.

They would talk about this race until their dark hair turned gray, well past the long shadows of their autumn. Jimmy and the Ellison car reached a higher plane on this night, perhaps each surprising the other with performance that teetered on perfection.

Jimmy's emotions got a lift—as if he needed further motivation—within thirty seconds of the start, when a sudden plume of smoke enveloped the field far ahead of him. He blinked through the acrid fumes to see an oil-soaked Steve Graffan piling from the Strong sprinter almost before it had rolled to a stop, the bottom end of the engine scattered across hell's half-acre.

Now it was Graffan's turn in the bad-luck barrel…about damned time.

When the race resumed Jimmy put the Ellison machine on the cushion and planted his right foot on the belly pan. He moved past cars so quickly that it was almost an optical illusion, because most were having trouble with the tall ledge that had developed.

Harvey—along with just about everybody else—had been

wrong about this race track; the cool air brought the moisture up tonight, and everybody found their setup to be tight, tighter, or "uh-oh."

Jimmy found that the harder he pressed the Ellison car, the better it liked it. While others became cautious amid the treacherous conditions, Jimmy blasted by them on the outside, sometimes getting all four wheels over the cushion. Each time he kept his foot planted to stay off the wall, flirting with certain trouble but moving forward.

By the halfway point he trailed only Rick Wagner, who offered token resistance when Jimmy challenged. He quickly took command and stayed hard on the throttle, ripping past slower cars as though they were orange pylons on the highway.

He could see the crowd waving and jumping, could feel them reach through the din and the dust and infuse him further with their energy.

He knew he had the race won, and the mature man inside his brain began chirping.

"Slow down, fool," the voice cried. "You're gonna wad this thing into a little ball!"

But the kid inside the brain, the restless boy who never got enough excitement, began to shout down the reasoning.

Gas it up! It likes it...you ain't gonna turn over, because you're Superman. Nothing can touch you, Jimmy. You're the man. Invincible.

In the waning laps he began to have some trouble getting into turn one. He tripped on the cushion and the car bicycled wildly, slamming back down on its wheels, tires churning through the loose stuff and sending clods 40 feet into the air. The crowd responded with a roar of amazement and relief, and on the next lap Jimmy did it again, exactly the same.

As he saw the white flag, the mature voice in his brain shouted loud enough to get his attention, and he took the edge off but was still strong enough to get past two more lapped cars, realizing one of the cars was Harry Bell's No. 2 with Sammy Caldwell behind the wheel.

He eased off the throttle as he sped past the checkered flag, a sense of relief sweeping over him. It was kind of odd, really;

despite giving these guys a complete thrashing, Jimmy felt only modest satisfaction, tempered by the embarrassment that he had allowed himself to lose focus earlier tonight.

Jimmy rumbled to a stop on the front straight as the crowd rose in a loud and raucous ovation. Jimmy rapped the throttle hard a couple of times, smiling to himself that the car seemed to relish the abuse.

Some horses cower under the whip; others are born to perform best under the toughest of conditions. More than ever before, as the car fell silent he realized that the Ellison sprinter was indeed a very special machine.

Jimmy pulled the helmet from his head, gently unbuckling his harness. A couple of officials and the PA announcer approached the car, grinning with excitement as Jimmy offered a subdued smile.

He climbed from the seat and waved to the crowd as they saluted, and saw Harvey and Slim hurrying across the track.

Jimmy looked intently at Harvey as he approached, an amazed grin plastered across the big man's face. Jimmy folded his arms as he spoke with a soft, firm voice.

"Did you say something about a candy ass?"

"Hot damn, now THAT'S how you race!" Harvey bellowed, grabbing Jimmy in a bear hug and lifting him off the ground. "I ain't never seen a car go like that! Hot damn!"

The announcer moved alongside with the microphone, giving Jimmy a nice introduction that brought another roar from the crowd.

"What an amazing run," the man grinned. "From 15th to win, lapping all the way to fourth place! And with Steve Graffan out early, this might be the break you needed to get back in the hunt for the championship! Jimmy, do you think you can catch Steve at this point?"

"I don't think it, I know we can," Jimmy said in a matter-of-fact tone. "Write it down…we're *gonna* catch him. This is just the start."

The man nodded, enjoying the moment. "Jimmy, what a turnaround for you tonight. You struggled earlier, and just barely got the last transfer to get in tonight's feature. Obviously, it looks like Jack Harvey figured out what was wrong."

Jimmy eyes twinkled as he turned to look at Harvey.

"He sure did," Jimmy nodded, hearing his voice echo from the crowded grandstand across the way. "Harvey made a very important adjustment right before we rolled out to race. He knew exactly what we needed. No doubt about it."

Chapter 32

"You see the paper this morning?" Jimmy breathlessly asked Sonny Ellison, closing the office door behind him. "Matt Coffman is big news now, that's for sure!"

Sonny looked up and nodded, reaching for the morning edition and sliding it across the desk. "Front page news," he said, shaking his head. "I sure hate it for Matt."

Jimmy looked again in amazement at the headline: "TAX TROUBLE FOR SOUTHSIDE ASPHALT OPERATION." Under the main head was a sub that added more intrigue, "Owner nowhere to be found, believed to be in Mexico."

"It's like a mystery movie at the drive-in," Jimmy said, sliding into a chair. "What do you make of it?"

"Oh, Matt's got himself in a jam…there have been rumors floating around all summer, but you can always hear things like that. But based on the newspaper, it looks pretty grim."

"Man, this is perfect Coffman," Jimmy laughed. "It isn't enough to owe back taxes, but he has to be front page stuff."

"I have a feeling he's drinking a Mexican beer right now and waiting for things to cool off," said Sonny.

"Does it affect us?" Jimmy asked. "I mean, we've had his name on the car all season."

"I don't think so," Sonny assured him. "My deal with him was pretty simple, he gave me some money this spring and that was for the whole season. He was going to come across with another grand if we won the championship, but obviously that's out of the question at this point."

Jimmy's eyes twinkled. "You don't think we can win it?"

Sonny smiled, leaning back in his chair. "I don't think I'll get any money from Matt."

Jimmy laughed, nodding his head. They were quiet for a moment before Sonny spoke again, his voice growing more excited.

"I'll bet I've had a dozen phone calls from guys who were at Bluegrass this past weekend…you must have driven the race of your life, Jimmy. Wish I'd been there."

Jimmy couldn't help but smile as he recalled the night, and for a moment felt the same rush of emotions he felt in victory lane.

"It…it was really cool. I can't explain it, everything just fell together perfectly. You know, Sonny, this sounds goofy, but something tells me we are meant to win the championship. I just feel it in my gut."

"Say…do you really think we could catch Graffan? Boy, wouldn't that be something…after all we've been through this year, I figured the championship was out of the question. But I have to admit, you've gotten close enough now to make it interesting."

"Graffan's got to help us a little," Jimmy admitted. "With four races left, I have to win and he has to struggle. And don't forget about Sammy…he's right there with us, and they're running good."

"Nah…Sammy's jinxed. He's a great racer, but he's tried to win the title for 15 years and never done it. I don't think it's in the cards for him. No, I think it'll boil down to us and Graffan…just the way you like it."

"Give me a break," Jimmy groaned. "You'd think by now I'd be over it, but there's still something about him that gets under my skin."

"Is that why you tried to knock his head off this spring?" Sonny grinned. "I figured once you guys finally got the fistfight out of your system, you'd be best buddies."

"That'll be the day. Next thing you'll tell me is that we're going to a two-car team, and you're hiring Graffan."

"Maybe I'm hiring him for my one-car team," Sonny needled, studying Jimmy for a reaction.

Jimmy raised his eyebrows, then realized Sonny's game. "That would be good, you and Graffan," he replied. "That would mean me and Bob Strong would have to team up…man, he's got some pristine race cars, doesn't he? And spares for everything! Wonder what that would be like, racing for a high-buck deal like that… makes a guy think, doesn't it?"

Sonny laughed, then winced, reaching over to hold up the newspaper headline.

"I'd buy all those spares too, but they keep running my sponsors out of town!"

The air turned chilly at Franklin on Sunday afternoon, but a huge crowd poured into the stands to watch the USAC sprinters in action. It was only fitting that the final events of the season would take place on the series most stalwart tracks: Franklin, Jackson County, Shoe's, and Sunset Park.

Jimmy and the Ellison team came into the event with an enormous amount of confidence. On the flip side, you didn't have to be an expert to see that Bob Strong's team was in turmoil: Steve Graffan and his red-haired crew chief, Billy Hobbs, even had a heated shouting match as they prepared to qualify.

Jimmy and Harvey watched from a few stalls away, grinning in spite of themselves.

"Harvey, would you look at that?" Jimmy said, his expression turning serious. "Look at how that mechanic is being so abusive to his driver. Isn't that awful? He ought to be banned for life."

"Well, his driver probably had it coming," Harvey said, nodding his head. "After all, race drivers ain't got the sense God gave a goose. But it sure is nice…while they're yellin' at each other, they ain't paying attention to their race car."

"Hey, did you hear the news about Coffman? He's in big trouble for dodging his taxes…big write-up in the paper this week."

"Yeah, I heard. Can't say I'm surprised. He's a real piece of work, him and that sleazy wife of his. Guys like that, you can spot 'em a mile away…big mouth, flashy jewelry, know-it-all. Can't trust a one of 'em."

"Isn't it weird how they wore us out at the first few races of the year, then all of a sudden, we never saw 'em again?" Jimmy recalled. "I don't miss 'em in the least, but it's kind of funny how they just stopped coming around."

"That's because she was hot for your tail, boy. But you shut her down…you saw that look in her eyes, and you ran for the woods like a scared rabbit!"

"You're crazy," Jimmy objected. "I did no such thing."

Harvey roared with laughter, enjoying the exchange. "Yeah, you run off and hid! I think you figured she could hurt you, boy…

and she probably could! She definitely had the kind of experience that matters. But, hey…ain't no education like an older woman."

Jimmy just shook his head, starting to walk away.

Harvey roared again with laughter.

"I got it right, didn't I, boy! Ran off and crawled under the porch is what you did! Afraid you'd lose your virginity!"

Jimmy couldn't help but grin as Harvey cackled. A couple of USAC officials paused as they walked past, looking with amused curiosity at the sight of Harvey guffawing loudly.

"Ignore him," Jimmy said, pointing at Harvey. "He hit his head earlier this year, and…well, you know. He ain't right."

Everybody who wandered past the Ellison pit stopped to visit with Jimmy, and he could sense a genuine sense of excitement about the points race. Barry Kane, the writer who covered the series, had a whole range of scenarios worked out.

"If you win all four races, you're gonna be close no matter what," Kane explained. "If you fall out of one race, you'd just about be finished. And if Graffan can win a race, it would be awful tough to catch him."

"I think you predicted we'd finish fifth or sixth in points this year," Jimmy said, enjoying the way Kane's eyes widened as Jimmy gave him a hard time. "I'm glad we could exceed your lowly expectations."

"Aw…I just call 'em like I see 'em," Kane stammered. "It's nothing personal."

"I understand," Jimmy kidded. "But if we happen to win it, will you pick us to win it again next year?"

Kane hesitated. "Listen, here's how it is…Bob Strong has all the best stuff, Billy Hobbs is an excellent wrench, and Steve is a top-notch driver. As long as they're together, the title is theirs to lose. Nothing against anybody else, but those are the facts."

Jimmy listened, and he couldn't dispute anything Kane said. "I guess that's why it feels so good when we beat 'em."

"I'm sure it does. You want to hear something amazing? I stopped by their shop a couple of weeks ago, and Hobbs showed me around. Man, they've got a spare of EVERYTHING, but listen to this: they don't just have one spare engine, they have TWO! Isn't that incredible?"

"Dang," Jimmy mused. "We don't even have one. Not put together, anyways."

The feature race was a good one, with Jimmy in the middle of a three-way fight with Rick Wagner and Rusty Fernandez. His spirits soared when he saw Graffan parked on the apron in turn two in the early laps, but it looked like he restarted. Jimmy had no idea where Sammy was running.

Not that he had a spare moment to watch, anyways. He had his hands full with Wagner and Rusty, and the three snarling machines bucked and bounced as they plowed through the usual holes and ruts that you could expect at Franklin.

After Graffan's early yellow the race went green the rest of the way. Around the midway point Jimmy sensed he had enough momentum to finally dispense with his two challengers, and for several laps they faded out of earshot.

Whether he got worse or they got better he didn't know, but with five laps to go he suddenly found them snapping as his tail once again. He tried changing lines a couple of times, and found a nice exit off four that seemed to help him. Wagner was suddenly very good on the outside, and Rusty found something on the bottom, and as Jimmy saw their rear bumpers he knew he had to try something different.

He moved to the cushion, leaving a heartbeat of space behind Wagner. They took the white flag, and Jimmy made a hard run into one, watching as the space between he and Wagner disappeared. He cut the wheel to the inside, driving across the middle of the groove, his tires finding enough traction to make it three wide as they exited the corner.

They roared down the backstretch as Jimmy realized he had cleared Wagner, and he moved to the outside once again. As they hit turn three Rusty worked the inside to perfection, but Jimmy managed to gain momentum as they drag raced to the flag. The Ellison sprinter screamed as they came off the corner, and Jimmy fought the wheel as the tires scratched at the dusty surface.

The car lurched just enough that the right rear tire banged hard against the outside wall, and for an instant Jimmy thought he might tip over. But he kept his foot in the gas, and he was pretty sure he had beaten Rusty to the flag.

He felt the car vibrating badly as he slowed through the east turn, and he knew the rap on the wall had knocked something askew. He and Rusty rumbled back to the front straightaway, where starter Mike Rydman pointed his checkered flag at Jimmy as the official winner.

Jimmy stopped the car and quickly climbed out, acknowledging the crowd's roar with a wave. He pulled his gloves from his hands as he hurried around the car to look at the right rear.

The wheel was clearly bent, and he looked more closely. The suspension looked okay, but he couldn't tell if he had bent the rear end as well.

Harvey and Slim hurried over, excitedly whooping and hollering.

"You beat him by less than a car length!" Harvey yelled. "Attaboy! Way to hang in there!"

He saw Jimmy looking at the rear end. "What's the matter? What you lookin' at?"

"Banged the right rear on the wall there at the finish," Jimmy panted, smoothing his sweaty hair with his hand. "Got the wheel for sure…hope I didn't get the rear end. Hit 'er pretty hard."

"I'll look at it tomorrow. Hey, helluva win, boy! Two in a row!"

"Where did Graffan finish?"

"Toward the back!" Slim offered. "Spun out there at the start and didn't go anywhere after that."

"How about Sammy?"

"Third," Harvey said glumly. "Passed Wagner right at the end."

The bright sunshine made the cool late-afternoon air tolerable as Jimmy greeted fans on the front straightaway, savoring the moment. People buzzed with excitement, offering encouragement.

"Two in a row!"

"You're gonna catch Graffan, I know it!"

"Way to go, Jimmy!"

Jimmy looked up to see a special-needs kid rushing toward him, bursting with enthusiasm. Jimmy guessed the kid was in his middle-teens, and he politely stuck out his hand as the boy approached. But the kid grabbed him in a huge hug, rocking him backwards and shouting, the torrent of words coming so quickly Jimmy couldn't understand a thing he was saying.

A middle-aged guy Jimmy guessed was the kid's father smiled and he helped calm the kid down.

"His name is Jimmy," the dad said. "We were at Bluegrass last week, and when he heard your name on the PA he got all excited, because you have the same name. He cheered for you at Bluegrass, and he insisted that we drive over today because the 49 is 'his' car."

"My name is Jimmy too!" the boy shouted. "Your name Jimmy!"

"Yes, I'll call you 'Little Jimmy,' how's that?"

The boy shrieked. "I little Jimmy! You BIG Jimmy!"

Jimmy laughed, feeling a little awkward because he didn't exactly know how to deal with a kid in this situation.

The kid said something else, but Jimmy struggled to understand him.

"He says he's your good luck charm," the father explained. "Both times he's seen you, you've won."

"Well, there you go," Jimmy grinned. "You'd better come down to Jackson next week…I'll take every little bit of luck I can get."

"Yeah!" the boy shouted, then suddenly turned to his dad. "We go to Jackson? Where's Jackson? Is it California?"

"No, it's here in Indiana, a couple of hours from home," the dad explained patiently.

"If you promise to come to Jackson and bring me luck, I've got something for you," Jimmy said, reaching into the seat of the car and hoisting today's trophy. "Here you go, take it home with you."

The kid was so excited he squealed, jumping up and down.

"That's awfully nice of you," the dad said, growing serious. "Are you sure you want to give such a nice trophy away?"

"Sure," Jimmy assured him. He didn't bother to tell the guy that when you live in a tiny dump of a trailer, you don't have room to keep any trophies anyway.

Jimmy had never felt quite comfortable at Jackson, and all week he worried. Even though the track was a high-banked half-mile paved track very similar to his all-time favorite, Sunset Park,

Jimmy had never figured the place out.

He was grateful that his last-lap adventure with the Franklin guardrail had resulted only in a bent wheel. Even when you win, if you bend the car you're going to hear it from Harvey. But the big guy was in great humor…when you're on a win streak that mood comes easier.

Jimmy tried to ignore all the rattling in his brain about the point race, but there was no escaping it. Every person he encountered at the track brought it up, offering encouragement and advice. As Slim helped him buckle in for the feature, he tried in vain to quell the butterflies in his belly.

But once the car was fired his emotions quickly settled down and he focused on matters at hand. The race immediately shaped up as a three-way fight between the point leaders: Graffan, Jimmy, and Sammy. The veteran Sammy had a ton of laps at Jackson, and he used every ounce of his experience to keep the younger men at bay.

They got into dense traffic, where Sammy was particularly skilled, and Jimmy had to hustle the car to keep up. Graffan seemed to have the stronger car early on, but as the laps clicked away he began to fade and it became a two-man race.

The Ellison sprinter was very good, and Jimmy had to drive it perfectly to keep up with Sammy. He stayed right on the back bumper of Harry Bell's No. 2, desperately trying to figure out how to make a run at him.

His lucky break—and Jimmy couldn't call it anything but—came when they encountered a lapped car as they saw the white flag. Sammy was committed to the outside, and as they hit the front straightaway the slower car hesitated for a moment before swinging wide at the flag stand. Sammy was forced to brake for an instant, and that was all it took.

Jimmy was on him like a dog after raw meat, knowing this was his only shot. The Ellison car swept alongside Sammy and used the slower car as a pick, rolling into the lead as they hurtled toward the first turn. Jimmy flogged the car for all it was worth coming off, knowing Sammy would not go easily.

The veteran came right back at him, pulling to Jimmy's inside as they approached the final turn. The two screaming cars were side-by-side, but Jimmy had a much better line into the corner on the outside. He heard Sammy breathing the throttle slightly as the fought the tighter inside lane, and Jimmy pulled him by a car length as they flashed under Mike Rydman's checkered flag.

Three in a row, Jimmy mused, catching his breath. *And this one was kind of a gift...hmmm, maybe there is something to Little Jimmy being my good luck charm. You never know...*

He thought for a moment about points: Sammy was second, so he didn't pick up much. Plus Graffan had hung in there for third, making it awfully tough to gain any ground. Still...a win is a win, and this felt good.

Jimmy greeted well-wishers on the front straightaway, standing alongside the cooling Ellison machine. He kept an eye on the line of people pouring through the opening at the flag stand, and he finally caught a glimpse of Little Jimmy and his dad.

The boy rushed toward him, screaming with excitement, nearly bowling him over in a hug.

"Listen, I sure hope you're coming to Shoe's next week," Jimmy grinned at the father. "I'm beginning to think this good luck thing is working!"

"We'll be there," the man laughed. "Are you kidding? All he's talked about for the past week was that trophy. He took it to school to show it off, and he keeps it right by his bedside. You bet we'll be at Shoe's...as far as he's concerned, you're the greatest!"

Chapter 33

Sonny eased the pickup truck into the parking lot at Ellison Paving, cutting off the engine.

"Thanks for coming along," he said to Jimmy as they stepped from the vehicle. "It's good to have some company at these equipment auctions."

"Aw, I love going to a sale," Jimmy nodded. "But I noticed you didn't open that checkbook today."

"Don't have any money," moaned Sonny.

"Then why'd you go?" Jimmy teased.

"Doesn't cost anything to look...kind of like women, Jimmy. Doesn't cost a penny to look over the inventory, even if you're not in the market."

Jimmy laughed. "Spoken like a married man."

They glanced up to see a small caravan of vehicles sweeping into the parking lot, pulling up near the race shop. A sheriff's car led the way, followed by a black sedan and a tow truck pulling a flatbed trailer.

"What's this?" Sonny said, eyeing the sheriff's car with concern. They hurried over as two men in dark suits climbed from the sedan.

Harvey and Slim came walking from the shop, eyeing the group. As Sonny and Jimmy approached the sedan a short, stocky guy in a dark suit reached into his breast pocket and flashed his identification.

"I'm agent Pickens, and this is agent McConnell," he said, nodding to the other suit. "We're with the Internal Revenue Service."

Sonny looked suspiciously at the two men. "All right...what's this about?"

The short guy continued, producing a sheet of paper. "We're here to take into our possession property related to the Coffman

Materials Company, 6815 South Bluff Road, Central City. On behalf of the Federal government of the United States of America, certain property is to be retained by our agency until tax liabilities owed by Coffman Materials Company are satisfied."

Sonny's expression was a mixture of confusion and irritation.

"Well, you're standing on the property of Ellison Paving and Construction, Inc. This company has nothing to do with Coffman Materials other than we used to purchase a considerable amount of asphalt material from them. I hate to tell you this, gentlemen, but you're barking up the wrong tree. I suggest you go back to Coffman's place. You won't find any of his property here."

The short guy cocked his head and gave a smug laugh. "No sir, that isn't correct," he said. "According to documents filed by Matthew Coffman earlier this year, you have in your possession an asset and/or assets related to his company. And we intend to remove those assets from the premises as part of an ongoing action against Coffman Materials to satisfy a tax liability."

Sonny shook his head. "And what 'asset' would I have that belongs to Coffman?"

The agent nodded toward the open door of the race shop, where the Ellison sprinter sat in silence.

"You have a racing car, number 49, white with red and blue trim. Mr. Coffman specifically listed said item in an inventory sheet filed as part of a loan application with American Fletcher National Bank on May 18 of this year. Said property has now been duly located and is to be removed pertaining to liquidation proceedings to begin within the next two months."

The Ellison group—Sonny, Jimmy, Harvey, and Slim—nearly came unhinged. All four began talking at once, instinctively moving themselves between the agents and the open shop door as a parent would protect a child.

The agents raised their hands for quiet, and by now Sonny was shaking with anger.

"Mister, you have no idea how wrong you are," he charged. "I don't care what Coffman listed…this car belongs to me and I've got the papers to prove it."

The short agent walked into the shop, and the group followed.

The man pointed to the lettering, "Coffman Asphalt" on each side of the hood.

"If it's not Coffman's car, how do you explain that? Looks pretty official to me."

Sonny immediately pointed to the lettering on the side panel: "Ellison Special."

"There's my name…doesn't that look official, too?"

"Listen," said the taller agent, speaking in a low, calm voice. "You say you've got papers. Let's see 'em."

"I don't have them here, they're at my accountant's office. I can have them here first thing in the morning."

"No good," said the shorter agent. "We're under an order from the United States government to seize any assets related to this case as soon as they are located. No exceptions."

"But if you'll just be patient, I can sort this whole thing out!" Sonny said, growing more exasperated. "This is all a misunderstanding, I'm telling you!"

"Yeah, right," the agent said with a laugh. "It's always a misunderstanding. You'll have your chance to prove your case."

"He shouldn't have to prove it!" Jimmy objected. "You can't just come on a man's property and take something just because some crook said it belonged to him! That's nothing but legal stealing!"

"Look, maybe you're right about this being your car," the taller agent said sympathetically. "But don't worry…just come to the hearing with the ownership papers, and if they're legit the judge will release the car to you."

"When is the hearing?"

"November 18. Federal building, downtown."

All four men groaned.

"That's no good," Sonny offered. "We're in the middle of a race for the championship, and we have two more events over the next two weeks. You can't take the car now…our whole season will go up in smoke!"

"We have no choice but to take the car," the taller agent said. "We don't make the rules, we're just following them."

Sonny looked at the deputy, a younger guy he had seen around town.

"Is this legal?" he asked. "These guys can come onto my

property and take something that's mine, just because somebody else misrepresented themselves to a bank? How can that be right?"

"They've got the papers," the deputy said, shaking his head. "Nothing I can do…legally, they have every right to take the race car. It's all laid out in this repossession order, signed by a federal judge. We don't want any trouble, Mr. Ellison. I suggest you cooperate fully with these men."

Sonny was beginning to accept the inevitable. "Then something is wrong with the law," he said angrily. "You haven't heard the last of this, I promise you."

The men stood looking at each another, and the body language said it all. The two agents were flushed with a growing sense of victory, while Sonny and his guys began to sag with the realization of the inevitable.

"Well, let's get this done," said the short agent, walking toward the car. He reached into a folder for a black and white photo, holding it up to look at the car.

"Okay…a white race car, number 49…yes, this is it."

"May we see the picture?" Sonny asked.

The agent handed him the photo.

"Looks like Western," Slim said, pointing to the background.

"Say, we were loose!" Harvey said. "Should have tightened 'er up a hair."

Sonny handed the photo back to the agent, who nodded at the tow truck operator.

"Let's get this thing loaded."

"Hey, wait a minute," Jimmy spoke up. "You've got to let us get the motor out."

The agents looked at him in confusion.

"Can I see that bank document?" Jimmy asked. The agent shuffled in the manila folder and produced a sheet of legal paper. Jimmy scanned the list of assets and found the description. Sprint car, white No. 49.

"Okay, it says sprint car. But it doesn't say anything about the motor."

"What are you talking about?" the agent said, his eyes narrowing.

"Everybody in racing knows that a car and a motor are two

different things…you say you've got the right to take the car, fine. But notice how Coffman didn't list the motor…that's a separate asset. Just because you've got a right to the car doesn't give you the right to the motor. Let us take it out, and you can be on your way."

The taller agent looked at his colleague with uncertainty. Now they were off-balance, and the short agent looked at the document and the car, his lips drawn.

"Well, c'mon," Jimmy pressed. "You have no right to the motor, because it's not listed here. Give us an hour and we'll have it out."

Harvey took the lead and stepped toward the toolbox.

"C'mon, Slim, let's get to pullin' it," he said, sliding open a drawer.

"Hold it right there," the short agent commanded, stiffening up. "The motor is an integral part of the car, no matter what you say."

Harvey began to remove the hood, oblivious to the man.

"Don't touch the car!" the agent commanded, his voice growing louder. "We are taking this car as is. Nothing is to be removed."

Harvey shrugged and stepped away, tossing the wrench back on the bench.

The agents and the tow truck guy moved to the front of the car and leaned in to push it outside. That's when Jimmy noticed that the upholstery seemed different…it was more of a dark brown instead of black. He glanced at the dash, and immediately spotted that the gauges were different than he remembered.

He shot a glance at Harvey, who was studying Jimmy from across the room. The big man offered a slight shake of his head, and Jimmy looked back at the car in confusion.

The agents tried to push the car, but it was obviously in gear. They stepped back, looking lost.

"Uh…how do you release the brake?" the tall agent asked.

"You smart guys work for the government," Harvey cackled. "Figure it out."

The short agent was losing his patience. He turned to the tow truck driver and growled, "Put a cable on this thing, and drag it outside. I don't care if you tear off every wheel, just get it on the trailer."

The man nodded, and began walking toward the truck.

"All right, take it easy," Harvey said. He reached in to take the car out of gear and stepped back.

The three men rolled the Ellison sprinter outside, and in a moment had it up on the flat trailer.

"I want a receipt," Sonny insisted. "You can't take it without a receipt!"

"It isn't your property," said the short agent, tossing the manila folder in his car. "I don't have to give you anything."

They watched as the men climbed into the sedan, and the tow truck driver began to pull away. The two cars followed him off the property, with the deputy bringing up the rear. Soon they disappeared down the street and the scene was quiet.

The four men stared off in the general direction, saying nothing. Jimmy's mind raced with emotion…it was three days before the race at Shoes, and they had nothing. How could it come to this?

He looked over at Sonny, who stood in heartbroken silence. Jimmy had never seen his friend so distressed. But Jimmy's feelings of sadness and confusion were quickly swept aside, replaced by anger and determination.

Nobody—not even the United States government—was going to stop them from winning the championship. That much he knew.

Chapter 34

Jimmy clenched his fists in anger; everything they had worked for this season was gone. The injustice was burning in his heart, tinged with frustration that the legal system could work like this.

"Well, there it goes," Sonny finally spoke. "Boys, I'm sorry…I never thought Matt Coffman was capable of something like this. I'm sorry we're in this mess because of someone I thought was my friend."

"It's not your fault," Jimmy reassured him. "Besides, we're in this together. We'll figure something out. You'll see."

Sonny replied with a deep sigh.

"That's pretty optimistic…how can we possibly come up with everything we need to build a new car in three days? Actually, two days, when you get right down to it. Plus, what about a motor? Face it, boys…we're done."

"Aw, cheer up, Sonny!" Harvey called out, offering a loud laugh. "Look at the great tax deduction they lined up for you!"

Sonny and Jimmy shot an angry glance at Harvey. This wasn't the moment for jokes, or laughter. But the big man just grinned broadly.

"You've got rotten timing, Harvey," Jimmy snapped. "They just took our race car, and you're making a joke. Knock it off!"

"Hey, you're wrong, boy!" Harvey countered, a gleam in his eye. "They got our car…but they didn't get *OUR* car."

Jimmy and Sonny stopped and stared at Harvey in confusion.

"What are you saying?" Sonny finally spoke.

"Well, let's just put it this way…maybe those smart ol' government men didn't exactly get what they thought they were getting."

Suddenly Jimmy remembered the different upholstery, and the different look of the gauges on the dash as the agents rolled the car out of the shop. A rush of exhilaration swept through him.

"Holy crap!" he exclaimed. "Harvey…are you saying that wasn't our car?"

"How many times I got to tell you, boy…man's got to get up mighty early to put one over on ol' Harvey."

The men were so excited they could hardly contain themselves, everybody talking at once. Sonny held up his hand for quiet.

"Harvey, tell me exactly what just happened. And don't leave out anything."

"Well, it's like this…I saw in the newspaper about 'ol Coffman gettin' his tit in the wringer with the government. I been thinking about it, just about all the time, worryin' that some of his stink might drift over our way. Made me nervous, havin' his name on the car.

"First thing this morning when I come in, a slick-lookin' lawyer type was parked in front of our shop, sittin' in his car lookin' through some papers. When I unlocked the door, he comes walkin' over, real easy-like, but I could tell he was up to something.

"He says, 'Say, is that a sprint car in there?' I says, 'Who wants to know?' Well, he hem-haws around a bit, and asks if he could see it. I let him have a look, and he says, 'Number 49. That's it.' Then he thanks me and hurries out to his Cadillac and wheels out the driveway. Right then I knew something was up.

"I didn't like the smell of this deal, 'cause all of a sudden I had a hunch they were lookin' for this car. Now, we know this car don't belong to nobody but us, but they don't know that. And no way could I let 'em take what is a hundred percent ours.

"At first I figured I'd just take the car out of sight, but that's no good. They'd just wait till we showed up at the race track and that'd be all she wrote. So I got to thinkin'…them government boys ain't gonna know one race car from another. Right about that time Slim comes rollin' in, and we put the car on the trailer and headed for Sid Johnson's place. That's where our car is, right now."

Sonny and Jimmy stared at each other in disbelief.

"You stinking genius," Jimmy said, barely able suppress a laugh. "I could almost kiss that fat, ugly face of yours."

Harvey cackled. "Ain't I told you I'm smart, boy? Ain't I?"

"Harvey," Sonny said, trying to sort it all out. "If that wasn't *our* car…what car was it?"

"Remember that car Harry Bell built for Sammy, probably five years ago?"

"Six years," Slim corrected.

"It was five," Harvey insisted. "It was about the same time we got our car together. Well, Sammy turned it over at Shoes, and Harry sold it to Fred Otley. Rick Wagner twice got on his head in the car, and they replaced about half the frame. Never could get it workin' right, and it wound up with some young boy from Ohio.

"The kid was down on his luck and Sid felt sorry for him, so he let the kid trade him the frame for some wheels and a rear end—"

"It wasn't a rear end, it was a steering box," Slim interjected. "He said it was a steering box."

"It was a rear end," Harvey argued. "Anyhow, a couple of years ago Graffan crashed Sid's car up at Sunset, and they dragged this old frame out and got it going as a backup. Sid said the car was so evil it probably couldn't fall out of a tree by itself, so he rolled it back in the barn and ain't touched it since."

The men stared at Harvey, still in complete shock.

"Anyways, that's the car they got. It's a junk frame, with a motor that don't run, a bent rear end, and our tank and body work. I figured we better use our body just in case they had pictures. Which them sons-a-bitches did."

They looked at each other for a moment, then burst out laughing. Their cheeks flushed with color, they shared the joy of men spared from the gallows at the last moment. They began to regain their composure, when Sonny suddenly turned stone sober, the color draining from his face.

"Wait," he whispered. "Oh, boy, wait."

"What's the matter?" Jimmy quizzed.

"Guys, think about it…we just defrauded the federal government. This is no laughing matter."

Jimmy let out a low, slow whistle. "Leavenworth, here we come."

"To hell with them!" Harvey bellowed. "They got no right to take what ain't theirs!"

"Something tells me those two agents wouldn't see it that way," Sonny insisted. "I don't think they'd enjoy being had."

"Especially that smart-mouthed little prick," Slim nodded.

"Listen very carefully," Sonny instructed. "Nobody—and I mean absolutely nobody—can know about this. The four of us, and that's it."

"What about Sid?" Jimmy asked.

"Hmmm…Harvey, how much does Sid know? What'd you tell him?"

"I just told him I was in a jam, and had to leave our car there. I also said I needed to borrow that old heap he had in the barn. And I said he ought not to ask any questions, 'cause I couldn't answer 'em."

"Well…what did he say?"

"Aw, you know 'ol Sid. He's all right. He just told me to take what I needed. Even helped me and Slim swap the tank and bodywork."

The seizure of the Ellison car was the buzz throughout the pit area at Shoes, particularly since a news story had appeared in the Central City newspaper. Everyone came by to see the "new" car; flat black body panels with a white number 49 on the tank, a far cry from the pearl white and gold leaf paint job they were accustomed to seeing.

Barry Kane was one of the many who stopped by the Ellison pit. Taking notes for his story in the racing papers, he nodded to Jimmy as he drew out a pen and a pad of paper.

"Anything interesting happen this week?" he kidded.

"Oh, pretty uneventful," Jimmy smiled.

"When did you know they were taking the car?"

"Wednesday, when they came and got it."

"I'll bet it was a shock."

"That's putting it mildly."

"How…I mean, how could you guys possibly get another car together so quickly? Two, three days? That's amazing."

"Jack Harvey is the greatest when it comes to preparation," Jimmy explained. "He's always ready for whatever comes his way, no matter what it is."

"So you guys had another car ready? A backup?"

Jimmy smiled coyly.

"Remember, we're running for a championship," he said carefully. "You've got to have contingency plans…just in case."

Kane nodded. "I still say it's amazing that you're here, and you've got a car. Pretty cool story."

"I think you're missing the story," Jimmy offered.

"What do you mean?"

"Well, the deal with our car was just one of those weird things that happen. We'll get it back, and it will all be forgotten. But the real story is what happens on the race track. You've got three guys separated by just a few points with today and one more weekend left to go. That's a heckuva story, in my opinion."

"Oh, you're right, that's the story," Kane quickly agreed. "But you've got to admit, getting your race car taken away by the IRS, that's big news."

"Nah," Jimmy said, smiling and shaking his head. "That's just a misunderstanding. You'll see."

Soon all attention turned to the high-banked half-mile dirt oval for the first of two 40-lap features. It was almost like a script, with Jimmy lined up fifth right behind Steve Graffan. The man he was chasing for the title was right in his sights, with the third man in the scenario—Sammy Caldwell—alongside Jimmy.

Sammy asserted himself right away, and went straight to the front. Jimmy locked into a hot duel with Graffan, the two cars fighting for traction on a surface that was drying out under the October sun.

It was another of their great confrontations; each man was a good racer in his own right, but each would especially get up on the wheel when challenged by the other. It was about more than money, or finishing position, or points. This matchup always boiled down to pride, and emotion.

Graffan was working the middle groove, and Jimmy was on the cushion. As they came off turn two Jimmy had a nice run to his outside, but Graffan drifted high. Jimmy moved the Ellison car dangerously close to the fence, but it was too late. Graffan's momentum carried him into Jimmy's groove just as the Ellison car swept alongside.

The two cars banged wheels, and Jimmy fought to maintain control. In a moment he was back on the throttle, and Graffan disappeared from view. After taking a moment to settle himself, Jimmy concentrated on running Sammy down.

As the laps clicked away Jimmy inched closer, and was soon on Sammy's bumper. The Ellison car was working very well, and Jimmy studied his quarry, sizing him up for a weakness that meant opportunity. But Sammy was strong, and Jimmy realized that it would take a perfect move to get past him.

With five to go Jimmy made a run off turn four, pulling to the inside as they roared past the flag stand. They entered turn one hub-to-hub, inches apart, with Sammy refusing to yield an inch. Jimmy realized he didn't have enough momentum to make it work, and as they came off two Sammy pulled back in front.

It took Jimmy a couple of laps to regain his momentum, and he knew he was almost out of time. With two laps remaining they encountered heavy traffic as they cleared turn four.

Three cars were racing hard for position, using the entire race track. Both Sammy and Jimmy had no choice but to check up slightly.

Like a summer re-run, this one played out exactly like the race at Jackson County one week earlier, with Sammy again on the wrong side of racing luck. His natural line was the outside, where there appeared to be an opening. But one of the slower cars swung wide on the back straightaway, forcing Sammy to lift. In less than a heartbeat Jimmy shot into the opening now looming in the middle groove.

The Ellison car cleared the traffic as they took the white flag, and he hustled the car as much as possible. In a moment Jimmy flashed under Mike Rydman's checkered flag and eased off the throttle.

Jimmy's confidence soared, and he felt certain they were destined to win the championship. How else could you explain it? This was four wins in a row, and nobody had an answer for them. They were fast, they were ready, and more importantly, luck had been running their way.

His mind raced, already consumed by the second feature race coming up. The track was definitely getting slicker, but how much? The invert was six for the next race, so they would certainly need to pass some cars.

Jimmy climbed from the Ellison car on the front straightaway for photos and a quick interview. The PA guy pointed to the car.

"Jimmy, folks are probably a little bit surprised with the appearance of your car. It's usually a beautiful white, but this is a brand new car. Lots of stories circulating about what happened this week, do you care to tell us about it?"

Jimmy grinned and nodded. "Why, sure," he began. "Pretty simple, really. We loaned our car to the government."

A cascade of laughter echoed from the grandstands, and a smattering of applause. The PA guy began to laugh before composing himself.

"What do you suppose the government is going to do with it?"

"I think the President wants to go sprint car racing," Jimmy continued. "You never know, he might be in the car at Sunset next week. Come out to the track and see!"

A push truck rolled him back to their pit, where Harvey was waiting with arched eyebrows.

"Did that damned Graffan run into you? I oughta wring his neck!"

"Nah, he just moved off the middle, and he couldn't have known I was there. We just banged wheels and tried to get away from each other…no big deal."

"He must figure differently," Harvey said, nodding down the way. "Here he comes, and he don't look happy."

Jimmy saw Graffan storming in his direction, surrounded by a throng of people.

"What's your problem??!!" Graffan hissed, waving his arms like a maniac. "You ran right over me!!"

"You're crazy!" Jimmy countered. "You're the one who moved…I had the line and you came out into me!"

"I'm sick of you hitting my race car!!" Graffan ranted, so animated he was flinging spit through the air. "You've ran into me every other week this year, and it's over, do you understand??!! Lay off me!!"

Graffan moved so close that Jimmy could see the tiny red blood vessels in his eyes, and feel the heated air from his breath. It was obvious Graffan was about to explode, and Jimmy knew it couldn't just be from such a marginal issue as the wheel-banging. Was it the heat of the points race? Was Graffan finally cracking under the pressure?

Jimmy seized the opportunity to throw gasoline on the fire. He slowly smiled, a grin spreading across his face and a laugh rising from his throat.

Graffan's voice raised another octave. "Don't you laugh at me!!" he screamed. "I'll knock your head off!!"

Jimmy just kept laughing, knowing that would surely send him over the edge.

Graffan suddenly drew back to swing, but several officials and a couple of Graffan's crew grabbed him and wrestled him away.

"That's enough!" Al Petrov barked to Graffan's guys. "Get him back to your pit! NOW!"

As they dragged him away Graffan wrested free for a moment, pointing his finger at Harvey.

"Mister, I'm gonna wreck your race car!!" he blustered. "You hear me?"

Harvey straightened up, his eyes boring directly into Graffan's, his voice calm and even.

"That's fine, boy. But just remember, you touch my car, I'm gonna stomp your puny little ass into a mud hole. And it ain't gonna take me two seconds to do it. Keep that in mind."

In a moment the excitement had abated, with all but a few stragglers dispersing from the scene. Jimmy looked at Harvey with a sheepish smile.

"You sure pushed his button," Harvey nodded. "I thought he was gonna blow a gasket!"

"Aw, he's losing it. That's good…if his head is all screwed up, he's not gonna race very well."

"Listen!" Harvey said suddenly. "What's the idea of wasting all that time chasing Sammy? You got to him and then just rode around…how many times I got to tell you, boy; you ain't gonna beat a man by following him! You lucked out when that traffic held him up."

Jimmy shook his head. "You're about as goofy as your buddy Graffan. If I could've passed him, I would have. But he was too good to get a run at him…I tried that one time, and I didn't have enough."

"When you caught him you were still real nice in the middle, and you could have drove right past him. Or you could've run it harder into the corner and cleared him before you got to the cushion. It was plain as day, boy. You just got to be more aggressive."

Jimmy rolled his eyes. "Yeah, and you've won every race you've watched…listen, all you've got to do is have 'em make a seat big enough to fit your fat ass, and then you can drive it any way you want to. Until then, it's me."

Harvey harrumphed mightily, and both he and Jimmy realized they had only a couple of minutes before the next feature.

"How much were you spinning your tires coming off?" Harvey asked quickly.

"A little bit. We better tighten it up some, because it's definitely gonna get slick."

Harvey leaned over to look at the right rear tire, studying the tread. He looked up again at the track, and then glanced at the sunny sky.

"That's what everybody is thinking," he said. "So I'm gonna leave it alone."

Jimmy's gaze widened with concern.

"You sure? We'll be awful loose at the end."

"Yeah, but you'll be damned good at the beginning. You and Sammy were the fastest cars on the track a minute ago. We're goin' racing in a couple minutes, and the track didn't change that much. Everybody else will tighten theirs up, and they'll be junk at first.

"Here's what you gotta do, boy: Get after it on the start, and get to the front. It's probably gonna end up one lane on the cushion. If you're up front, you can run up on the cushion even if you're loose. By then they won't have enough race track to get a run at you."

The officials were calling for cars, and Slim quickly poured another jug of fuel into the tank. Harvey went over the car, banging the wheels tight and rechecking the tire pressure.

Jimmy hurried to add a couple of tear-offs on his visor, and then climbed into the car. In a moment they were fired, and as the field shaped up he found his starting spot on the outside of row three, with Sammy to his inside.

As they roared to life Jimmy moved past Jack Underwood and Rick Wagner in the first corner, and swept past Rusty Fernandez on the backstretch. He could see the other cars fighting tight conditions, and he realized Harvey had been right: The Ellison car was very good now.

Now it was Graffan that Jimmy chased. The Bob Strong sprinter was also good, but Jimmy found enough momentum to beat him off the corner, pulling alongside on the straightaway. The Ellison car got to the next corner first, and Jimmy slid to the cushion, now claiming the lead.

He heard another car to his inside, and figured Graffan was coming back at him.

"Ain't gonna work, Stevie-boy," he said aloud. "Your car won't work down there."

When a nose poked into his range of vision to his left, he was surprised to see that it wasn't Graffan, but the Bell Trucking sprinter of Sammy Caldwell. Sammy had found enough traction in the middle to get a nice run at Jimmy, who could only watch helplessly as Sammy pulled into the lead.

Within a dozen laps the track had turned to a skating rink, much more slippery than Jimmy had anticipated. The thin cushion was treacherously close to the guardrail, but Jimmy was too loose to dare try the middle. He carefully navigated the cushion, pedaling the throttle delicately, knowing that a miscue would bring disaster.

Others weren't quite as fortunate. Rusty Fernandez miscalculated as he entered turn one, and his right rear got over the cushion, banging the guardrail. The front end sucked to the right and the rail grabbed his right front, vaulting the Moore sprinter into the air, flipping it wildly across the track and down the steep banking. The red light blinked on, and the field fell silent.

Jimmy caught his breath as he sat parked in turn three, trying to think of something that might help him get past Sammy. He heard the crowd cheer their approval and he figured whoever had crashed must be okay.

Twice more the same scenario played out. The slightest miscue sent a car into the rail, leading to a bone-jarring flip and another red. The last one came with 10 laps to go, and Jimmy was growing more frustrated. Sammy had given up the middle and was also married to the cushion, and his car was no better than Jimmy's.

The Ellison machine could follow right behind, but passing him was another matter.

As the final laps clicked away Jimmy wrestled with a powerful temptation. Maybe he could get enough momentum to slide under Sammy into the corner, and could beat him to the cushion and take the lead. But the margin for error was so thin it was almost non-existent; he had visions of smacking the rail and going for one of those rides that makes your head hurt till Wednesday.

He ran through the fallout in his mind. A wrecked car, and a wrecked shot at a USAC championship that was still very much in the balance. He imagined the conversation with Harvey as he tried to explain how he maybe threw the entire season away.

So he followed Sammy home, figuring half a loaf was better than no loaf at all…although at the moment he sure as hell wasn't interested in bread.

He rolled to a stop in their pit and cut the fuel, allowing the engine to fall silent. He tugged the gloves from his hands, feeling his fingers trembling from fatigue and tension. He climbed from the car, realizing he was tired.

Harvey stood with his hands on his hips, and Jimmy offered only a glum shake of his head as he walked toward the back of the pickup with his helmet and gear. He took a long swig of water, and used a towel to wipe the sweat and dust from his face.

"I didn't dare try," he said finally. "That cushion was thin as hell."

Harvey shrugged, pulling a rag from his back pocket and wiping his hands.

"Aw, I guess it wasn't a bad day," he said grudgingly. "We'll take a first and a second."

"I know this much," Jimmy offered, "I hate points racing. I'll be glad when this thing is over."

Fans began pouring across the track and into the pit area, and among the first was Little Jimmy, the special-needs kid he had befriended some weeks ago. Instead of bowling him over with his usual boisterous hug, the kid was much more subdued today.

He walked up to Jimmy and stared, their faces only inches apart. Even through the boy's thick glasses Jimmy could see the confusion in the teenager's eyes.

"You didn't win the race," the boy said, shaking his head. "How come you didn't win the race?"

Jimmy began to laugh, shaking his head.

"He didn't win," the kid said to his dad, who offered a gentle smile. "Big Jimmy didn't win!"

"I can't win 'em all!" Jimmy protested. "I wish I could, but it doesn't work that way! Hey, hang on, I've got something for you."

He stepped over to the truck, reaching in the bed for the trophy from the earlier race.

"Here you go, take that home."

The boy shrieked his approval, jumping up and down.

"You're spoiling him," his father chuckled. "He thinks you win every race, and he gets the trophy."

The boy was obviously excited, and he spoke in a torrent of words that Jimmy couldn't understand. The father coaxed the boy to slow down, and Jimmy could make out something about a giant.

"He wants to know if you get a giant trophy for the championship."

"Big as the sky!" the boy shouted, clapping his hands and laughing in a roar. "Big as the sky!"

Jimmy held out his hand to indicate how big the trophy might be. He began raising his hand higher and higher, until he was on his tip-toes and his arm was extended as far as he could.

"Big as the sky!" the boy squealed again, and he grabbed Jimmy in a powerful hug, rocking him backward.

Jimmy's mind was made up. He was going to win this championship. As the kid hugged him for all it was worth, Jimmy realized it wasn't just he and Harvey and Slim, and Sonny Ellison. There was something else, something he couldn't explain. He wanted to make this kid happy. That seemed like an awfully good thing to do.

Chapter 35

The brisk wind brought a chill as Jimmy pulled the collar of his jacket against his neck, sitting on a stack of tires in the pit area at Sunset Park Speedway. The gray skies darkened the mood as Harvey and Slim puttered with the Ellison sprinter.

It had been a long week, the hours and minutes crawling past. With the harvest season getting underway in earnest Jimmy spent most of the week in Gene Morrison's semi-truck, hauling grain to the local terminals. It had been a good diversion, but not enough to keep his mind from constantly thinking of today's showdown for the USAC championship.

The scenario was so tight it screamed with tension. Steve Graffan held a lead of just eight points over Sammy Caldwell, who was two points ahead of Jimmy. Somebody was going to win this thing, and the other two guys were going to spend the winter thinking of a thousand ways it might have been different.

And it was going to be decided today. Not tomorrow, not next week, not next month. It all came down to two 40-lap features that would end the season.

Man, what a season it had been. Matt Coffman driving them nuts in the beginning, throwing everybody off balance. Harvey and Slim getting hurt badly in the highway crash, and Jimmy throwing in with Sid Johnson to keep the No. 49 alive. The cauldron of emotions in May as Jimmy made his first start at the Indianapolis 500. Harvey finally got back on his feet, right about the time Bobby busted his leg. Then came the terrific west coast swing that went well, but ended with Jimmy crashing violently. If he turned his head a certain way his neck still hurt from that one. His favorite girl, Elaine, exited because Jimmy's life was too consumed with racing. Then the IRS entered the picture, causing all sorts of controversy. Now came a nail-biting afternoon to decide the USAC championship.

Sheesh. After this Jimmy was ready for a vacation.

"Don't think so hard," a voice called out. "You'll give yourself a headache."

Jimmy looked up to see Sammy Caldwell approaching, wearing his usual smile.

"I've already got a headache," Jimmy joked. "What's goin' on, Sammy?"

Sammy eased himself onto the stack of tires, looking at Jimmy with a knowing smile. "Been thinking about it much?"

Jimmy shrugged, feigning a look of indifference. "Nah," he replied.

"Oh, really? You're a lyin' dog."

They began to laugh, and Jimmy slowly nodded. "All right, maybe I thought about it this week. A couple of times."

Sammy grinned at the younger man. "I'm just ready to get it over with," he said. "Let the best man win, and all that."

They sat quietly, and Sammy looked around. "Sonny didn't come over? It's not like him to miss a race at Sunset."

"He's up in the stands," Jimmy smiled. "He wasn't coming with us when we got going good the past few weeks, and he didn't want to jinx us by coming with us now. Oh, believe me, he's here. He loves this place."

Sammy nodded. "Me too," he said. "It's bit me a time or two, but I still love it. Guess I don't know any better."

Jimmy studied his friend, noticing the deepening lines on his face and a hint of gray hair along his temples. His respect for Sammy was enormous; the man was a great racer, yes, but it was more than that. He was one of those guys who carried himself with class, as straight-up as they came.

"How long you been doing this, Sam?"

"Oh…22 years. Too damn long, I'm afraid. Sprint cars are for young men. I don't know how much longer I can keep up."

"Oh, sure," Jimmy scoffed. "You took me to school last week at Shoes, remember? Don't be telling me how you can't keep up."

Sammy smiled, and he fell silent for a few moments, staring straight ahead. Finally he spoke.

"What was it like, winning it a couple of years ago? The championship, I mean. Did it feel…different?"

Jimmy was astonished at the question. Here was one of the most admired guys in the sport, asking him what something felt like. He mulled the question carefully, because he wanted to give him a square answer.

"Honestly, it made me want another one," Jimmy finally replied. "It was a rush at first, for a couple of days. Then it starts nagging at you that you've got to defend, you know? I guess your pride kind of gets in there."

Sammy smiled, and nodded. "Pride is a powerful thing," he said softly. "When I watched you win the title the first year you came, I was jealous. My first year in USAC all those years ago, I finished second in points and figured it was a sure thing to win it the next year. Or the next, or the next, or the year after that.

"Five times I've finished second in points. Then I quit thinking about it because it wasn't meant to be. So this year Steve stumbles a little bit, and you guys had your bad luck, and here I am. And it feels just like it did all those years ago...you get your hopes up even though you know how rotten it feels when you fall short."

As Sammy walked away Jimmy noticed the Otley sprinter parked a few spots down. He strolled that way and saw Bobby talking with Fred Otley out by the wall. Jack Underwood was putting a couple of tear-offs on his visor.

"What's up?" Jack called out. "Ready to get everything settled today?"

"More than ready," Jimmy nodded. "How about you? You and Fred talk anything about next season?"

"I'm done here after today," Jack said matter-of-factly. "Bobby's back in the car next spring."

"You sure?"

"Sure I'm sure. That's what Fred told me when he hired me."

"Kind of a tough spot, when we fill in for somebody who got banged up," Jimmy smiled.

"Yeah, kinda. Listen, I'm as ruthless as the next guy...I'd steal a good ride in a heartbeat. But I don't want to slide in under a guy when he's laid up. Nobody feels good about that."

"Nope."

"How about you? You're back with Sonny next year, I assume?"

"I assume," Jimmy smiled, then laughed. "You know how it is in this business...NO ride is guaranteed. When your butt slides down and hits the bottom of the seat, that's when you're sure you've got the ride. But not until."

"Ah, you'll be back. You guys are good together."

"I don't think anybody else could stand working with Harvey," Jimmy grinned. "I must have an unusually high pain tolerance."

"I'd be glad to work with Harvey," Jack said, his eyes twinkling. "So don't slip up, buddy...I'm always right here, ready to steal your seat."

"I'll keep that in mind," Jimmy nodded.

He looked across the way at Bobby. All the worrying his friend had done since his crash, fearful that he'd be replaced. Turns out Fred was a man of his word after all. Jimmy was glad. Somehow that seemed right.

"Well, I hope you get something lined up for next season," he said to Jack. "I like racing with you."

"Same here," Jack waved. "Good luck today."

Jimmy climbed into the Ellison sprinter, fumbling with the belts as he settled in. Why was he so nervous? The butterflies in his belly had multiplied, and he felt his fingers trembling with tension.

"You got a good starting spot, just be patient at the start," Harvey coached. "Take it easy on your tire the first half of the race, and don't wear yourself out. Watch for me down in one, I'll give you a wave when it's time to go."

Jimmy stared straight ahead, holding his helmet in his hands. After a few moments Harvey reached his big paw inside the car to jostle Jimmy's shoulder.

"Hey! Boy! You hearin' me?"

Jimmy looked up quickly. "Yes, I heard you!" he said sharply. "I'm not deaf!"

"Yeah, but you sure are dumb!" Harvey said, guffawing at the joke. "Get it, boy? Deaf...and dumb? Ain't nothin' like a good joke to settle you down!" He guffawed again, obviously quite pleased with himself. Jimmy responded with an annoyed frown.

"Relax, boy!" Harvey insisted. "You got this in the bag...them other guys can't keep up with you here at Sunset...you're a sure thing!"

Jimmy nodded grimly. If he had it in the bag, why did he feel like he was about to drive off a cliff? He tugged his helmet in place as Harvey and Slim rolled him forward to be pushed. Harvey reached in and gave him a rap on the helmet as he stepped away.

The push truck moved into place, and in a moment the car burped and fired. Jimmy felt a wave of panic...was that a stumble? Is there something wrong with the ignition? What if they got some bad fuel? He gently pressed the throttle on the backstretch, picking up his revs and listening intently to the engine.

Everything felt fine, and he began to breathe again. The simple black paint job surely looked out of place on these familiar old banks, but the car itself was as good as ever. The field began to shape up, and Jimmy found his way to the second row inside, right behind Underwood.

The butterflies were gone now, replaced with a powerful combination of focus and determination. Now he was in his realm, where he knew he could make a difference, and make it all work.

As the field rolled into turn three the pitch of their engines began a steady rise, with Jimmy's right foot taut with anticipation. His eyes locked onto the back of Underwood's car, and he perfectly matched the moment in which Underwood accelerated.

The Ellison sprinter wiggled under the powerful burst of torque, and Jimmy fought to keep the car straight. In a flash they were across the length of the front straightaway, with Jimmy holding the car to the inside as turn one rushed toward him. Rusty Fernandez was inches to his right, their tires nearly touching as their cars danced a potentially lethal ballet.

Jimmy felt his tires slip, and Rusty had the better line off the corner. He watched helplessly as Rusty hustled Virgil Moore's sprinter to the advantage, and as they hit turn three Jimmy fell in behind his friend as they worked the fast but treacherous high groove.

Underwood wrestled the wheel in Fred Otley's machine, and Rusty and Jimmy both rushed past him on the straightaway. Jimmy hustled to stay with Rusty, then remembered Harvey's warning about using up his right rear too quickly. Rusty was obviously not in the mood to conserve rubber, so Jimmy debated: Take it easy, or stay with him?

He decided to ease up, allowing Rusty to steadily pull away. They would surely draw a caution sometime in the race, which would erase Rusty's lead and play into Jimmy's hand.

For the next 20 laps Jimmy second-guessed himself. What if they went green-to-checkered? Rusty now led by a full straightaway, and Jimmy knew it would be tough to run him down now. His eyes darted to the left as he rolled through three and four, looking for Harvey. He spotted the big man standing on the hill near the pit entrance, waving his arm.

That was the sign: Jimmy could almost read his mind as he flashed past. Give it hell, boy. He picked up the tempo, feeling the Ellison car surge as if it were a great stallion allowed to have his head.

Jimmy nearly shouted in relief as he spotted a slowing car on the backstretch. It was Underwood, and the California driver had steered to the apron with his right arm outside the cockpit in warning, the engine on the Otley sprinter popping and cracking. Would he make it to the pits? Jimmy waited for the yellow, holding his breath in anticipation.

But the green light stayed on, and Jimmy's heart sank. Underwood had obviously made it off the track, and no yellow was coming. As the laps clicked off he could see that he was catching Rusty, but without a yellow...it was going to be difficult.

With five laps to go he was on Rusty's back bumper, looking for a way past. He could see that Rusty was now very loose, no doubt out of right rear. But the tire on the Ellison car was also giving up, and Jimmy's wrists and foot began to work in unison as their traction steadily diminished.

They soon flashed under Mike Rydman's white flag, with Jimmy still hoping desperately to make a run. But it took everything he had to keep up with Rusty, and any hopes of getting a shot at him were futile. As they took the checkered he could see Rusty pumping his fist, celebrating his first win at one of the most demanding tracks in the nation.

As Rusty slowed Jimmy pulled alongside and offered a thumbs-up. Jimmy breathed deeply as the Ellison car continued to slow, and immediately began thinking about what they needed to do for the final race.

Chapter 36

"Just a little bit short, boy," Harvey called out as the engine fell silent. "I can't believe ol' Red still had any tire left, the way he was burning it up early on. If we woulda got a yellow it would have been a different race."

"Where did Graffan and Sammy finish?" Jimmy asked.

"Fourth and fifth, but I ain't positive," Slim offered. "They were racin' each other the whole time. They were behind you, though."

"Geez," Jimmy muttered. "Wonder what the points are now? Gotta be even tighter."

Jimmy climbed from the car, stretching the stiffness from his legs, flexing his fingers to get rid of the tingling.

"How's come you took it so easy at the start?" Harvey quizzed. "You let him get away too far."

Jimmy looked at Harvey in surprise. "Because you told me to save my tire."

"Yeah, but not *that* much. He just drove away from us."

"Aw, whatever."

Jimmy walked to the grassy area behind their pit, reaching into the cooler for a sandwich and a jug of water. The nerves came rushing back at him as he eased into a lawn chair, wolfing down the food without tasteq. He watched as Slim poured fuel into the car, and Harvey bolted on a new right rear tire. Jimmy looked down the way as other cars were serviced, the pit area alive with movement.

Jeff Todd, the series PR man, came hurrying over, an excited grin spread across his face.

"Boy, it's close now!" Todd shouted. "Steve is ahead by two points, and you and Sammy are tied for second! Two points! Isn't that great??!!"

"Yeah, great," Jimmy said dryly. "How long before the next race?"

"Al said we'd have a 20-minute intermission. But first we're going to have a driver introduction on the front straightaway."

"Aw, why are we messing with that?" Jimmy griped. "Let's line 'em up and go racing…quit messing around."

"Listen, when they introduce you, they want an interview real quick. Is that okay?"

"No," Jimmy retorted. "I'm not in the mood to talk to anybody."

"The crowd wants to hear from all three of you guys before the last race!" Todd insisted. "C'mon, Jimmy, you can't be serious."

"No."

Todd stared for a moment before taking a seat in the lawn chair next to Jimmy. He offered an understanding smile as he spoke softly.

"Hey, I know you're stressed, and I understand…but be fair, Jimmy. All those people paid their money today, and we need to take care of 'em. This is a race they're going to remember for a long time."

Jimmy looked up into the crowded grandstand, his granite expression easing slightly. A few moments passed before he finally spoke.

"All right," he said quietly. "I'll do the interview. Just a short one, though."

"Great!" Todd said, jumping to his feet, reaching over to pat Jimmy on the back.

"Oh, one more thing," he called over his shoulder. "We'll need to get some photos of you three guys shaking hands, too."

"Hey!" Jimmy called out, his voice rising. "C'mon, man! No pictures!" But Todd laughed and pretended not to hear as his strides lengthened and he hurried away.

Jimmy's stomach fluttered wildly as he waited. A few minutes later an official began calling for the field to assemble on the starting grid, bringing another stab of nerves to Jimmy's belly.

Jimmy sucked in a breath and lifted himself from the chair, tossing the water jug back in the cooler. Harvey and Slim had already rolled the car out, and Jimmy suddenly looked around in a panic. His helmet and gloves…where are they? Damn it, they aren't here. Did Slim make sure his gear was in the seat just like always? Isn't this a fine thing, misplacing your stuff at a time like this. A big frown crossed his face as he began walking toward the group of drivers that had assembled at opening in the inside wall along the front stretch.

Jimmy didn't feel like conversation, so he sat alone on the wall a few yards away from the group. The introductions began, back to front, with each driver waving to the crowd as he headed for his car.

Rusty Fernandez would start sixth, and the big redhead offered a broad grin as his name was called. Jimmy would start alongside, and the PA man gave his introduction a nice bump as Jimmy slowly began to walk toward him.

"Lining up fifth in the Ellison Special No. 49, a championship contender originally from Greensburg, Illinois, please welcome Jimmy Wilson!"

Jimmy's heart was buoyed by the loud cheer from the grandstands, and he couldn't help but smile as he waved to the crowd. Jimmy felt the thumping inside his chest as the microphone drew closer.

"Well, Jimmy, this is it," the man began. "One final race to decide it all. Any thoughts?"

"Let's go racing," Jimmy said simply, sparking some cheers and applause.

"Just two points…will you be conservative, or go for the win?"

Jimmy looked at him in genuine amazement. "I'm here to win the race," he said matter-of-factly. "Same as always."

The man wished him well, preparing to introduce Rick Wagner. Jimmy stepped back toward him, indicating that he wanted to say something else. The man smiled and reached toward Jimmy with the microphone.

"I know there is a lot at stake here, but I wanted to mention something very important that Sammy Caldwell said to me earlier today," Jimmy began, his voice stone serious as the crowd fell silent. Sammy, leaning against the inside wall, looked at Jimmy with an expression of surprise and confusion, trying to figure out what he was talking about.

"Sammy wanted me to share this with all of you," Jimmy said, his voice echoing loudly from the big speakers. "Sammy said…that if he wins the championship, there will be free beer for everybody in the grandstands after the races."

The crowd let loose with a tremendous roar, their applause and laughter rolling across the scene. Sammy began to laugh, shaking his head helplessly, and Jimmy waved as he began walking toward his car.

"Go get 'em, Jimmy!" someone in the stands called out. "Go Ellison!" another voice yelled. Jimmy waved, feeling the tension draining from his body. What the hell…he was here to race, and that's what they were going to do.

Todd headed him off with a sheepish smile. "The photos," he reminded. Jimmy nodded and waited, and after Sammy was introduced he walked toward Jimmy.

"What a rat," he grinned, shaking Jimmy's hand. "Free beer… that'll be the day."

Graffan was introduced, and after his interview walked toward them. Todd positioned the three drivers together, having them reach forward to clasp right hands. The photographers moved in close, their flashbulbs flickering under the chilly gray sky. After a moment the three men said nothing as they parted and walked toward their cars.

Jimmy got to the Ellison machine and quickly glanced in the seat. His helmet sat waiting, with his gloves tucked neatly inside, and he responded with a sheepish grin as he realized Slim was watching him.

"What, you think I forgot?" Slim asked with a smile.

"You don't miss a trick," Jimmy replied, reaching his arm across his friend's shoulders. "I can always count on you, Slim."

Now the tension had finally caught up with Harvey, the big man wearing a grim expression as he paced around the car. Jimmy climbed inside, squirming his butt into the bottom of the seat. He pulled the submarine belt into place, then drew the side belts across his lap. His hands deftly reached for the shoulder belts, draping them along his chest, his fingers expertly placing everything together and closing the latch like he had done a thousand times before.

This time there were no butterflies; he felt a big rush of confidence that they were minutes away from his second championship. He couldn't stop grinning, and he noticed Harvey's stoic expression.

"Hey, Slim, look at Harvey," he laughed. "He's actually nervous!"

"No I ain't!" Harvey snapped. "Just payin' attention to stuff!" Jimmy grinned and shook his head as Harvey made two more frantic laps around the car.

"Fuel!" Harvey hollered at Slim. "We didn't fuel 'er!"

"Yeah I did!" Slim insisted. "Relax, will you? You're so excited you're about to slobber on your shirt."

"Listen, boy, don't take it so easy this time," Harvey implored. "Don't use up your tire, but go for it! Take it easy but get on the gas!"

"Make up your mind!" Jimmy grinned.

"Well, you can win this one...you got the car, boy. You got the car. You just gotta drive it right."

"How about if I just drive it like I always do?" Jimmy said, his thumbs hooked inside his helmet as he prepared to place it on his head.

"Yeah," Harvey said, nodding vigorously.

"Hey, how about a joke?" Jimmy offered, enjoying watching Harvey squirm.

"I ain't in the mood for a joke! Shut up and put your helmet on!"

"What did the elephant say to the naked man?"

"Huh? Elephant? I...hell, I don't know."

"He said, 'Mister, how do you drink through that thing?'"

Slim began to laugh, but Harvey just stared at Jimmy like he hadn't heard the punch line. Jimmy pulled his helmet in place and reached for his gloves.

The field rumbled down the backstretch, every nerve in the place standing on end. The autumn chill had deepened, and the crowd shivered as the final race of the season prepared to take flight.

It was simple, really; it would boil down to finishing position in this race. The championship hung in the balance and the field exploded in noise as Mike Rydman frantically waved the green flag.

Sammy got a great start, immediately edging into the lead.

Jimmy followed him closely, rocketing past Graffan and Wagner. The cars slipped precariously at the top of the banking as they blasted through the corner, inches from the rail.

Aside from his nervousness, Harvey had given Jimmy a great race car. He felt as good as ever on these old banks, the car building speed as the laps clicked off, Jimmy getting into a nice rhythm as he rode inches behind Sammy.

There was no holding back. Not at this stage; Jimmy was determined that he would stay with Sammy, knowing he could get him in the latter stages. This time the action was interrupted by a couple of cautions, a spin by a back-marker in turn four and a tow-in for Duke Moran.

As Jimmy saw the crossed flags he had a sinking realization. Although the Ellison car was nearly perfect, and Jimmy had exactly the line he wanted, Sammy was beginning to inch away. Could this be possible? Jimmy was the star here at Sunset, and at the moment was turning some of the fastest laps of his life.

But there was no doubt about it; Sammy and Harry Bell's No. 2 were a shade faster.

Jimmy grit his teeth in desperation. Traffic…if they could catch traffic, he had a shot. He guessed there were 10 laps to go when he spotted a pack of slower cars entering turn one as he and Sammy came roaring off turn four. Would they catch them? Was this the break he needed?

Suddenly Jimmy saw a puff of white smoke way down in the corner just as the yellow blinked on. His heart sank, and a bitter realization swept over him: With this caution, there would be no traffic. He saw the same back marker parked at the bottom of turn two as they rumbled past.

If he was going to beat Sammy, he would have to do it one-on-on, straight up.

Of the tens of thousands of laps Sammy had under his belt, he had never driven 10 more perfect laps than he did after the restart. Jimmy drove his heart out as he chased, pedaling the Ellison car on the razor's edge.

As Mike Rydman waved the checkered flag Jimmy stared at the tail of Sammy's car, his insides aching with disappointment.

He slowed to a crawl as he rolled down the backstretch,

watching Sammy pump his arms outside the cage, as if he wanted to leap from the machine before it had even stopped. Jimmy steered the Ellison car to the pit entrance, coasting to a stop as he reached up to turn off the fuel.

The engine sputtered and fell silent, but Jimmy made no effort to climb from the car. He was so utterly crestfallen that he almost felt like crying. He brought his trembling hands up to unfasten his helmet, realizing Slim was standing alongside the car. Slim leaned against the cage in resignation, slowly stepping back to take Jimmy's helmet from him.

Jimmy lifted his aching arms, pulling himself out of the seat. He was so tired he felt a little unsteady, and he caught his breath as he rested, finally managing a long, disheartened sigh.

He saw Harvey walking slowly toward them, his shoulders sagging. Harvey sat on the left rear tire and crossed his arms, the despondency evident in the big man's eyes.

They looked at each other, but nobody spoke. Jimmy leaned against the cage, looking toward the front straightaway where Sammy was engulfed in a huge mob of people.

He would have liked to have said he was glad for Sammy, but at this moment he really wasn't.

Jimmy glanced toward Bob Strong's pit, where Steve Graffan had climbed from the car and was sitting on the ground, a towel draped over his head while his crew stood in stunned silence. Sure, Graffan had it worse; they went from a big lead to watching the title slip away over the past two months of the season. Jimmy and the Ellison team weren't even supposed to be contenders by this stage. But none of that made the huge lump in Jimmy's throat any smaller.

"Just a little bit short," Harvey said, his voice so low he could hardly be heard.

Jimmy nodded and pushed himself away from the car and began walking slowly toward the celebration.

The mob parted as Jimmy drew closer, offering him words of praise as he nodded blankly. Sammy grinned uncontrollably as he acknowledged the crowd's cheers and shouts, with Harry Bell standing alongside. Somebody had mussed up Harry's carefully combed gray hair, but the older man just shouted riotously along with the others. Several people in the crowd were crying openly, overcome by emotion.

Jimmy stepped toward Sammy, who saw Jimmy and reached out to him. Jimmy draped his left arm across Sammy's shoulders, pulling him close as the two men shook hands. The look of joy on Sammy's face eased Jimmy's heartbreak just a bit, and he squeezed Sammy's hand.

The two men said nothing, holding the handshake. Jimmy saw the photographers crowding toward them, and he tugged Sammy's hand to pull him outside the mob of people, facing the adoring crowd in the grandstand.

Jimmy lifted Sammy's right hand as a boxer would salute his foe, while the crowd roared their approval and several photographers scrambled to capture the image. After a moment Jimmy released Sammy's hand, leaning close and offering an admiring grin.

"You're the man," he said simply, seeing Sammy swallow deeply as he blinked away the flood of emotion in his eyes.

Jimmy slowly walked back toward their pit. Harvey and Slim had begun to gather up their things, and both men looked up at Jimmy as he approached. Harvey had obviously gotten over his disappointment pretty quickly, as he worked with determination.

"Sit down here, boy," Harvey called out, pointing to the fender over the trailer tire. "You too, Slim."

Jimmy and Slim exchanged a curious glance before taking a seat. Harvey put his foot up on the trailer rail, crossed his arms and glanced indignantly toward Sammy's victory mob.

"Let's get somethin' straight right now," Harvey began. "Boy, I don't want to hear any crap this winter about you driving somebody else's car next season. You hear? You're gonna stay with us, and we're gonna come back next year and give 'em an ass-kicking they ain't gonna forget. You just put that in your pocket and carry it till spring."

Jimmy laughed. "What if I don't want to stay?" he quizzed. "Don't I have a say in the deal?"

"Nope," Harvey said. "You need me on your ass to keep you thinkin' right, and that's what I'm gonna do. When I was layin' in the hospital after our highway wreck, I figured I had to pull through because if I wasn't here, you'd never win another race. That's a lot of pressure on me, boy. So we're gonna come back better than ever next year, all three of us, and we ain't gonna come up short. You hear?"

"You thought I'd never win another race? What a load," Jimmy laughed, feeling a little better. "All right, boss, if you're in for next year, so am I. And you're right…we aren't gonna come up short."

Jimmy rose from the fender, looking up to see a stream of people pouring across the track and into the pit area. He had thought about a quick change of clothes and slipping away unnoticed…well, maybe greeting some of the fans would be okay.

People quickly surrounded Jimmy and the Ellison car. He was buoyed by their energy and affection, each person congratulating him on a great season. Several people commented how nice it was that Jimmy had taken the time to pay homage to Sammy in victory lane, but he just smiled and shrugged. He hadn't done it to impress anybody; it was a genuine tribute to somebody he respected and admired.

His heart sank when he saw Little Jimmy approaching, the teen-aged special-needs kid that had become his ardent follower. The past couple of weeks he had given the kid his trophy, and he felt badly that today he had nothing to offer.

Little Jimmy crowded past the people surrounding the car, staring intently at his hero as the boy's dad hurried to keep up. As he drew closer Jimmy could see tears streaming down the boy's face, and his heart sank.

"I wanted you to win," the kid said, stumbling on the words.

He threw his arms around Jimmy, hugging him tightly. Jimmy felt the heaving of the boy's chest, his muffled sobs soaking into his uniform. Several onlookers looked on sympathetically as they watched the scene unfold.

Jimmy held him close, patting the boy's shoulder affectionately.

"Go right ahead and cry," he whispered to the boy. "That's just how I was feeling."

After a few moments the boy began to quiet, and Jimmy put his hands on the kid's small shoulders and had a look at him. His thick glasses were askew, his face covered with tears, his lip trembling.

The boy's father reached toward him with a handkerchief, and Jimmy took the cloth and began wiping the boy's face.

"Look at that face!" he smiled. "You're a mess! But we'll be all right, won't we? We've gotta be tough...that's part of racing. We just got beat today...and when you get beat you gotta take it like a man."

The boy's father gave Jimmy a hearty handshake, drawing him close.

"Listen, we appreciate how you've been so nice to us," he said. "It's meant so much...he just can't stop talking about you. You've really made an impression on him. And me, too."

Jimmy didn't know what to say, and his face reddened. "Aw... he's a nice kid, and I like having him around. Say, we'll have next season, you know. I hope you guys will still come around."

"You can count on it," the father said, shaking Jimmy's hand again. He took the boy and gently began to guide him away. The kid followed obediently before suddenly turning to point at Jimmy.

"Who's number one?" the kid shouted, grinning.

"You are," Jimmy called, and the kid clapped his hands and squealed as the people surrounding the car laughed.

The infield was nearly empty, and Jimmy watched as the last few stragglers made their way toward the parking lot. Most of the teams had loaded and gone, with the chilly wind sending people on their way a little quicker than usual.

The Ellison car had left nearly a half-hour ago, but Jimmy lingered to chat with a few friends after changing from his uniform. Sammy's big party had moved out to the grassy parking area, the celebrants oblivious to the cold wind and the approaching darkness.

Jimmy hoisted his helmet bag across his shoulder as he made his way across the track, walking through the wide opening in the fence. Some teen-aged kids were picking up trash under the grandstand, laughing and chattering as they worked. He paused and watched them for a moment, then turned and walked along the pathway that led to the old wooden bleachers.

He began walking up the aisle. One, two, three, four rows, then five, six, seven, all the way to the top, where he placed his hands on the metal railing. He felt the chill in his hands, slowly turning to sit on the top row, leaning back against the railing to look across the great old track as the night edged in close.

The gray clouds had disappeared, leaving a crisp and beautiful autumn evening. The tall, stately trees behind the backstretch were now nothing more than a dark gray wall, their leaves nearly gone and the limbs reaching out their crooked fingers like an ominous giant.

The cold wind buffeted Jimmy's face, biting his ears. He blinked from the sting, but stared stoically across the landscape.

He felt empty and sad, knowing how close they had come. But he felt proud, too, because they definitely gave it all they had.

As far as he was concerned, winter couldn't come quickly enough. He was so sick of all this he didn't care if it snowed for a year. Yet his stomach was knotted with hunger; why couldn't they start all over again tomorrow, and this time they'd…well, they'd do it better.

Sure. Do it better, that's all. He and Harvey and Slim, and Sonny Ellison, they were a team. A feuding, fussing, fighting bunch that couldn't get along more than 10 minutes at a stretch, making each other miserable all the way. But that's how it is. And he wasn't ready for it to be over.

Other books in the Jimmy Wilson series

SPRINT CAR SALVATION

First of the series, covering Jimmy's first "season" of racing. Discover the origins of the series, and meet the characters who gave the series such staying power.

Hardbound, 240 pages

FAST AND FEARLESS

Second of the series. The saga continues with Jimmy and the Ellison team's continued adventures. Additional characters and lots of new scenarios.

Hardbound, 288 pages

Also by
Dave Argabright...

LET'S GO RACING!
with Rex Robbins

This is the amazing story of the American Speed Assn. as told by series founder Rex Robbins. A lively and fun read!

Foreword by Darrell Waltrip

AMERICAN SCENE

A collection of nearly 100 columns and feature stories from 1988 to 1997, from auto racing's well-known storyteller. The stories you have loved for years, in a book to be enjoyed forever.

EARL!
with Earl Baltes

A one-of-a-kind book on the life of one of the greatest racing promoters in history. There's never been another like "EARL!"

Foreword by H.A. "Humpy" Wheeler

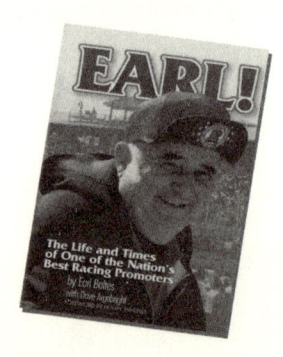

LET 'EM ALL GO!
with Chris Economaki

A history of auto racing by the man who was there...the greatest racing journalist of all time, Chris Economaki.

Foreword by Roger Penske

LONE WOLF
with Doug Wolfgang

An articulate and haunting look at life and sprint car racing, told through the eyes of a survivor. A book you'll never forget!

Foreword by Steve Kinser

FAST COMPANY
with "Speedy" Bill Smith

From one of the most successful car owners and businessmen in racing history comes "The World According to Speedy Bill!"

Foreword by Ken Schrader

STILL WIDE OPEN
with Brad Doty

One of the most popular racing books of all time...in an updated second edition with bonus material.

Foreword by Steve Kinser

Dave Argabright has covered auto racing since 1981 for a variety of print publications, including *National Speed Sport News, Sprint Car and Midget Magazine, Speedway Illustrated, Road & Track, DirtOnDirt.com, On Track, OPEN WHEEL Magazine, Car and Driver,* and *AMI Auto World*. His broadcast background includes the Indianapolis 500 Radio Network, CBS Sports, SPEED, MustSeeRacing, MAV TV, Versus, ESPN, and TNN Sports.

His professional honors include the "Frank Blunk Award for Journalism" from the Eastern Motorsports Press Assn., the Dymag Award of Journalism Excellence, the "Outstanding Contribution to the Sport" award from the National Sprint Car Poll, and the Hoosier Auto Racing Fans "Media Member of the Year" and "Gene Powlen Fan Appreciation Award." He is a six-time recipient of the "Media Member of the Year" award from the National Sprint Car Poll. Dave is also an inductee of the Hoosier Auto Racing Fans Hall of Fame, the Dayton Auto Racing Fans Hall of Fame, the National Assn. of Auto Racing Fan Clubs Hall of Fame, and the Little 500 Hall of Fame.

Dave resides in Fishers, Ind.

Ordering information:
American Scene Press
P.O. Box 84
Fishers, IN 46038-0084
(317) 598-1263
www.daveargabright.com